MORGAN MALONE

AN AFTER 50 DATING MEMOIR

*Cock*tales

Cocktales
by Morgan Malone

Copyright © 2015, Deborah Sabin Cocktales
Media > Books > Non-Fiction > Body, Mind & Spirit Books
Biographies & Memoir, Religion &
Spirituality/Spirituality/Inspirational/Relationships, Dating,
Women, Men, Transformation, Personal Growth

Trade Paperback ISBN : 978-1536960624
Digital Release: July 2016

Editor, Deelylah Mullin
Cover Design by Calliope-Designs.com
Painting/illustration by Lorraine Callan
Author photograph by Jessica Kleemann, jlkPhotography

All rights reserved. The unauthorized reproduction or distribution of this copyrighted work, in whole or part, by any electronic, mechanical, or other means, is illegal and forbidden.

This is a work of nonfiction. Names of people or places may have been changed by the author. The events related are the author's experiences and written from the author's best recollection.

Interior format by The Killion Group
http://thekilliongroupinc.com

DEDICATION

To all the women who made this book possible. You know who you are, but especially to CKS and ADG for being my safeties, the Posse for joining in and making some of the misadventures into lasting memories, the Yentas for listening, Susie for being my late night phone call, and DWR for the kids. My gratitude to Robyn Ringler for teaching me to stop writing like a lawyer, Writing Women's Minds (Maggie, Sharon, Posey, Jean and Kathe) for giving me a comfortable and safe place to craft my stories, the two Sues for being the best Beta readers ever, and Dee, the most talented and empathetic editor I know.

TABLE OF CONTENTS

The Beginning	1
Pause Here	3
Ten-Inch Tim	8
John Number One	17
Karma Chameleon	23
John Number Two	27
Bad Boys	32
Crazy	34
Phone Sex	36
The Rabbi	41
Richard	47
Friends With Benefits	52
Boyfriend Bob	58
Hot-Tub Ken	65
Mr. Less Is More	71
Pepsi-Can Ken	75
Déjà Vu	79
And So It Goes	84
The Professor	86
Georgio	90
Jewish Marks	96
The Wine Critic—First Encounter	101
The Wine Critic—Part Deux	105
The Wine Critic—Adieu	109
Sir E	114
Yalie	122
Men	131
The Felon-What Was I Thinking?	135

The Felon-This Is Not Going to Work, Is It	140
The Felon-Will This Ever Be Over?	145
Jamie—Fact or Fiction	150
Jamie—Lake Placid & Kinderhook	155
Jamie—Boudoir Gymnastique	163
Jamie—Battle Lines	169
Jacob	179
Surrender	184
Married Men	186
Tom—Everything Old is New Again	191
Tom—Fourth of July 2009	196
Tom—Mariposas	200
Tom—The Irish in Me	203
Tom—Intimacy	208
Tom—What I Did For Love	210
Tom—Men in Kilts	215
Tom—Segue	222
Cocktails	226
Epilogue	228
Questions for Discussion	

COCKTALES

Eight years, Eighty Men and Not Quite 8000 Orgasms: A fifty-ish woman's journey through the world of Internet dating, to find lust and love later in life.

I was married to the love of my life at twenty-five and widowed ten years later. Approaching my fiftieth birthday, I sent a small, selfish prayer to Heaven: I wanted to feel something, preferably an orgasm, just one more time.

My friends laughed at my wish. What man in his right mind would want a fifty-year-old woman, overweight, scarred, graying and out of practice in the ways of love? I took the challenge. I was not looking for a marriage, a long-term relationship or even a short-term liaison: I just wanted to get laid. *Cocktales* chronicles my journey from lust to love to hope.

In *Cocktales*, you will meet a sampling of men I dated, and some will make you laugh until you cry. The "bad boys" will make you hurt until you cry. And a few will just make you sigh.

Cocktales is my story, told through my encounters with many men over the last decade. I've grown from an isolated, lonely widow to a woman who has faced many fears and fantasies, gathering some practical advice and some hard-earned insight along the way to becoming the woman I want to be.

THE BEGINNING

Right before my forty-ninth birthday, I asked my husband if he minded if I had sex with another man. He didn't answer me, so I persisted.

"Listen, I'm almost fifty years old, I know. Who would want me? I've had two kids and a hysterectomy. I've got stretch marks, scars and cellulite. And I know I need to lose at least fifty pounds."

No response.

"It's been a long dry spell, you know. Almost fifteen years. I think I'm entitled to at least one more orgasm that doesn't come from something powered by a nine-volt battery."

Still nothing.

"Okay, then, I take your silence to mean I am on my own in this. You don't have an opinion one way or the other. Right?"

Silence.

It was March and the Yankees were still in Spring Training so I knew so there were no distractions from current league standings or the pitching staff. His side of the bed was ghostly quiet. And empty. He had been dead for almost fifteen years.

I talked to him all the time. Not every minute of the day, but an ongoing dialogue in my head where I kept him informed of the day-to-day minutiae of our lives. I announced major developments then I waited for an answer. Call me crazy, but there were times when I heard his response in my head as clearly as if he had just spoken directly in my ear.

Sometimes, like now, there was nothing. *Figure it out for yourself.*

So, I turned out the light and sent a silent prayer Heavenward. "God, just once before I am over fifty, let me have sex with a man who wants me, let me remember how to do it. And let me *feel*. Amen."

PAUSE HERE

My religion and my husband were my second, albeit best, choices.

I was born and raised a Catholic in a middle-class family in the far northern reaches of New York State. The third of five children, I had an older brother and sister and two younger brothers. My father was a contractor and my mom was a legal secretary. She stayed home when we were little and then went to work for the County Treasurer. My parents were practicing Catholics; my mother was almost a saint.

I had been fascinated by Judaism since I was five, when I met my three favorite friends in kindergarten, all of them Jewish. After that, I celebrated Hanukkah and Passover with them, loving the tradition and history of their beliefs. As I grew older, their history and traditions began to speak to me on a deeper level, as though my soul was reaching out for their ancient beliefs.

In high school, I dated a bit, but I was in love with a boy named James who was two years older than me. He was Irish Catholic, brilliant and politically active. I think I loved his brain as much as I loved his unruly brown hair and wicked smile. He taught me to think…and to question. By the time I graduated from high school, teenage rebellion and the cruelties of war, poverty and discrimination that I nightly witnessed on the news, had caused me to question the faith of my parents. *How could God allow such things?* I was whittled down to a Sunday Catholic, almost agnostic.

I went off to college and met the second great love of my life. A nice Catholic boy from New Jersey, his name was also James. He graduated from Colgate at the end of my freshman year and left for law school in Baltimore. We saw each other as best we could for the next two years. But when I moved to Washington, DC, for the first half of my senior year, we were finally able to spend almost every weekend together in Baltimore. That included Mass every Sunday morning. As the weeks passed, I found I couldn't do it, not when I had begun to have doubts about my religion and our relationship. I loved him, but I was no longer *in* love with him. That

meant everything he did or said was starting to annoy me, including dragging my tired butt out of bed early every Sunday morning for Mass and Communion, after drinking and fornicating mightily the night before. I cracked right before Christmas, and that was the beginning of the end. Instead of getting engaged by the New Year, I had broken up with him.

My last semester of college was a whirlwind of studies, law school preparation, and inappropriate men. I graduated with honors and headed off to law school, determined to live the single life for the next three years.

I met my husband the day before law school began. He had become the roommate of the older brother of my best friend from home. And he was Jewish, as was my friend. As much as I had loved my college sweetheart, my feelings for him paled in comparison with the love I felt for my husband. We were almost instantly connected and were rarely apart for more than a day. He was tall, dark, handsome, funny and smart. A Reform Jew from Long Island, he was more a cultural Jew than a spiritual Jew. He had no problems dating a *shiksa*, a somewhat derogatory term for non-Jewish females, especially non-Jewish females who date Jewish males. His family was not thrilled with me at first, and my parents were a little taken aback, but seeing how right we were together, our families became pretty accepting of our relationship. We married three years later, after graduating from law school and taking the NYS Bar Exam. Our wedding was in my hometown, on the putting green of the local golf course, officiated by my priest, a rabbi-for-hire and my husband's former roommate, an Episcopalian divinity student at Yale.

My husband joined a small law practice in Mechanicville, NY; I went to work in Albany as a hearing officer for a small

NYS agency. Promotions and raises followed, and soon my title changed to Administrative Law Judge. I loved being a judge, even if all I presided over were administrative proceedings involving varied labor law issues.

Three years after our marriage, as we waited for the birth of our first child, I converted to Judaism. It was like coming home. The last piece of my puzzle fell into place. Our son was born three years after our daughter and our lives were complete. Or so I thought.

Work was complicated because I was a mother. At first, I was the only professional woman at the agency with small children. As is often the case with working moms, there were times when the demands of family wreaked havoc with my schedule. Surrounded by men whose wives stayed home with their children, I was often the target of criticism because of the juggling my husband and I did to care for our children and handle our jobs. But, life was still good.

In 1987, I was diagnosed with cervical cancer. Scary, at first, but with a great doctor and a loving husband, I got through the initial procedures, ending in a hysterectomy, and was pronounced cancer-free. I thanked God, knowing everyone had in their lives some tragedy, some misfortune. I was so grateful my brush with death had left me with nothing but a bad scar and profound thankfulness to be alive and well.

In 1988, my husband suffered a tragic accident and was in the hospital for thirty-two days. He died just days before our tenth anniversary. He was only thirty-five. I was left with two small children, ages six and three. And a mortgage. And no one to rely on anymore. I was alone. Things worsened at my job; one of my co-workers made a pass at me. I laughed it off, but he took my rejection seriously and began a twenty-year long vendetta. Being the sole caregiver, even with the help of au pairs and baby sitters, I took a lot of time off from work. I was now the only single mom on the professional staff, and my supervisor repeatedly commented negatively and without good reason about my frequent absences. In 1993, I gratefully accepted a title change from Administrative Law Judge to Assistant Counsel to the Board. I moved away from my male coworkers, down the long hallway, to the Board level at the office. And my travel away from home for work virtually disappeared. But throughout my tenure, there was a constant tension caused by those male co-workers who I now referred to as the "boys" because of their childish, bullying behavior. It was not just me; they were not happy about any woman who was an equal and not a subordinate.

Money, too, had become an issue, with huge childcare expenses, psychologist bills, private school and the cost of trying to distract my children from the loss of their father with gifts and trips. My husband had not carried much life insurance, and my salary, though constant, saw few increases during some of the State's lean budget years. I did what I could to stretch my government paycheck to fill all our needs, and the needs of my aging parents, but most months found me juggling to balance income with outlay.

I managed. I survived. I focused on my children and my job. I taught Hebrew School. I socialized only with my friends with kids and a few ladies from work. Over the next fifteen years, I gained almost one hundred pounds. I did not wear make-up, and I dressed in matronly clothes that made me look as old as I felt. And I felt I had aged fifty years.

My children grew up. My daughter went off to college, followed four years later by my son. As I turned forty-nine, I realized that soon I would be an empty nester; my only company my beloved, but aging, yellow Lab. I would be alone.

With my husband's death, religion had taken on greater importance and deeper meaning for me. Every night, my prayers echoed against the floors of Heaven. How many nights had I cursed the Almighty for my great loss? How many nights had I pleaded for understanding? How many nights had I prayed to turn back the hands of Time and return to my wonderful life with my husband? All those prayers went unanswered.

Now, after almost fifteen years, I was reciting different prayers. Not for another great love. I knew my heart had died with my husband, shriveled to almost nothing in the blazing heat of August 1988, when I recited the prayers of mourning at his grave. I was certain I would never love again, save for the love I felt for my children. I believed my heart was too scarred for anything else.

So, I prayed for a man who would want me one more time. Just once was surely not too much to crave. I just wanted to feel wanted again, to feel desire again, to feel that momentary release that wipes all thought from your brain, all cares from your soul. Believing I could never have love again, I prayed for lust. A small prayer, I thought, one that had some slight chance of success. I told no one I had pleaded with Heaven for earthly pleasure, certain this prayer, like so many others, would not be answered.

After all, how was I going to even meet such a man? It would take a miracle.

TEN-INCH TIM

It was a cold Sunday morning about two weeks after my impassioned prayer to the Almighty. I was bundled in a really old flannel nightgown, my glasses perched on the end of my nose. During my monthly visit to my mother's house, I was sitting in my youngest brother's bedroom using his computer to check my bank balance. I got on the Internet using AOL, the only connection available. As usual, the difference between what was on screen and what was in my checkbook register stymied and annoyed me.

Hello.

The message popped on my screen.

The ping made me look over, unsure of what was going on, new as I was to the world of Instant Messaging. The greeting was from "Tim." *Hmmm. My big brother has become computer literate?*

Hi back.

How are you this fine Sunday morning?

I'm at Mom's trying to balance my damn checkbook.

Oh, too bad.

My older brother was the most technologically challenged man I knew. I was amazed he had figured out Instant Messaging.

What are you doing and when did you get on the computer?

I'm getting ready to go to Mass. I've been on AOL for a while.

I am stunned and amazed. Did one of the kids show you how?

I double-checked the last entry in my checkbook and the balance on the screen. Still miles apart.

My son got me started.

I didn't know Mark was around that much anymore.
Mark who?

Was he that dense, I thought, or had I missed something while trying to make sense of the morass my checkbook was becoming?

Your son. You really are getting senile, bro!

It took a few minutes for the *ping* from AOL to announce he had replied. My head was down, staring at my checkbook. How could I be overdrawn when I still had checks? I chuckled to myself at how apt that clichéd saying was to my situation.

Who do you think I am?

Now, I was totally confused and more than a little suspicious.

What? You're my big brother Tim.

I nervously awaited his response, hoping this was one more of his lame attempts at humor.

No, I'm Tim from Clifton Park.

I was stunned and immediately typed one word,

WHAT?

I signed off before he could reply, appalled I had been speaking to a strange man while in my nightgown. That's how naïve I was about connecting on the Internet.

Apparently, when I had created my AOL account some years earlier with the help of one of my girlfriends, she had created a profile for me. It was pretty basic. Female. Born 1953. Widow. Saratoga County.

Tim e-mailed me later that day and said he had been looking through the AOL profiles and came across me. He wanted to apologize, though he wasn't sure for what. Then, he wrote:

I am forty-eight years old. I've been divorced for a couple of years. I have one son. I work for NYS. I am just looking for a nice woman to spend some time with.

With some trepidation, I wrote back.

I am forty-nine years old. I am a widow with two children. My daughter is in college and my son is finishing high school, so he still lives at home. I also have a huge yellow Labrador Retriever. I've worked for NYS for almost twenty-five years. I have not dated since Gerald Ford was President.

I stole some of my best lines from the movies. He was amused by my reply; I correctly guessed he had not seen *Sleepless in Seattle*.

So there was the answer to my prayers. God works in mysterious ways. I was still feeling my way through the technology of the Internet and the niceties, or lack thereof, of online communication. Lack of punctuation and capitalization bothered me, and I was lost with some of the acronyms used in e-mails and instant messages, or IMs as I learned to call them. But, we managed to communicate online over the next several days.

After a few more e-mails, I had a pretty good image of Tim. He was still smarting under the terms of a particularly nasty divorce, but he was a down-to-earth guy: a guy's guy, who drove a Suburban and was employed by NYS as supervisor of blue-collar workers from whose ranks he had risen. He was not intimidated by my law degree; he was amused by it. He was enamored with the title of Administrative Law Judge. Even though I explained I had been an Assistant Counsel since 1993, he insisted on calling me "Judge." Little did I know he was only the first of many who would use Judge as my nickname, a turn-on and a term of endearment.

He sent me his picture first. Dark hair, starting to gray. Dark moustache, which I really liked. Dancing brown eyes and a mischievous smile. A well-toned physique. I was stymied about what picture to send him. I was older than he was; he was in better shape than me. I had "mom" pictures, "sister" pictures and pictures with my kids. I finally sent a photo of me from the previous year, taken in Lake Placid. I was all blond hair and big smile, wrapped in my mink coat. I didn't look like a mom or a Sunday school teacher, and the mink camouflaged those extra pounds.

I began to look forward to his e-mails and IMs throughout the day. He made me laugh and was a total flirt. First thing in the morning, he would give me a letter of the day to spin out fantasies of any sexual activity that began with that letter. Our e-mails took on a passionate tone late in the evening. I was warming to the idea of playing out sexual fantasies on the computer. After all, no worries about my hair, make-up, soft tummy, laugh lines. No mess. And no real attachment.

Tim took it a step further early one Sunday morning. He was horny and wanted to play. Fairly graphic messages were popping up on the screen as my son slept safely in his room down the hall. My bedroom was heating up behind the closed and locked door.

Touch yourself. My cheeks were burning. But my fingers strayed as if of their own volition to my breasts and below.

Tell me what you feel. I was a little embarrassed and incredibly aroused. I was feeling things I had not felt in years. Muscles I had forgotten I possessed tightened. And I swallowed my shyness and told him. In graphic terms, I told him what was hard and what was wet.

I am touching you. I could feel his hands on me. It was my hand, but it had become an extension of Tim and his wicked mind.

There. And there. My nipples, my inner thighs, my lips. I was panting.

What do you want? I felt lost. In an erotic world of Tim's making. I felt as though I had found myself or at least a part of myself that had been missing for so long. I wanted to feel it all.

What will make you feel how I feel? Him being inside me would probably do it, I thought.

It was then I realized I was rushing down a one-way street to actually have sex with this man. I knew then that we would be lovers. But for now, I wrote I wanted him, all of him.

I am so hard. He was so turned on by my few halting messages, my compliance to his commands, my reaction to his directions. He wanted us to find release together.

God. Baby. Suck. Fuck. His messages became a staccato of one-word commands. Then, finally: *I want you to come. Now!*

I did. Wave after wave of release swept through me. My first non-solo orgasm in years. To my complete and utter astonishment, his words, his directions, had me melting helplessly. I think I bit my lip until it bled to keep from making a noise. I could not believe it!

Cybersex. I had just had cybersex! I had heard the phrase before and thought it was ridiculous and impossible. I could not get my head around how in the world you could achieve an orgasm from words flashing on a computer screen. And how could you respond? If you were doing all the touching required, how could you type a response or even want to? I knew I was not good enough at typing to do it. And how did you know if your partner was faking it. Or worse, sitting around with his buddies laughing at your typed moans and groans. *Oh, baby, I need you. Oh God, I'm going to come. Yes. Yes! Oh, God, oh God!* For all he knew, I could be doing my nails. For all I knew, he could be ironing.

Well, I wasn't and neither was he.

From his messages, Tim appeared to be as shaken as I was. *Dear Jesus God! That was unbelievable. I can't believe that just happened. Wow! You are so incredibly sexy. What just happened here?*

By that evening, he was insisting we meet. I had some trepidation about that. More than mere reluctance, I was scared to death. I had not had a date since 1978. I had not kissed a man I was not related to for fifteen years. I had stretch marks, for God's sake.

He was smooth, I'll give him that. Tim had been divorced for a while and had been dating—had been having sex with other women, to be accurate. He was proud of his accomplishments in this area. From the braggadocio that began appearing in his messages and our phone conversations, it seems he fancied himself quite the lover. In his most impassioned plea for a meeting, he mentioned his penis was ten inches long. I fell out of my chair when I read that.

My friends and I had been discussing that very topic just the month before. I had read an erotic romance novel, where the hero had a twelve-inch long penis, which caused the heroine to swoon after several splendid orgasms. We actually pulled out a ruler and stood there staring at it, trying to imagine a vagina long enough for it to fit into. We looked at each other and burst into laughter at the ludicrousness of the notion all that muscle would fit inside the average woman.

Tim's endowment became the source of much discussion among my friends. I insisted he was probably exaggerating, as men do about such things, but vowed to bring a tape measure along on our first date. They dared me to use it.

It was assumed our date would involve *sex*, the wheres and hows I left up to him. I had a son at home and so did he.

So, there I was two weeks later, waiting in the K-Mart parking lot for a black Suburban. I had dressed in black, lots of layers of black. I figured black was slimming—don't all the fashionistas say so?—and layers of clothing would conceal some of my fat and would slow him down if he simply intended to just rip my clothes off (which I secretly hoped he would do, removing any decisions or awkward movements from me). I had bought new sexy black lingerie, covered it with a camisole and a loose open knit cotton sweater. Black pull-on linen slacks so there would be no tight marks around my middle and black wedge flip-flops, for ease getting off and no lines from knee-high hose.

My friend Georgeann had the pertinent details about Tim and the *date* in a sealed envelope I had given her before I left the office and my promise to call her at ten o'clock that night to report I was safely home. I even had condoms in my purse, just in case he forgot.

He was better looking than his pictures: salt and pepper hair and moustache, strong build. He pulled up next to my car, and I got out, trying to look calm and in control. My stomach was doing flip-flops and my heart was hammering.

What was I getting into? I am going to get laid!

Fifteen years without sex was a powerful incentive to overcome my reticence and send me sauntering over to meet him. We shook hands through his car's window and he told me to get in. I hesitated.

This is nuts. What was I thinking? Getting into a strange vehicle with a strange man?

Who I knew wanted to get me naked as soon as he could. I almost bolted.

He quickly got out and rounded the front of the Suburban. Tom was taller than me, dressed in a black T-shirt and jeans. He touched my elbow, and steered me closer to the door. He opened the door for me, and I froze. My fear must have been painted on my forehead: *Crazy, nervous, middle-aged woman too horny to think straight, too afraid to move.*

"Judge, what are you worried about? You know everything about me, including my social security number." That was true. I made him give it to me the night before on the phone. "We're going for a ride, so we can talk. We're just going to talk unless you want more."

This seemed reasonable to me, so I climbed up into the Suburban. He closed my door then got back into the driver's seat. He leaned over to kiss me. He was a talented kisser. My toes were curling, my breath caught and my undisciplined nipples turned into rocks. *Oh, yeah, I was getting laid.*

We drove to a corner of his property a few miles away. I could see the lights of his house across the field. Trees surrounded the spot he pulled into, a small clearing on the side of the road. He turned the engine off and kissed me again. *Damn.* The man could kiss. The windows steamed up, I was leaning across the console, letting him devour my mouth, while his hands roamed over me. He pulled away and said, "Scootch in the back there, so we can spread out."

Scootch? At my age, I didn't *scootch* anywhere, I told him. Sighing, he got out, opened my door, and then opened the back of the Suburban. I followed him and paused again. I was forty-nine and overweight. Just as *scootching* was beyond my physical capabilities at that time, so was climbing into the back of an oversized SUV with any semblance of grace. So I sat on the back edge facing him and swung my legs up and to the side. I was able to execute a not-too-awkward slide to the right. He climbed in after me. He had spread out a sleeping bag, silky side down, flannel, deer-in-the-wood print side up. I stared at him for a minute, not sure whether to recline or lean in for a kiss. He solved my dilemma by wrapping his arms around me and lowering me to the sleeping bag as his lips descended on mine.

Did I mention he was a helluva kisser? He was. His tongue swept into my mouth, taking my breath away. He was teasing my tongue with his. I discovered then I had not forgotten how to do this. I kissed him back. I had been a helluva kisser too in my day. Our kisses grew deeper and deeper, as if we were trying to climb inside each other.

His hands slipped from my face to my arms, then my back and then to my aching breasts.

My hands were under his T-shirt, feeling hot male skin, his chest dusted with just the right amount of hair, his nipples tiny hard pebbles under my fingers.

In minutes, kissing progressed to foreplay. He had my sweater off and was making fast work of the camisole. I was a little self-conscious, not willing to lose this opportunity I had prayed for, but I didn't want to take off the camisole yet. So I eagerly, if not without some finesse, reached for his waist and got his jeans unzipped, as he was pulling my trousers off. He kicked out of his jeans and sat there in gray briefs showing off his enormous erection. I stared. He smirked. Then he pulled off his underwear to reveal his pride-and-joy.

Whoa! It really was ten inches long. I swear it reached his navel. *I swear!* I stared at this boa constrictor-like penis. I salivated. Then I grinned. I looked up at his face. He was grinning now, too.

"I didn't lie," he said a bit too smugly.

"I'm a lawyer. I need proof," I said as I reached for my purse and my tape measure. He gulped in disbelief, I am sure, but then laughed good-naturedly.

"Go ahead. Did you bring a camera?"

"No, just this," I murmured as I stretched the limp fabric measure from the tip to base of his really hard length. He never wavered and there was no perceivable shrinkage due to my scrutiny. I wondered if he had ever been sized up like this before, but the thought died in my head as I looked at the tape measure's answer: ten inches.

"Are you done?" he asked.

"No, I think we've just begun." I smiled and bent my head to salute his sword with a kiss.

I was on my back in seconds.

Tim's fucking was by the book. He liked the missionary position, and he didn't spend too much time on kissing anything other than my lips. But I wasn't about to complain. It had been a long time, too long a time, since I had felt what he made me feel. And it felt damn good, even though there was a little too much of him for me to handle. And I received the answer to my prayers with a long, slow, rolling orgasm that left me gasping for breath—then a deep throaty laugh of pure satisfaction. That laugh was to become my trademark. He laughed, too.

We were still laughing as he drove me back to my car. He kissed me goodnight and asked me to call him when I got home, to make sure I arrived there safely. *How sweet*, I thought. *And how very, very good.*

And it was good, for a while. We met secretly every few days for sex and small talk. We chatted on our cell phones at different times during the day. I was terrified anyone would discover I was having sex. I was afraid of the reaction of my kids, especially my son. I had been *just Mom* for so long, I did not know how he would react. Hell, *I* didn't know how to react. And, I will admit Tim, even though a funny, sexy, and smart man, was a bit rough around the edges. He carried a chip on his shoulder against the legal establishment for the treatment he received in his divorce, and he was still bitter about his ex-wife's infidelity.

Through the spring and early summer, Tim answered my prayers. Sex was easy if unexciting, as unexciting as sex with a man with a ten-inch-long penis can be. Seriously, what was the problem with that? I was certainly satisfied after each encounter. But I began to feel as if more was expected of me than of him. He brought the penis to the table, or the back of the Suburban or the motel room, but that was it. Innovation was on me.

So I practiced on him. It was like riding a bike or swimming: you don't forget the moves, your body remembers, almost instinctually. And I had a good memory. But, I wanted him to do more than just fuck me; I wanted him to make an effort.

Tim didn't have it in him. He had relied on his equipment for so long that he had never developed any seduction skills. I made the mistake of complaining one night that, for a change, he should do what I wanted. He blew up. The epithet "lawyer bitch" was used, and we drove back to my car in silence. As I left the Suburban, he muttered, "I'm sorry." Too little, too late.

I watched him watch me drive away and knew it was over. Too soon.

JOHN NUMBER ONE

I could do this. I was an educated woman, how hard could it be? Even two of my idiot brothers had ventured into this new world of cyber-romance. That one brother, happily married, was online posing—just for the hell of it—as Jamie, a thirty-two-year-old divorcée, wondering if she should get her breasts enlarged, shouldn't stop me. My baby brother was finding romance and some sex in northern New York pretty much as himself. He had posted his picture, thinning hair and all, and had plenty of offers. Even though many were immediately dismissed as illiterate or outside of his age requirement—they had to at least know who Grand Funk Railroad (those chart-topper singers of *We're An American Band*) was as proof they had grown up in the 70s like him—I wasn't discouraged.

These two younger brothers had given me a crash course on computer flirtation and assignation. First, I had to change my screen name. Any screen name that contained "mom" was not going to garner any serious attraction from the opposite sex. My new screen name had to be "hot," even though they both snickered at the notion anyone would find their fifty-ish sister "hot." Second, I had to ditch AOL and sign up for the Internet through another carrier because, my brothers announced in unison, "AOL is for losers." Third, I needed to go into some chat rooms to relearn how to flirt. Being female, I had assumed flirtatiousness was inherent, but I was assured this was the new millennium, and things had changed. I was, however, cautioned to stay out of any chat rooms that were identified by initials. I knew what SM stood for, but BDSM (bondage, domination, submission, masochism) had to be explained to me. While I thought I might fit into the criteria for the BBW (big, beautiful women) room, my brothers once again announced I should not go there.

So there I was, trying to figure out a new name, a new persona, and a new Internet site. I joined Yahoo; the name suggested *party* to me. My much younger secretaries gave me my screen name; because I was intelligent, attractive and dyed my hair, I became "smarthotblondie."

The profile was easier. I had been reading trashy romance novels for decades and trying my hand at writing one for the last year.

So, I wrote a witty and sexy little piece:

"Lookin' for love in all the wrong places"
About me
I am intelligent, blonde (no blonde jokes, please), curvy, not into playing games, except for those intimate games involving two consenting adults. Have been a widow for years raising two children, and now I have time for me. I don't think I am looking for marriage or a long-term relationship yet. I work hard as a government lawyer, hard as a mom, hard as a romance novelist and want to play with the same intensity I bring to everything else. I have a rather high profile job, so a photo is available after you make contact.
I'm looking for:
An intelligent, sexy, funny man, who is secure enough to look at the possibilities of life, and who likes women as people. A man who is a human being first, then a friend and lover and is comfortable with the man he is and the man he almost is. (Yeah, I know it's from a movie...but which one? You get points for the right answer).
The most important thing in my life is:
The most important people in my life are my children. The most important thing in my life is honesty. And, then, of course, the Yankees.
I spend my free time:
I have great friends. I love to spend time with them drinking, dancing, dining out, going to the movies, Yankee Stadium, concerts, etc. I also like my alone time with a hot chai and a

good book and, when I have the time, the Sunday NY Times. I try to write a little erotic romance every day to offset the hours spent writing dry legal treatises. I cook when the spirit moves me, exercise because it hurts so good and have been known to boogie to the Dixie Chicks, though I prefer Springsteen. I am into Picasso, not Dali; Seurat, not Monet; Clancy, not Grisham; Beethoven and Mozart, not Wagner and Bach; Garth and Faith, not much other Country; Clapton and Rodin. I will hike up mountains, skyscrapers and national monuments. I'll walk anywhere, but my running days are over. I can't carry a tune (I'm a helluva hummer though), but I will carry your sports equipment, camera bag or picnic basket.

I thought I had done a fairly decent job of describing who I was and what I was looking for, but I worried still no one would want me. Would my words be enough? I needn't have been concerned; I immediately received numerous requests for my photo, a date and/or various sex acts. I blushed and didn't know what to do with all the attention. I thought about becoming a nun again. "In for a penny, in for a pound," my mom would say about tentative beginnings—so I forged ahead.

One night, about a week or so after I posted my profile, I found John's message. It was pretty straightforward. *Do you want to have a drink?* I looked up his profile. He lived in my town, having recently retired from the Navy as a Chief Petty Officer, and he was a few years older than me. I liked the photo of a tall, dark-haired man with a nice smile, standing next to the requisite mid-life crisis sporty red convertible. I could forgive him that because he had written a funny, clever, and very sexy little paragraph about himself in his request for a date. Though I was not crazy about the IM-type usage.

I lack a Master's by three classes, so I seek someone of intelligence as well as wit. Sounds like we are in sync with each other. Must tell u that I am very sexual and far from a quickie kind of guy. I do, however, need the communication and physical just as much as sex. Humor is very important to me too. Like u, I am not looking for a roommate (sleep over PJ parties once in awhile are ok). U will find me to be very secure with myself, so I am far from possessive, owning or controlling. Like u, I enjoy my privacy and space, so I can respect others wanting and needing. U will find me to be extremely open and honest. so ask and I'll be more than happy to answer.

We e-mailed a few times that evening. I was sufficiently interested to call him the next night. His voice was very deep and sexy with a slow drawl—a Pittsburgh accent, he told me. Before I knew it, we had a date for the following evening.

Nerves were getting the best of me all day; I kept planning to cancel because of a cold, the flu, the plague. I tried on and discarded at least a dozen outfits between the time I arrived home from work at five-thirty and quarter to seven, when I walked out the door to meet him. Jeans and a red top that matched my sparkly flip-flops and my nail polish were the result. I had showered, washed my hair, and even shaved my legs, though that meant ridding myself of the one foolproof guard against sex on a first date.

The bar where we had decided to meet was under a gazebo, behind a local bistro: quiet, intimate, a nice breeze, and the added bonus of not having to walk through a crowded restaurant and chance running into well-meaning but nosy acquaintances. I saw the red Miata he said he would be driving in the parking lot and smiled. Though it was a cliché, it was a hot little car, and I had an immediate image of myself with the wind blowing through my hair as we sped along some coastal highway.

There he was, sitting at the bar, a longneck bottle poised halfway to his lips. The tropical print shirt and jeans gave him the look of a Jimmy Buffet wannabe, but there was nothing wrong with that; he was, after all, a landlocked sailor. My heart was beating a little faster as I approached him. I deliberately slowed my gait and tried to appear cool and collected, but I was nervous as hell. I had only walked into a bar to meet a man a few times since embarking on my quest, with no small measure of success, but I was still basically shy about entering a room, any room, alone.

John turned and smiled at me with real appreciation, and most of my nerves disappeared.

He really did have an appealing smile. As I came up to him, I extended my hand. His hand reached for mine, he pulled me in. Not to be outdone by his familiarity, I leaned toward him to plant a warm, wet kiss on his cheek. I found this opening kiss established me as the one in control. And besides that, I got a good whiff of the cologne or aftershave—always a turn-on.

I heard his voice welcome me as I bent to kiss him. I smiled to myself, thinking this was going to be a very productive evening. Then I froze, my lips centimeters away from his face.

Oh. My. God! He had the dirtiest ear I had ever seen! It was not "oh, I was changing the oil in my sports car, painting the bedroom, cleaning out the attic, and I missed a spot of something that got in my ear temporary *schmutz*." This was "a Q-tip has not seen the inside or even outside of this auricular cavity in many, many months, possibly years, filth."

What do I do? What do I say?

My immediate thought, after "Yuck!" was *what other body parts are covered with crud*?

I couldn't possibly have anything more to do with this man. Personal cleanliness, though inadvertently omitted from my *requirements* on my profile, was definitely a deal-breaker. I had just assumed, erroneously I now knew, all these men would be at least clean.

I was still standing there, my hand in his, my face inches from his face, starting to feel and probably look ridiculous. I straightened, withdrew my hand and, in my best faint female voice, said, "I am so sorry, I can't do this. It's just too soon. I'm not ready." I turned, but not fast enough to miss the red flush creep across his face, and walked away. I felt terrible for embarrassing John. I hurried out to my car and drove away as quickly as I could.

Then the shudders began. Pulling the car over, gulping for breath, waves of emotion swept over me. Regret for my abrupt departure? No, that ear was still making me gag.

Disappointment at the loss of a potential lover? No, I had only invested a few e-mails and telephone calls in this man. Astonishment that one person could be so dirty? That was partly it; I had never seen a body part so completely filled with grime.

Then I realized it was absurdity. The ludicrousness of the situation reduced me to helpless giggles, tears streaming down my face, as I rocked with hilarity in my car, whooping and gasping for breath. I couldn't wait to tell my friends. It was such a funny story.

He sent an e-mail the next day, calling me a "tease." I thought about sending him a box of Q-tips but adding his story to my repertoire more than made up for the insult.

KARMA CHAMELEON

You would never have known to look at me that I was leading a double life. Mostly, I appeared to be exactly who I was: mother, lawyer, Sunday School Principal. Saturdays would find me running around in jeans, sneakers and a sweatshirt from Disney World, at the supermarket, at the garden center, in the kitchen, in the basement doing laundry. Weekday mornings I'd be driving down the Northway in my suburban mom minivan, briefcase, and purse on the front seat, trench coat over suit jacket over simple blouse, over slip, over bra. Layers of clothes over layers of fat, hiding the woman within. For years, there was no blond in my hair, no make-up on my face. No sparkle in my eyes, no smile on my lips.

Then the cracks began to appear. I fell into an affair. No strings, no future, just feeling. Again. After years in hibernation. My life had started changing from the inside out. Now the outside started to follow.

Clothes. You can't meet a lover in elastic waist jeans and a Mickey Mouse sweatshirt. You can't meet a lover in a business suit and panty hose, tasteful black patent flats. Actually, you can, but I didn't know that then. What do you wear for a tryst in the back of a Suburban, parked on the country road behind your lover's property? There will be moonlight playing across your face; there will be the bright flash of the courtesy light as you open the front door to drive home. Underwear must match, should be black and lacy, should push up where appropriate and pull in where needed. No socks, no knee-highs, no panty hose. Jeweled flip-flops in warm weather, black patent *fuck me* heels the rest of the time. Jeans that fit, a black low cut sweater to draw attention to that cleavage and away from that midriff. A shorter skirt that cuts just at the knee, not mid-calf. Mascara to darken lashes, eyeliner to make you look mysterious, lip gloss in a deep pink instead of clear. And fragrance. Something from Victoria's Secret, nothing that smells like fruit or your spice rack. Something musky or oriental. Sensuous and seductive.

The small fashion changes began to creep into my real life. The underwear was the first infiltrator. I started wearing sexy lingerie to the office. No one could tell, but I knew. Those underwire bras give you a different profile; you have to stand a little straighter. My heels got a little higher, my skirts a little shorter. As did my hair—a little shorter and a lot blonder. Nothing inappropriate. But I knew my toenails were fire engine red or hot pink. I knew under my pink blouse was a pink lace bra. And lip gloss became an essential because I was smiling more, my lips actually stretching into a wide grin several times a day. And I laughed. I laughed out loud.

I started losing weight. I was too busy to eat; and as they say, the more you exercise, the less appetite you have and the more calories you burn. And sex is a great exercise. You burn the calories, you use muscles you haven't used in a while, and the cardio workout has you gasping for breath, your heart beating as if you've just run a mile. I was slimming down and toning up. Not that I had become a size four. But I had been close to two hundred fifty pounds approaching my forty-ninth birthday, and I had lost almost fifty pounds by the end of summer. I wasn't built like a fortress anymore; I had started to resemble a French chateau, interesting structure, graceful lines, age indeterminate but showing depth and character.

The physical changes had surprising side effects, sometimes at inopportune times. I would be riding on the elevator up to my office and it would stop at the fourth floor. The slight jolt would make me shift, and I would feel the remnants of the morning's loving in my muscles, in my gut, inside. So, I would enter the office with a slight smile of remembrance tugging at my lips.

To my Jewish girlfriends, the *yentas*, I was looking better, I seemed happier and I had more energy. To my co-workers, I was on a great diet, my kids were growing and giving me some space, and I had successfully made the move from the

Democratic Party to the Republican Party to save my job. No one had any idea I was leading a double life.

The boys at work were stymied. The rumor was I was having an affair with Gerald, our tech guy. He and I laughed about that because Gerald was gay, in a relationship with a construction worker named Bryan. Gerald had become one of my best *girlfriends*. And my women associates at work were becoming really good friends, too. My neighborhood friends and the *yentas* were mostly my age; married twenty to twenty-five years, with responsible jobs and grown kids, even grandkids. I couldn't confide in them that I'd had sex with a man I had met online, a man I had no intention of dating or getting into a serious relationship with, much less "settling down."

The craziness of my life was bringing me closer to some of my other girlfriends, though. Maureen was my age. Like me, she was a nice Catholic girl who had married a nice Jewish boy, converted, and had a great life until he died in her arms at fifty, leaving her life in shambles. We changed our organizational name from *shiksa sluts* to *widows-r-us* shortly after that, as we sought solace with each other. Maureen started dating a few years after her husband died, when her youngest was in high school. When I entered the dating pool a couple of years after her, she was full of practical advice and instructive anecdotes. We would put our heads together every Saturday morning over bagels at Bruegger's, sometimes laughing so hard at the retelling of our adventures on Friday night that we risked being asked to leave on more than one occasion.

Georgeann had been my first secretary when I started working for the State. She was twenty and I was twenty-five. I danced at her wedding, her younger sister babysat my kids. She loved my late husband, whose practice was in her hometown, like a big brother. Georgeann remained one of my few friends with whom I could share memories of him without being lectured about "moving on" or "leaving the past behind." She and Maureen were my confidantes; it was with one of them that I would leave pertinent information before I headed out to meet a new *beau*. Safety in numbers and in that little white envelope that was sealed and resealed over time as I removed and added names and phone numbers of the men on my growing list.

It seemed as I opened up and became less rigid, especially in the office, my female coworkers did too. Soon, my secretary and I were chatting about more than the due date of my next decision; I was sharing romance novels with the administrative assistant and discussing new nail polish colors with our fiscal officer. A change in administration and a new boss for me certainly contributed to a more relaxed atmosphere. But I like to think we developed real affection for each other as we shared stories about the men or lack thereof in our lives over tea in the coffee room or lunches at our desks.

Gerald dubbed us "the posse," and soon thereafter, as some of our group joined the ranks of online daters with varying degrees of success, he changed our appellation to "the pussy posse." We stopped short of having sweatshirts made with our new team name.

If he was the court jester, then I was the princess. If Gerald remained in the closet to most of our co-workers, I was like the butterfly emerging from a cocoon. Integrating my new easier personality with my former almost dour demeanor, a chameleon no longer.

JOHN NUMBER TWO

Tall, dark, and handsome. Well, okay, medium height, brown-haired, and good-looking.

He would do.

Six months after I dove into the world of online dating, and my expectations were still pretty low. I was trying to be inclusive and nonjudgmental in my search for romance. The *must have* requirements I had listed in my head were damn easy to meet: not married, not an axe murderer, and not a hunchback. Amended recently to include clean, of course.

Cupid.com was my venue of choice because it was free and was easy to navigate. I was still only slightly above computer illiterate on the scale of technological abilities and did not want my ineptitude to cast dispersions on my chances for success in the world of cyber-romance. In my almost cyber-virginal state, I thought what my profile looked like was as important as its contents. I didn't realize the fact that I was breathing, employed and not interested in marriage all but guaranteed my success.

My profile was witty and wise, sexy and savvy and used a lot of alliteration. That more than made up for the absence of a photograph as far as I was concerned. Given my profession and position at the time, I did not want to be too easily recognizable to the lawyers who appeared before me, and who, I was discovering, were cruising the online dating sites in droves. I described myself fairly accurately, though, giving my real age, height and build—okay, I described myself as "curvy" rather than as a dropout from Jenny Craig, Weight Watchers and Slim-Fast. I had learned "curvy" translated to "needs to lose a few pounds" (and I still did), just as "athletic" was a man's way of saying he wanted a thin woman.

What a thrill it was to fire up my computer at the end of a long day to discover the men Cupid had sent my way. Everyday brought me at least a dozen inquiries from gentlemen in the greater Northeast. I use the term *gentlemen* loosely—I discarded without reply the married, vulgar and/or grammatically incorrect. That left me with four or five prospects each night.

One evening in early September, there was John, asking if I liked to sail. His photo showed a smiling man, leaning against the rather thick mast of what had to be a large sailboat, blue sky behind him, sun shining on a rather impressive chest. His dark brown hair was receding a bit, but still thick and wavy. I told myself the wrinkles fanning out from his brown eyes were due to the sun's glare rather than age, and I was probably half-right, even though he said he was only forty-five. He had an engaging smile and, best of all, a moustache. I am a sucker for a moustache.

John was divorced with sole custody of his adolescent son. He included a few too many details of his messy divorce, but I was used to that, probably because I was identified as a legal professional in my profile. Owning many properties, he spent his time managing real estate holdings and acquiring more. He assured me he was financially well-off. Even so, I wasn't ready to accept his invitation for a moonlight sail on Lake George. After all, this was only the first salvo in our own personal battle of the sexes. I parried with a flirtatious response about how traditional movie love scenes always culminated with waves crashing on the beach—think Burt Lancaster and Deborah Kerr in *From Here to Eternity*—and asked his opinion about making love on a beach as opposed to the deck of a sailboat.

The next night there was a photo of the sailboat in the moonlight and an impassioned plea to meet. It was a big beautiful boat, and he used full sentences and words of more than one syllable. I was so impressed I sent him my photo, the carefully chosen shot of me in my mink coat on a snowy street in Lake Placid. I almost always used this photo because it was a full- length picture of me, my hair was really blond against the dark mink, a quiet statement of my socioeconomic status, and I was heavier in the photo. If a man was still attracted to me at my chunkiest in recent years, then I had some wiggle room on the weight issue. He took the bait.

A blonde, in a mink, who mentioned sex in a literary context in the first communication, is a lethal combination on the Web. The only thing that could have garnered more interest from John was if I had mentioned I was thinking of getting my breasts enlarged. By the third night, he was begging for my phone number.

Because you never give your home telephone number to a man you are flirting with online, I asked for his phone number. I called John after pushing *67, so my number would not be revealed if he had Caller ID. He had a really deep voice, rough with some heat. He seemed a little nervous but resolute that we meet soon. Eager but not pushy, he was moving up on my *this might work out* scale.

John was taking his son to Lake George for a week's vacation, and they were leaving in two days. He was worried I might meet someone in the interim, and he would lose me before he had a chance to sweep me off my feet.

I told him the Jewish holidays were upon me, and I didn't have a lot of spare time between work and cooking, cleaning and baking for Rosh Hashanah. But he was so sweetly desperate that I took pity on him and agreed to a drive-by the next night.

We would meet in Sonny's parking lot at Exit 11. I would know him because he would be wearing a Yankees cap, big points for that, and driving a blue Miata, no points for that cool-car-diminished-by-the-midlife-crisis factor. We would just see each other, chat for a few minutes, maybe one small kiss in parting. I was starting to look forward to our chaste little tryst.

A clean fuchsia T-shirt and a jeans skort, fake tan legs and hot pink flip-flops, French manicure and pedicure, and spiked blond hair—I was ready to meet John the next night. Sounds like a lot of fuss to run out to the market for golden raisins, which was the excuse I gave my son for my departure right after dinner, but when you are almost fifty years old and easing back into dating after a decade and a half, you need all the props you can muster. Besides, my daughter and her roommate were on the way home from college, and I knew they would be expecting noodle pudding. The golden raisins were a necessity, not just an excuse.

And there he was. I pulled into the parking lot in my minivan - I was still such a suburban mom - several parking spots away from the bright blue mid-life crisis Miata. John turned to me and smiled—he had a really nice smile, all white even teeth. The chances for success were getting better and better.

John got out of his car and started walking toward me. Keeping the door locked, I rolled down the window on the passenger side of my minivan, so he could speak to me. He waved and called out to me, "Hi. How are you?" Same deep husky voice, but something was wrong. A wave of unease swept over me. *What was not right with this picture?*

He was at the passenger door and, as he leaned in the open window, I realized he was reaching up to rest his elbows on the doorframe. Reaching way up!

He was a midget!

Well, maybe not a midget. But he was short, *really* short. He could not have been even five feet tall. I was only five-foot-three, and I can easily lean into an open minivan window without reaching up. John must have been standing on his tiptoes to be able to see over the window ledge.

I'll have to include "not vertically challenged" in my list of requirements. Now what am I going to do?

I was not proud of myself for being so shallow. I realized that even as short as I am, I have a height requirement in men. They had to be taller than me. John was smiling at me and talking, and I couldn't hear him because of this conundrum ringing in my brain. *How am I going to get out of this?* I then realized, fortunately, my cell phone was also ringing. Grateful for the temporary reprieve, I answered it.

"Hi, Mommy, we got home early." My daughter's voice sang into my ear. "Can you bring us some pizza, we're starving!"

"Of course, honey, that's okay. It will be all right." I assured my confused daughter. "I'll be right home."

I disconnected the call and turned to John. I told him how sorry I was I couldn't stay, but my daughter had just gotten home from college, and there was a problem that required my immediate attention. I assured him we would talk when he returned from Lake George. Leaving him open-mouthed and gaping at me, I sped away.

I was disconcerted enough to drive all the way south to Exit 9 of the Northway to pick up pizza, certain he would somehow turn up and catch me in my lie. It wasn't until later that night as I reread his profile that I stopped beating myself up and started to get angry. He listed his height as five-foot-eight He had lied. *Did he think I wouldn't notice?*

When he called a week later, I felt no compunction in telling him I couldn't see him because I had gotten engaged.

BAD BOYS

Why is it we love bad boys? Where is the justice in that? We complain men are dogs, yet we always head right for the mongrel cur waiting in the corner, knowing we'll come to him, as we bypass the vigilant German Shepherds, the loyal Collies and the hard-working Sheepdogs.

The mongrel cur waits around every corner, tempting us with his lack of respect, luring us in with his easy, sleazy gaze and we come.

Good men complain women really don't want them, and they are probably right. It must be the Eve gene we inherited from the first woman, the desire to reach for that which is just beyond our grasp, to taste the forbidden fruit, to push the acceptable into the prohibited.

My sister-in-law has always called me a "stray-dog-magnet." She would always say, "Girl, you walk into a room with ten men, all equally good looking, well dressed, and all smiling. Nine are good guys and one is a bad boy. You unerringly head for the bad boy every time. It's like a magnet." It's true; save for my husband, my heart has always been given to the bad boy, the rebel, the felon, the unattainable married man.

It's their eyes. I know it is their eyes. It's the twinkle, but it's more. In the brown or green or grey depths, I see everything that could be but shouldn't. My shrink says it's because I was raised to be the good girl, and I *was*; the good wife, and I *was*; the good mother, and I *was*. And what did it get me? I was the least favored in my parents' home, I was almost popular in high school but never the prom queen, and when I finally was rewarded for my good behavior by getting a great husband, he was taken from me. My affinity for bad boys was my small rebellion against the strict rules of my life under which I have always chafed.

And the fun. Why are bad boys so much fun? Is it because rules make us humorless, social constraints tie us down, but bad boys flaunt the rules and thumb their noses at social mores? They take us along on the roller-coaster rides of their lives. The highs are so high we think the lows, which are so low, will be nothing in comparison.

But the bad boys get off the ride without warning or care and leave you with just a queasy stomach and a bad taste in your mouth.

And still, it was the bad boys I responded to time and time again.

CRAZY

Summer makes me crazy. Raised in Northern New York, I have a low tolerance for heat. Still overweight and in those *menopausal* years, heat and humidity were my worst enemies. And my husband died in August, after thirty-two days in the hospital. I could still remember what happened to him on each day of his hospitalization, paralyzed from the neck down. On this day, his heart stopped. On that day, he ran a fever. On the next day, he could feel a burning in his fingertips. From July 8 to August 10, my mood swings from depressed to angry to fatalistic.

I make my worst decisions in the summer. And that first summer of online dating was no different. As I emerged from my cocoon, I seemed to shed my caution and my good judgment as easily as I was now shedding my clothes. And most of the time, I didn't care. The psychologist whom I had seen on and off since my husband died in 1988 opined it was a response to my near- perfect behavior for the last fifteen years. I had been so good, for so long, now that the shackles of my self-imposed loneliness were off, I was rebellious and reckless.

But my recklessness did not include engaging in unprotected sex. In every encounter, I insisted upon the use of condoms. And that was quite a difference for me, after years with my husband when they were unnecessary. But, that was one of the conditions for sex in the new millennium, and while I was willing to take some risks, I was not willing to risk contracting HIV. Every three months or so, I showed up at my doctor's office for a blood test. The first time I asked him to include STD and HIV testing in my semiannual blood work, he almost fell off his stool. When

I explained why, he hugged me and said, "About time!" All of these requirements that had not been present the last time I dated (in the 1970s) were not enough to deter me.

It was my deficit in orgasms that was the focus of my attention at the time. During all of those years alone, I figured I had missed out on approximately seven thousand orgasms. I believe that was a conservative estimate because my husband and I had enjoyed what is euphemistically known as "a good sex life" in the two years prior to his death. Loss of weight and loss of uterus had been powerful incentives to make up for the early childbearing, infant and toddler stages of our marriage. Those years when the act of sex was often messy, inconvenient or impossible to accomplish for days and weeks on end. My husband was a willing participant in any intimacy I had a mind for, and I had a very fertile mind, given the impetus from the romance novels I devoured. We loved loving each other.

And I missed his touch every day. I missed everything about him, especially in the summer. So, now that there were interesting, available men who were pursuing me, I took my gloves off and entered the arena. I was determined to make up for the lost years, for the lost intimacies. I was a little crazy, and I just didn't care.

PHONE SEX

I got sucked into phone sex the same way I got sucked into most other madcap adventures I have embarked upon in recent years—impulse, curiosity, and I'm a writer.

My stupid cell phone was acting up, so I dialed 611 for customer service. I got a friendly male voice on the other end. I described my dilemma, and friendly-male-voice, who by now had given me his name and work location, started on the problem. We chatted while he delved into the computer mysteries of Verizon Wireless. My issues quickly solved, I thanked him for his assistance and was about to end the call, when he said, "I hope you don't mind me saying this, but you have a really lovely voice."

I always thought my voice sounded thin and weak, but I thanked him nonetheless.

He responded by telling me lots of women used their cell phones to conduct "business" while going about their daily chores, such as laundry, ironing, cooking.

"I know many women who use their cell phones to make a little extra cash from home."

"Really?" As a single mom, with a mortgage, college tuition, two kids and a State paycheck that hadn't seen a raise in two years, I always needed extra cash.

"Yes, while the kids are napping or they are doing chores, they have phone sex."

Really!

"Some of them call customer service from time to time, and I have to tell you that you have the sexiest voice I have ever heard on the phone. If you ever think of setting up a 900 line, give me a call, and I can walk you through it. I think you would be great!"

Right!

Once again, I thanked friendly-male-voice and hung up. *Grinning.*

At that point, I had been having phone sex for quite a while. Not for money. For research.

The men I met online, in chat rooms or dating sites were as varied as the shoes strewn across my closet floor. Some practical, some frivolous, some sexy, some sturdy, some totally inappropriate and some just about right. How was I to know who would be the man for me?

A test drive. You look at a new or used car, you take it for a test drive before committing to anything. You plan to have sex with someone, you test the waters first. I could have gone on the requisite coffee date, then the wine date, then the dinner date, then the why-don't-you-come-back-to-my-place? date. But, at my age, I didn't want to waste the time. How many good dating years did I reasonably have left? I figured ten, maybe fifteen years tops, before my knees gave out, my boobs sagged below my waistline, my vagina dried up and my libido disappeared. I was meeting about ten men a day online. Narrowing the field down to two or three was easy: I eliminated the married ones (at least the ones who admitted they were married, and more than you can believe were up front about that), the ones who could not write a complete sentence and the ones who had photos of their proudest part, and I don't mean their hairline, posted on their profile. I eliminated some after a few computer chats: too much detail about the ex-wife, too much focus on their wants and desires, too religious (you would be surprised by the number of men who hold themselves out as devoutly religious who are interested in some really nasty sex...or maybe not, given Jimmy Swaggart and Jim Bakker) or just too boring.

Then we progressed to the telephone. A few lost their chance with me because of an irritating voice or poor phone manners ("Let me just take this other call, hold on." Or, "I have the game on, you don't mind, do you?"). But, if they were interesting or funny, intelligent or politically correct, they made the first cut. I bent the rules if they had really sexy voices, voices like Alan

Rickman, Clark Gable, Jeremy Irons or my psychologist. Some I readily agreed to meet after one or two phone calls. They were the ones who I either knew for certain I was going to have sex with or who had piqued my curiosity enough to fast-forward them to the in-person first kiss. But, I would never get to first base much less that coveted home run, if I vetted them all in person.

The ones who had made the first cut and progressed directly to "Go" had to pass the phone sex test at some point. They were no match for me; I had studied with the best.

When I first went online, my brothers had urged me to practice in chat rooms. That and changing my screen name had been their best bits of advice. I had so many questions then. Was flirting still the same? What was the current vernacular? What were fifty-five-year-old men interested in from a fifty-year-old woman? But, how was I to find out? Online chat rooms! There, I had found interesting men at all hours of the day and night. Some were just lonely. Some were just horny. Some were just like me, back into dating after decades away from the game, trying to find their way. Some were in California, Washington, Colorado, Chicago, Florida, DC, England; some were in Albany, Saratoga or Lake Placid.

I practiced on the faraway ones; it was not likely I would be flying to LA or Naples or London for sex.

Michael-on-the-beach had the sexiest voice and the sexiest body; he was 30, a traveling sales tech manager from Florida. He called late at night from the road, his voice urgent and deep, full of naughtiness, as he talked me through one incredible peak after another. His sharp intake of breath and low moan let me know that we had lift-off.

Tony wrote for the *Chicago Tribune*. He had just broken up with his long-time girlfriend and was a lonely thirty-five-year-old. He called just as the sun was rising; he had to be at the paper by seven-thirty in the morning. He was full of practical advice for dating in the new millennium: blocked phone numbers, condoms, and pineapple juice to sweeten the taste of you-know-what. He groaned into a climax, low, deep and gritty moans. And then a short, relieved laugh and wishes for a good day.

Michael-slow-and-deep, a fifty-year-old lawyer from Seattle, told stories—erotic short stories—designed to tease and titillate. He drew it out, prolonged the experience, digressed into discussions of the legal or political issues of the day, and then slid back into eroticism as easily as I imagined he would slide into me. He chuckled at my gasps then echoed my sighs with his own. The next morning, he always sent a gorgeous photo he had taken of a beautiful flower or a shimmering sunrise.

Darren was the precocious twenty-seven-year-old from London who called for a bedtime story. I always had to tell it in the first person: "I was out with my friend, Georgeann, and we met a guy who couldn't choose between us, so we..." He would swear at completion, four-letter- word expletives mixed liberally with references to God and Jesus, but almost laughing throughout, so great was his glee at the ending of another trip through my wickedly creative mind.

Donald, from Edinburgh, was like listening to a very naughty Sean Connery detail one bawdy adventure after another, interspersed with concerned questions about my progress and well being. He was the only one of my long-distance telephone lovers who I ever met in person and let me just say I was not disappointed.

Shaved Snake was a screenwriter living in a beach cottage on Cape May. His name was Rick, and he wrote incredible erotic short stories about the two of us in a mountain retreat, on the beach, driving along the highway to nowhere. I melted at each story. And his voice, when we finally spoke, was dark and dirty. He was a demanding and dominating lover on the phone, his years in the military giving his voice a command tone even when he was whispering erotic endearments. He was the one who got away, the one phone lover I always longed to meet but never did.

So, the first date wannabes had stiff competition in measuring up to the standards set by my unseen, deep-voiced seducers. And, sadly, some of them just did not make the cut. Most needed very little urging to slip under the spell of my seductive voice. I might mention I was wearing black silk or perhaps nothing at all. That was usually enough. I might seek input into a particularly erotic scene in my yet-to-be-published first novel. That was pretty much all I needed to reel them into my net of dark images and forbidden pleasures. I admit to often being a bit detached from the conversation. I was testing them; I already knew what my interests and my limits were. I knew what my voice was like at the moment of completion, breathy, reverent, repetitious, ending in a slow, deep-throated chuckle. It drove them mad.

Their voices floated through the phone lines, each one different. I labeled them: shouters, moaners, sighers, irreverent, prayerful. Laughter and groans were fine, heavy breathers were okay, too. Some went too far. Gary, the cop, who called me a bitch at his final moment, was never spoken to again. Neither was the man who called out, "Mommy, Mommy!" Or the one who was reduced to grateful sobs. Some made it to the home run club, despite their rather bizarre exclamations.

So, after several months of cybersex, phone sex and the real thing, I had to chuckle when Verizon Wireless's friendly-male-voice told me I would be great at phone sex. *Great!* I was Dina, Warrior Princess. I was fan-fucking-tastic!

THE RABBI

I don't think of him very much anymore. Only when something jostles my memory, shaking the dust off the box I put him in, loosening the ribbons I tied in a neat bow on top when I put him out of my mind and my heart. If I am at services when the Torah portion for Bereshit is read, I think of him. When someone begins the Blessings before the Haftorah, I start. And one day, in the car as I returned from early morning services, listening to *The Yiddish Policeman's Union* read by Peter Riegert, I heard the name: Menachem, called Mendel, called Mendele as a sweet nickname. The exact pronunciation of his name, followed by the nickname said in just that way, coupled with the echoes of Hallel from the morning's service, pulled the lid off the box and put him front and center again.

It was summer of the year I jumped back into the dating pool, the year of my most acute attack of craziness. Careening from one man to the next and back again and then into the arms of a third, I was at the apex of my power. Dina, Warrior Princess, was on the prowl, taking names and kicking ass up and down the East Coast. There was no man I could not have, and very few I wanted for very long. I haunted the chat rooms, practicing my lines, my approach, satisfying my curiosity about what was new, what was available. I was smug and smutty and very much above it all. Not looking for love, not looking for a long-term relationship or even a short-term relationship, I was almost masculine in my approach to dating: love 'em and leave 'em. Move on, move forward, do not look back.

I think it was in the self-pleasure chat-room on Yahoo that we first met. People talked about what they wanted and what they needed and sometimes derived some measure of release from the discussion. After my first cyber-sex experience with Ten-Inch Tim, I had learned quickly. Now, I found it all vaguely amusing…that my words would get some guy off, all while I mimicked his need and desire with my typing of "oooh" and "aaaah." I thought, *how did they think a woman managed it?* Typing furiously, moving the action along, all while I was supposed to be touching here and there? I was not that coordinated and frankly, didn't want to get my keyboard messy. So, I scripted passionate trysts in cyber-space, taking notes about wants and needs, sometimes laughing, sometimes sighing; finishing my evenings with writer's cramp and vague longings.

And then there he was. His screen name was Mendele, so I assumed he was Jewish, and he was. I was forty-nine and he was forty-five. He lived on the Jersey Shore, managing his family's deli. He was separated, he said; his wife had moved out and left him with the children. He was funny and sweet. We chatted for a long time, agreeing to exchange pictures via e-mail. I had a decent picture for online romance now. In it, I was sexy and blond, at night in the darkness of my bedroom, all soft lights and a hint of black lace. Mendele's photo showed soft brown hair, big gray eyes and a full brown beard. He was wearing a purple T-shirt and purple plaid boxer shorts, and I noticed his nice legs. He sent me his telephone number a few days and numerous e-mails later. I called around ten o'clock one evening, after my son had ensconced himself in his room. Mendele's voice was low, deep and musical. I fall in love with voices, and I fell almost in love with his.

Soon, we were talking every night, about everything…being Jewish, having kids, living alone after years of living with another, the world, music, movies and the Yankees. I liked him, I was beginning to really like him.

Now comfortable with him, I began a phone conversation one evening by teasing him about his screen name; joking that we had both chosen old-fashioned Jewish names for our aliases: Dina for me, Mendele for him.

"But, that's my real name," he said, sounding somewhat confused by my assumption it was an alias.

"Mendele is your real name?" I squeaked, because this made no sense. "But, that's an old Jewish name."

"So?"

"So, your parents must be Orthodox if they gave you such a name."

"They are."

From what I knew of the Orthodox world, I could not believe it was possible he was still Orthodox and chatting up women on Internet dating sites. So I asked.

"How do they feel about you not being Orthodox anymore?"

"I'm still Orthodox."

"Right. How can you be Orthodox and be fooling around online?" I was becoming suspicious, really suspicious.

"I'm not fooling around online. I just wanted to meet a nice woman."

"Really?"

"Yes, really. And I found you." I was beginning to have some doubts, but before I could voice them, he continued.

"Listen, I have something else to tell you. Are you sitting down?" "Yes. *What?*"

"I'm not only Orthodox, I'm a cantor and a rabbi."

Okay, that is when I knew I was going to Hell. I had been flirting with an Orthodox rabbi.

A separated Orthodox rabbi. I had been having cybersex with a semi-married cantor. *Damn.* I told him this could not be happening. How could he expect me to believe what we had was anything more than a lark for him, given who he was and what I was not?

He made protestations to the contrary. It would be fine. I was so smart and so funny and so Jewish. I was perfect. He cared for me. And I believed him.

Our telephone calls became a mixture of passion and prayer. He was a trained cantor. I was a convert who had never attended Hebrew School as a child and never made my Bat Mitzvah. Now, the old guys from my synagogue thought I could set a good example for other women in our congregation who had not been able to or had not wanted to make a Bat Mitzvah at the age of thirteen, by becoming Bat Mitzvah in the year I turned forty-nine. I had just started studying when I met Mendele online and was struggling with both the Hebrew and the melody. In between breathy sighs and explicit language, he helped me learn my Haftorah portion (the prophetic text accompanying that week's Torah reading, traditionally chanted by the Bat Mitzvah as part of the ceremony) and the blessings. It was insane and intoxicating. And inexplicably spiritual.

Mendele professed love for me. I derided him. I am not a lawyer for nothing. I wanted him to love me, but I couldn't believe he did. I argued that Orthodox men can only marry Orthodox women if they want to maintain an Orthodox home. A Conservative convert was no better than a non-Jew in the hierarchy of his world. In that world non-Jewish women were only good for one thing and it wasn't marriage.

He objected. He believed I was a good and pious Jew. He also believed I was the answer to his prayers after a long bout of celibacy during his separation from his wife. He talked about the future. I was filled with longing.

We decided to meet. I was to spend a few days at the shore with my friend Rachel, a nice Jewish girl who now lived in New Jersey. I would meet him at a Sheraton on my way home. My friend protested my plan.

"They are all liars." She doesn't much like Orthodox men, comparing them to the men she had met growing up on Long Island.

"No, he's modern Orthodox. He's different," I explained.

"He doesn't believe you are a Jew. You know what that makes you to him."

"He knows I am a Jew. He's even helping me with my prayers."

Well, that made her laugh. My Bat Mitzvah preparations were a source of great amusement and pride among my friends, as I was to be the first woman to be a Bat Mitzvah in our congregation. And I was the convert; many of them, born Jewish, had not had a Bat Mitzvah at the age of thirteen. And here I was, forty-nine years old, the most recent convert and the most devout, practicing my prayers with my cyber-lover. It was the stuff of a Michael Chabon novel!

I arrived at the hotel first. I hopped into the shower and changed into a negligee. Black silk with gold lace. After a few days on the beach, I was actually somewhat tan and really blond. My nails were blood red.

Mendele called from the parking lot. "Are you there?"

"Yes." I gave him the room number. "Leave your tallis in the car."

"Why?"

"I'm not kissing with you while you're wearing a prayer shawl." I didn't want to tempt fate.

There was a knock on the door. I opened it to find a sweet-faced, totally Orthodox-looking man smiling at me. White shirt, black trousers. Black yarmulke. Curls tucked behind his ears. He looked like a rabbi.

The door closed softly behind him as he took me in his arms. He was a great kisser. He had just come from the deli where he worked and tasted of onions and salt. Like a bialy. I laughed. He jumped into the shower and emerged wrapped in the hotel white terry robe. We fell onto the bed in a tangle of terry cloth and silk. The condom was quickly employed, and we slid into each other, damp and demanding. A touch. Another and another. Then completion. *God.*

He rolled off me and onto his back. I rolled onto my stomach, gasping. *Damn.* Laughing, I raised my eyes to his. And froze.

He had that *deer-in-the-headlights* look. I knew that look. "Tell me," I demanded.

"What?"

"Tell me. Tell me that you aren't really separated. Tell me I just had sex with a married man."

"She moved back on Monday. I didn't know how to tell you." I was so pissed, I almost snarled at him.

"You didn't know how to tell me and still get me to fuck you."

"Don't hate me."

"I don't hate you. I'd have to care to hate you." A lie, but soon to be true, as I felt all feeling for him die in me.

I made him leave, but not before I made him satisfy me one more time. Already damned, I supposed. And I made him call the front desk and confirm the room was billed to his credit card.

I felt dirty and disappointed. I showered again, washing him off me and out of me. If only I could erase him from my soul as easily as I removed any trace of him from skin and hair.

Wrapped in my beach jammies, I settled in. My cell phone rang. It was Rachel. "Tell me you haven't slept with him yet."

"He just left."

"Oh, my God, he's married!" We said it at the same time.

Rachel had asked the president of her shul if he knew a Mendele Silverman, explaining that she had a friend who wondered if Rachel and Mendele were related since they had the same last name, saying her friend didn't realize that Silverman was as common a name among Jews as Smith was among Gentiles. The man replied that of course he knew Mendele. Mendel. *Mendele* was his son-in-law and the father of his eight grandchildren. His daughter, Mendele's wife, had been away most of the summer with their children at Orthodox summer camp in the Catskills where she worked as a counselor to defray the camp tuition.

Mendele had the nerve to call the next day to ascertain if I was angry with him. I was not. He had damaged my heart and my pride, but I was no longer angry. God, on the other hand, was, I so informed him. Then, I told him what I knew. He was terrified. I told him he was stupid; he had risked not only his marriage, but, given his background, he could have lost his children, his job, his place in the community…everything to have sex with me.

"It was worth it."

I was pleased to hear it but not appeased.

"You are a fool. And you're going to Hell."

"*What?*"

"You might have fooled everyone. But, you didn't fool God. You committed adultery with a *shiksa*. You are damned. I, on the other hand, am unmarried and, by your standards, an ignorant outsider. God will not punish me. But, you lied, you cheated and you fornicated with a heathen. You are going to Hell." I paused.

"Oh, and next time you fool around online, change your name. The next *shiksa* you fuck might not be as forgiving as me."

I made my Bat Mitzvah months later. I thought of *Mendele*, briefly, as I chanted the prayer after the Haftorah reading…the one he had taught me. Rachel caught my eye and smiled a secret smile. I knew what she was thinking: *he* was in temple, chanting the same prayer. And he was remembering me. He would always remember me. I smiled back.

RICHARD

Absolutely, baby! But say it with an Oklahoma drawl—yes, they do have a distinctive drawl in Oklahoma. A bit more country and less in-your-face than Texas. Not twangy, kind of sexy, really.

The first time I heard Richard say, "Absolutely, baby," I grinned. Then I smiled for the rest of the day every time I thought about it. You have to love a guy who will put a smile on your face. And I did. I slipped into cyber-love with a fifty-three-year-old, white-haired, bespectacled, retired Army sergeant, now San Francisco detective, as easily as a sailboat slips into a deep-water, rocky cove.

I had been practicing my flirting skills in one of Yahoo's chat rooms—probably the "over fifty and loving it" room, although it might have been the more intrepid "self-gratification" chamber. It was a Sunday morning, and I was cruising. And then, there he was. He was "Topcop" and I was "Dina, Warrior Princess." His opening line was "Hello, baby!"

I wasn't looking for love; I was looking for fun, distraction, and maybe a healthy dose of self-esteem. I had decided it was time to finally emerge from my cocoon of sadness to see if I could feel *anything* for a man again. And after Mendel, I had found I could feel not just physically but emotionally, too. I was hesitant and still safeguarded my heart, but I had really liked some of the men I had met. I was still totally taken aback by the response of men to me— and my response to them.

I had developed an addiction to the thrill of all those hello messages popping up every time I signed into a chat room. I got so good I could flirt with four separate men at a time. Lest I confuse names, I called them all *Darlin'*. It worked.

Richard was separated from his wife Janie (yes, Dick and Jane). His son had followed him into the military police by joining the Army right out of high school. His daughter had suffered a traumatic brain injury in a car accident, and his wife had withdrawn into the care of their daughter and an obsession for support groups. And the church. Richard (I just couldn't call him Dick) was adrift and looking for a flirtation too, while he decided what direction his life should take. I learned all this in the first half hour of chatting with him online. My rule was married men were off-limits. But he said he was separated, and we had developed an immediate rapport given his law enforcement background and my judicial status. And he liked my boobs.

In the chat rooms, I never showed a picture of my face. If I liked someone, and I felt comfortable, they got the *red lace* picture. Just my chest encased in a gorgeous Victoria's Secret red lace bra. No one except my gynecologist could identify me from that picture. And I got a real ego boost from the barrage of complimentary expletives that always followed immediately after I pressed the *send* button. Yeah, Richard was hooked by the red lace bra.

What followed were several months of e-mails, phone calls, letters and packages. He would call at seven in the morning. Pacific time, just as he signed onto his computer at work. I took my tea break then, shutting the door of my office as soon as I heard his cheerful "Hello, baby!" It was a lovely start to the day. There were other calls later depending on our workloads. We talked on my drive home from work and then three or four hours later on his drive home. He started sending cute cards to the office (my son was still living at home, and he brought in the mail, so nothing was sent to my house). Then packages started arriving. He often shopped at the Post Exchange at the local airbase and knew I loved chocolates. The first two-pound box of Godiva arrived about one month after we *met*. I called him from the office, dark chocolate truffle melting down my throat, to express my thanks and that of Cecilia, my secretary, who was in on the secret. She scouted out the mailroom early every morning to grab anything from Richard so the mail clerk wouldn't open it. The next week, there was perfume from Victoria's Secret, another box of Godiva for me and a small one for Cecilia. She and our friend, Georgeann, started showing up in my office around ten o'clock every morning to say hello to Richard. Sometimes he would put us on speaker phone, and the three blondes from New York would greet the morning shift of the San Francisco Detective Division, Fraud Investigation Unit, with a cheery "Hello, baby!"

We played one-upmanship for a while: he sent me Godiva, I baked him oatmeal raisin cookies; he sent me a Starbucks card, I sent him a coffee mug. He gave me a life membership in the NRA, I retaliated with one for the ACLU. The high point came one fateful morning when a rather large package arrived from California. Both Georgeann and Cecilia came slithering into my office just after nine o'clock with a big box and even bigger grins. I closed the door and tore it open to discover small boxes of Godiva for both of them, another small one for my daughter, and a golden five-pound box with a silk rose for me. Tucked around the candy were bottles of Passionate Kisses perfume, lotion and bubble bath. At the bottom was a small, flat, square package wrapped in tissue. It felt too heavy to be jewelry, but it was. *Steel bracelets*, otherwise known as handcuffs. The man had sent me Smith & Wesson official police-issue handcuffs!

Engraved with my name, I saw as soon as I slid them out of the box. Then I did what every woman would do in the same situation: I slipped one cuff on my wrist and snapped it closed. Unfortunately, Cecilia grabbed the dangling cuff and followed suit. There we were, handcuffed together in my office, door closed, giggling. Then Georgeann sagely observed that we didn't have the key. Panic set in!

The phone rang. "Hello, baby!"

"Hello, Richard."

"I sent you a big package this time."

"We just opened it. The girls thank you for the chocolate."

The red-faced ladies in my office chorused their thanks in rather strangled tones.

"There's a surprise in there for you."

"I know. I found it."

There was a pause on the other end of the line. I heard him switch on the speakerphone. "You read the instructions first, didn't you?"

"What instructions?"

My phone was filled with whoops of male laughter. "Are you wearing them now?"

"Well, I'm wearing one. My secretary is wearing the other." Now there were chortles and catcalls.

"Let me get this straight: there is a blond judge and a blond secretary handcuffed together in a NYS office, and you don't know where the key is, do you?"

"Officer, this has ceased to be humorous. Where's the damn key?" I responded in my best judicial voice.

Oh, California was having a field day with this one. The detectives were howling in San Francisco.

"Baby, they're in the same little box, taped inside a piece of tissue."

Georgeann fished the key out of the box and unlocked us just before she, too, collapsed in laughter.

"Ladies, you made our day! We're on our way to a stakeout and it's pouring rain. The image of two sexy blondes handcuffed together will keep us warm for the rest of the morning."

"Well, I'm glad we could be of service." I gave in to a giggle.

"Absolutely, baby!"

I wish I could say our entire affair was as light-hearted and fun. But I fell in love with him on the phone. He fell in love with me. We came to depend on each other as sounding boards, friends, and cyber-lovers. We didn't mean for it to happen, we were supposed to be just distractions, but we became more. We even talked about meeting. In San Antonio so he could buy me red cowgirl boots. In Las Vegas so we could gamble and eat and make love at all hours.

Then the e-mail you never want to see.

I'm Janie, Dick's wife. I found your e-mail address. I know he told you we were separated, but we are getting back together. A lot of it was my fault, but some of it was his. He told me that you kept telling him that he had to work as hard on his marriage as he was working on flirting with you. He promised me that he would never talk to you again. Good-bye. And thank you.

He broke his promise to her. One last letter. He wrote Janie had revealed in counseling that she knew there was another woman, and it was breaking her heart. Richard hadn't believed she still had feelings for him. When he realized she did, he knew he had to make his marriage work. He begged my forgiveness. He told me there would always be an aging cop who thought of me every morning in his office as he drank from his *I Love NY* coffee mug, as he gazed at the small painting of a red sailboat I had made him at Christmas, and as he remembered that he had been lucky enough to be loved by two women in his lifetime.

I had foreseen this. On the back of the sailboat painting, I had copied a bit of verse from *For My Lover, Returning to His Wife*, by Anne Sexton, where she likens her lover's wife to being his must-have, a monument, reliable like a dinghy. Like the poet, I was a luxury, a red sloop, painted in watercolor. Easily washed off.

Absolutely, baby.

FRIENDS WITH BENEFITS

Fuck buddies are good to have around. There are times when all you want to do is get laid. You just want that mindless explosion to ease the tension, fill the void, calm your restless spirit. Who better to call than a willing man, tested and not found lacking, reliable and at the ready? Every woman should have a fuck buddy or two or five. I accumulated several over my first year of Internet dating. Some of them came and went, some stayed with me for several years, in between and sometimes, during, the relationships that followed.

Pitney-Bowes Ken was one of the first. Always eager, always ready to buy lunch or dinner, get a room at the Comfort Inn, and take care of me before I took care of him (unless the Red Sox had won). Then thirty minutes of tangled sheets and back to work, or back home to real life. He always patted me on the bottom as he left and promised me, "The Red Sox are going all the way this year…or next year."

Frank from Stillwater was not as flush as Ken but would gladly come over anytime I called, whenever my house was free of children, to delight in the pleasures of my "Rubenesque glory" (his words). He would rub my back when we were through, tucking me in before he left, making sure the front door was locked as he whistled his way out into the frosty night. A sweet thank you would be in my e-mail inbox the next morning.

Then there was "Zoomie," a retired Air Force pilot, now middle school teacher, from Glens Falls. All he needed was a phone call to shower, hop in his truck, and speed down the Northway for a booty call. Well, he wanted cookies, too. I would call around seven or eight or even nine at night, horny and needy, and tell him I had baked cookies. Ranger cookies, all soft and spicy, full of nuts and raisins, were his favorite. He once drove to me at midnight, in the dead of winter, on a school night, to minister to my needs, when he heard me say, "I have Ranger cookies cooling on the kitchen counter." He would grab two before he headed up my stairs. Services rendered, he would stuff his pockets for the trip home.

All nice men, all attuned to my needs, all available, all likeable, but men for whom I felt nothing more than sexual attraction and the easy affection you might have for your favorite handyman.

Friends with benefits are an entirely different species. They share the common denominator with fuck buddies: men who are ready for sex whenever you ask. But, that is where the similarities end.

Biff became my first *friend with benefits*. He was also my first *in-person* conquest, early in my dating adventures. The owner of a popular Mexican restaurant near my office, he was personable and sexy. Almost bald, with a bit of a gut from too many Dos Equis, he was still cute, with bright blue, dangerous eyes framed by thick black lashes and an easy, bad boy smile. The posse and I had decided to head over to his restaurant on Fridays for the generous lunch buffet and the cheap margaritas. Perhaps the second or third time we arrived, en masse, he stopped by the table to greet us. Then he stopped by again to make sure our drinks were okay. Then he stopped by again to ensure we had everything we wanted from the buffet. Always with a smile, a flirtatious wink, and a touch on the shoulder. My shoulder. I didn't think anything of it until our bill arrived with a credit for the margaritas.

"He didn't charge us for the margaritas. I wonder why?" I mused as I studied the bill.

"Duh!" Georgeann snorted.

"What?"

"He was hitting on you," Cecilia chimed in.

"No, he was flirting with you two," I protested.

"He was flirting with you, girlfriend!" Maxie and Chris agreed.

I was stunned. It was less than a year since I had jumped into the dating pool, and I still considered myself a minnow. Biff was definitely a barracuda. He was smooth, handsome, cocky.

As we left, though, he was there, smiling.

"Thanks for the margaritas!" we chorused.

"My pleasure, ladies, come back soon. Real soon."

He handed each of us his card, good for a free margarita on our return visit.

After that, we became regulars. Every Friday, there we were, same booth, same free pitcher of margaritas. Same Biff. I learned he was a workaholic, divorced, and he loved his two kids, his aging dad and his boat. He discovered I was a lawyer, had been a judge and wanted to be a romance writer. He gave me his e-mail address. I sent him a story about his boat and warm bodies. I was still more comfortable with written flirtations. And the phone. I did some of my best work on the phone. That quickly led to a date, of sorts. He worked every night, but we planned that I would come to the restaurant, late in the evening, just before closing. Then we would see. Cecilia accompanied me, and we perched on stools at the bar. Biff made us our favorite margaritas: blue for me, tangerine for Cecilia. He came over frequently to check on us, always with a touch on my arm, back, or waist. Cecilia had to leave at ten…two little kids to get up for soccer practice the next morning. I was fine at the bar alone.

The restaurant was emptying out. Chairs put up on tables, lights being dimmed. Soon it was just Biff and me alone in the bar. He turned out the neon sign and sank down on a stool next to me.

"What are you drinking?" I asked.

"1800 straight."

"I'll get it."

I slipped around the bar to play bartender. What fun! I served him as we chatted easily. By then we knew each other's kids' names, parents' names, last lover's name. Doing shots seemed to be the next logical step for the evening. And with my favorite Tequila: Sammy Hagar's Cabo Wabo Silver.

Like the Country song says, "tequila makes her clothes fall off" and mine did. We never made it out of the bar. Exciting because of the danger of discovery (huge windows facing

Central Avenue on a Friday night), erotic in the dim-colored lights, the cool leather of the booths arousing us. We drank and laughed and had tequila sex for hours. Then consumed huge amounts of tortilla chips and espinacha dip. Exhausted, I teetered out to my car on Biff's arm, a big smile still on my face. He made me call him when I arrived safely home. And so we began.

There were other lovers for me; I know there were other lovers for him. But, when I needed him, he was almost always there for me. Sometimes, it was a quick encounter in his office during lunch hour. When we could, we slipped into a room at the motel next door for an afternoon or evening of wild and crazy sex, tequila, and Mexican food. Biff would eventually see me through many bad times with my kids, my job and my other lovers. He listened and he shared: his opinions, his advice and his own stories. I trusted him with some of my darkest fears. He also fed hoards of friends and relatives at every party I hosted, with boxes of fresh chips and vats of his fresh espinacha. And at every lunch, there was a pitcher of margaritas.

His restaurant is now closed and he is gone, but I know if I call, he will answer.

Tom, who quickly earned the nickname "Critter," became my favorite friend with benefits; emphasis on both *friend* and *benefit*. We met online a year after I met Biff. He gave the cleverest answer to date to my break-the-ice-are-you-an-idiot question: name five Supreme Court Justices (You would not believe how many men did not know the answer to that question, or even how to find out the answer—Duh!). I had intended the answer to be five sitting members as a test of current events/law/politics, but my phrasing was not clear. So, his answer—John Marshall, Benjamin Cardozo, William O. Douglas, Thurgood Marshall and Whizzer White— caught me off guard and sent him to the top of that week's class.

Tom was an electrician, former International Brotherhood of Electrical Workers shop steward and then family court mediator. He had gone back to electrical work in his retirement. Bronx-born of a large Italian family, he was a Vietnam veteran and, as a result, a twice-divorced, recovering alcoholic. He was naughty, too. His profile had no picture. Later, he was to send me one: his penis. *A stalwart and sturdy member if I ever saw one*. I laughed and laughed when I sent that message to him and read his reply: *at your service, Judge*. I already liked him so much I let him get away with the penis photo, especially since the follow-up photo of a grinning Italian guy with dark hair and soft brown eyes was so sweet.

He didn't let me get away with anything in our first verbal encounters. He questioned my politics, my religion, and my sense of family. I was having a difficult time with my son, away for his first year at college, and Tom offered sage, if sometimes, harsh opinions about my methods for dealing with my son's escapades. I learned to appreciate his workingman, centrist, hard knocks advice. And then we met.

He looked like what he was, a tough guy who has lived a rough life. Until you saw the twinkle in his dark brown eyes and the dimple in his cheek. Average height, he has a prizefighter's face and build, salt and pepper hair, scars from his many battles. And a tender touch, a gentleness that transcends his rough-and-ready demeanor. As I was alone most nights, he would sometimes stop by on his way home from a job or a mediation. Tom's pick-up truck would slide silently into my driveway in the dark; he would leave before dawn lest the neighbors comment on a strange vehicle in my yard.

Tom required conversation from me as much as he wanted hard-driving, extremely physical sex. I was happy to accommodate him. The man could be insatiable. So could I. He matched me and surpassed me in endurance, yet sometimes I left him motionless on my bed, with only enough strength left to mutter "oh, my, my," in his sexy voice. I was a bit more limber than he was given his years in the military and construction; his knees gave out before mine. He appreciated my sexuality and sensuality. We called each other "Critter," the nickname he had given me because, as he said, I was such an animal in bed. At my age and weight, I loved the idea that I could be an *animal* about anything. And he rarely called me Judge, which at times I felt was overused by the overeager.

He traveled a lot for work and family, but when he was in town, he was mine for the asking. When he left for an extended stay in Florida, he made me promise I would not make any final commitment to any man until we had a chance to explore our feelings for each other, to talk about a future together. By that time, we had begun to feel a weird kind of symbiotic connection. I would think of him and within hours, if not moments, he would call me. A thought of me would cross his mind, and then he would find an e-mail or text from me, sent at almost the same time.

And he knew what I was feeling when he called. "Darlin', are you having a bad day?"

"Yeah, the boys at work are killing me. How did you know?"

"It just came to me that you needed me, so I called."

We had similar conversations at least a hundred times over the years, usually with one of us humming the theme to *Twilight Zone*.

He ended every conversation with the same line, delivered in deep, gravelly tones; it never failed to make me sigh in anticipated pleasure: *Oh, my ,my.*

Years later, when I was at the end of my time with a particularly bad choice in lovers, Critter came back to New York, out of the blue. We decided to meet…but where? It was the beginning of the Jewish holidays, and my kids were home. So, we got a room at a cheesy hotel downtown. Tom simply swept me off my feet and into bed.

Later, much later, I cried in his arms, pouring out my doubts, fears, and recriminations. He held me and soothed me, shook me and talked some sense into me. Then, he rolled on top of me. Propped up on his elbows, he looked down into my surprised face and said, "Say everything you have to say now because in thirty seconds I'm going to make you so stupid you won't be able to speak." And he did.

We left the room with the bed unmade, the keys on the table. And a smile on our faces. He is still just a phone call away.

"Darlin', I was thinking about you."

Oh, my, my.

BOYFRIEND BOB

His name was Bob. But, because my middle brother's name is Bob, and my immediate supervisor for many years was also a Bob, when I began dating him, he became Boyfriend Bob, lest I confuse friends and family when I spoke of him. I was just a year into my re-submergence into the dating pool and I was less comfortable with the intimacy of a given name than I was with nicknames. Plus, I was good with nicknames, especially for the candidates for flavor-of-the- moment that were still flooding my inbox every night with pleading e-mails: The Three Stooges—Tom, Ron and Don, The Midget, Dirty Ears, Shaved Snake, and the Construction Guys, most of whom had not made it past first base.

It had been a busy year. My first fling in April with Ten-Inch Tim was only the entrée to a new world of online flirting that frequently led to actual dating. And the dating had segued into a series of assignations, one-night stands and brief love affairs. My heart had not been broken, only bruised, by the lies and perfidy of the Rabbi. My spirit had been lifted by admiration and affection from the San Francisco Police Department.

Literate and slightly lustful, within the confines of Match.com, Bob described himself in his profile as very attractive and erudite, retired and well-traveled, with a bit of whimsy and a certain joie de vivre. He was multifaceted and eager to meet, but still I put him through my initiation process, one I had been developing during the first year of my dating experiment. The initial hurdle was written communication skills. I thought I was still only interested in racking up the orgasms, but Bob proved a challenge to that notion from our first communication. My tag line was "love the one you're with," and he responded with a bit of French prose. I was enthralled and gave in to his pleas for a telephone chat—the second level of my testing procedure. His voice passed the sexy and intelligent test; he was funny, too. Two down, one to go.

My son had just begun his senior year of high school and was not aware I had begun dating. Because I thought my experiment would be short-lived, I saw no reason to complicate his already complicated life with men who would not be around long enough to matter. And my mother was a frequent weeklong visitor, so my telephone conversations with Bob were whispered affairs on the phone late in the evening and early in the morning. We could talk for hours. He read at least four newspapers every day, he saw every indie movie as soon as it opened, and he plowed through the *New York Times* best-seller list with abandon. And he liked phone sex.

Good thing because, as I teased him late one evening, the night before we planned to meet for the first time, he exclaimed at the moment of completion, "You want this? You want this?" I was so taken aback, I almost dropped the phone; as it was, I had to put it on mute, so he would not hear my giggles. If I had actually been with him when I heard his orgasmic proclamation, I think I would have laughed in his face. Not a good start to an intimate relationship. He was definitely wobbling on that final, yet precarious third rung.

Nonetheless, I agreed to meet him the following afternoon at the Scotia Diner. He wanted to go for a walk in a nearby nature preserve. I was not stupid or eager enough to meet a strange man in a remote wooded area, so we compromised on the diner parking lot and decided to take it from there. I was a few minutes early and pulled in to a vacant spot on a clear Sunday afternoon. I was checking voice messages on my cell phone when I noticed a car pulling in two spaces over. Thinking it might be Bob, I turned with a welcoming smile on my face. Much to my surprise, the car was a Miata and the man behind the wheel was…John Number Two! He must have recognized me because he immediately got out of his car and headed over. I shoved my gearshift into reverse and hightailed it out of there. I hid behind a sign about a mile down the road, fearing he had followed me.

After several minutes, I pulled out and returned to the diner. I parked further away from the restaurant and waited.

I was looking for Bob's green Toyota. A dark sedan pulled in the next row over, and I craned my neck to see if it was Bob. Nope. An attractive redhead about my age got out of the car and started towards the diner. Just to the right of her, I spotted the Miata and John. He jumped out and went over to the redhead. He was speaking earnestly to her as they walked away.

Laughing, I sat at my wheel shaking my head. Then I noticed a white-haired man with a neatly trimmed moustache, in the car that had just pulled in, was staring at me and laughing. Even though we had not exchanged photographs, I knew it was Bob.

He got out of his car and came over to me. I was getting out of my car when he started laughing again. "I was hoping that woman was not you, I was so looking forward to your blond hair. Then I saw that guy tailing her, and I *really* hoped it wasn't you!"

"No, not me, though I know the guy. He's why I am a few minutes late. I spotted him when I pulled in before and had to drive away to hide from him. He is really persistent."

"Well, it looks like he met a nice lady. Maybe she's the one for him."

"I'll wager she is trying to extricate herself right now because he probably told her he was five-eight just like he told me. She's almost a foot taller than him."

"Maybe she likes short guys." This was said with a bit of a snicker, as Bob was over six feet tall.

"It wasn't the height that got to me as much as the fact that he lied about it."

Bob laughed again and nodded to the next row in the parking lot. Sure enough, the redhead was on her way to her car.

"Quick, hide me! He is probably right behind her!" We jumped into Bob's car, giggling like errant schoolchildren. It was the icebreaker we needed. I told him the complete story of too-short John while he listened intently. Laughing at my finish, he reached out and drew me to him. His kiss was damn near perfect. He smiled as he pulled away. "I think we are going to do just fine." I thought he was absolutely correct.

We had our walk in the woods, enjoying the crisp autumn air and the warm lingering kisses. We made our way back to his apartment in Albany where he thoroughly made love to me on the futon in the living room after plying me with a very nice pinot noir and sliced radishes, cheese, and crackers. I was prepared for his orgasmic exclamation and buried my face in his neck to hide my face. I am sure he assumed the shakes from my suppressed giggles were my own climatic shudders.

Thus began our relationship, kept secret from son and Mom, shared only with my girlfriends and my psychologist.

We met two or three times a week for movies, dinner, and sex. Sometimes he took me out for lunch; sometimes I arose very early and met him for breakfast in bed in his older apartment complex on a tree-lined street. His apartment looked like it had never been vacuumed since he had moved in two years earlier upon his retirement as Dean of Men at a local urban high school. He had been divorced for twenty years after a brief marriage, no children. His mother lived in Albany; he saw her once a week, called her every day. He rarely spoke about his family; his father was dead and he had no siblings. He visited cousins in Syracuse once a month. I never met his family or any of his friends, though he was eager to meet mine. He really was not posse material, but being age-appropriate and Jewish, he was a hit with the yentas and their husbands. Even my psychologist, not a fan of my one-night stands, was rooting for him, calling what I had with him, "a better than average later in life" relationship. I was not so sure, but since I was only looking for sex, and I had found a source of excellent sex in him, I was satisfied...almost.

It wasn't the dusty apartment or the messy car. It was not his reticence with speaking about his family or friends. It wasn't even his climatic outbursts. There was something remote about him, as if he was lingering just outside of us, observing our progress. And progress we did. We exchanged Hanukkah presents, something I had not done with a man since 1987. For his birthday in January, I surprised him with an overnight at a quaint bed-and-breakfast in rural Cambridge. It was there, in a big brass bed, under a fluffy down comforter, he told me he loved me. I was silent for a moment, as desperation washed over me. I believe I said thank you before I rolled over on top of him and expressed my feelings in the only way I could: I fucked his brains out.

After a few sessions of guilt and depression with my psychologist, I realized I cared enough for him to want to be careful with his feelings. I also realized I would miss him if he were gone from my life. So, a week or two later, I told him I loved him, too. It was the first time I had said it to a man since August 10, 1988. And it was the beginning of the end for us.

The death throes of our love affair had subtly begun. The messy kitchen, the rickety computer desk, even the hippopotamus collection began to annoy me. I could sense things were beginning to bother him, too. My schedule kept me from joining him on some impromptu day trips. He was afraid of dogs so he did not like being at my house with my beloved yellow Lab, Alex. And my son was now aware I was seeing someone, as I occasionally spent Friday or Saturday night at Bob's apartment. My son's demanding phone calls always came at inopportune moments with Bob. Resentment was growing in both of the men in my life. It came to a head when I agreed to journey to Maine with Bob for a long weekend in May. My son was outwardly okay but decidedly cool. Bob was impatient with my decision to meet him at his apartment rather than let him pick me up at home.

Our trip began with good weather, light traffic and a lovely late lunch in Ogunquit. Our motel was near the beach, and Bob delighted in showing me his favorite seafood restaurant in Wells. But, our room had double beds and, after brushing his teeth, Bob got into the other bed. I was stunned and speechless, hurt and confused and yet, said nothing. The next day was spent in Kennebunkport and Freeport, shopping and chowing down blueberry pancakes and lobster rolls. Again that night, Bob headed for the other bed. When I asked him why, he said his back was bothering him. I shrugged and rolled over.

Then, at midnight my telephone rang. It was my son. He had cut his hand; it would not stop bleeding.

"How?"

"I cut it on broken glass."

"What broken glass?"

"The garage door window."

I decided to stop asking questions as Bob was glaring at me from his bed. I went into the bathroom and sat on the toilet, while I instructed him to go to my friend's house. Diane is a registered nurse. I called to awaken and warn her. She still had a medical permission form for my children, and I knew she could handle the crisis. It was two o'clock in the morning before she called me to let me know my son was fine but had eight stitches in his hand. Bob's response was to tell me to get off the phone and go to bed. That was when I seriously started thinking about ending *us*.

I convinced myself I should dump him the next morning, when he didn't even ask me about my son. It was our last day, and we were heading home. I couldn't wait. I told Bob what had transpired as we headed south; his response was to detour to Nubble Light, adding two hours to our return trip. We barely spoke after we left the lighthouse; I was furious and he was oblivious. But I did not want to make a scene in the car during a four-hour drive, so I pretended to nap through Massachusetts. By the time we reached his apartment in late afternoon, I was exhausted from feigning sleep and hiding my emotions. After loading my bags in my car, he kissed me on the cheek and told me he would call later. I assumed I would never hear from him again.

At home, there was the expected drama with my son. All the relaxation from my vacation with Bob had disappeared in the last twenty-four hours, all the old worry and stress was back.

Surprisingly, Bob did call later. I was stunned when he asked how things were at home and suggested dinner later in the week. I put him off, not wanting to deal with breaking up with him then on the phone. I had no intention of seeing him again. But, after a few days of deflecting my son's mood swings and digging through the files piled up at work, I called Bob to tell him I would meet him for dinner on Wednesday. I felt better about breaking up with him in person.

Dinner was, as always, delightful. He had photographs of our trip for me, reminiscing about the fun recorded in each frame. He was attentive and affectionate. *Maybe his back really had been bothering him. Maybe he had been abrupt because he had no experience with children of his own. Maybe I wanted to delay my return to my house of woe.* I don't know what excuse I made that worked in my troubled mind, but I ended up back at Bob's apartment for a familiar and soothing bout of lovemaking. *So, I'll break up with him tomorrow*, I told myself late that night, as I drove home. It was to be my oft-repeated mantra over the next few months.

Summer with Bob was fun. We headed to Saratoga for drinks and dinner outside the bistros on Broadway, we listened to classical music from the lawn at SPAC, and we wandered around Cambridge and Schuylerville on Sunday afternoons. But, there was a tension between us. His impatience with my son, who was leaving for college in August, was more and more thinly concealed. My dissatisfaction with his increasingly infrequent lovemaking was making me ornery and horny. But, still he provided a refuge from the mess my life had become.

Nonetheless, I started looking for a replacement.

HOT-TUB KEN

There were so many Kens online that year that I had to name them. My psychologist still accused me of nicknaming the men I encountered, rather than calling them by their given names in order to avoid any commitment; but sometimes, the mothers of that generation had just not been original enough—weren't there any other good names in 1950 besides Robert, James, Kenneth and Thomas? So, in the summer of 2003, I encountered Choirboy Ken, Pitney-Bowes Ken, Pepsi-Can Ken, and Hot-Tub Ken.

As I have said, I don't do well in summer. Father's Day usually starts my doldrums. My son's birthday is July 4. My husband broke his neck three years later on July 8 and died on August 10. His birthday was August 21, and our wedding anniversary was August 26. I don't start coming out of my bad mood until after Labor Day and then the Jewish holidays, followed by the regular holidays, all centering on family, pretty much kick my ass until New Year's.

Valentine's Day, my birthday in April and Mother's Day in May are not good either. I'd say my one really good month is March; I don't tend to get into much trouble in March except on St. Patrick's Day.

In summer, I go a bit crazy, and that summer was no different. I'd had my adventures with quick and dirty sex and found I had an appetite for it. And there were plenty of willing partners-in-crime. It was like letting Imelda Marcos loose in a shoe store.

One Friday, in mid-July, I met Ken on Match.com. We flirted online when I got home from work. Our first encounter was fairly subdued—he was a fan of Crosby, Stills, Nash & Young and liked my tag line: "Love the one you're with," so we chatted about musical interests. Match was not the type of site where you jumped into a discussion of sexual preferences right off the bat. So, we danced. I told him I was in the process of leaving a relationship (soon-to-be ex Boyfriend Bob), and he talked about how his son might be moving back to his house now that he had finished college and had not yet found a job. Both of us had lives in transition. He lived on one of the quiet residential streets that ran between Sand Creek Road and Osborne in Colonie, a nice Cape Cod. With a big veggie garden. And a huge pool. And a hot tub.

The mention of a hot tub got the crazy cells started up. And I was bored. I painted a few erotic images for him. He was swift and explicit with his reply. He emphasized he was very oral. I suggested all men were oral—specifically, that all men were oral when they were on the receiving end. He insisted it was better to give than to receive, and he was a very giving man. I liked his reasoning. Within the hour, I had his phone number and called him a few minutes later. I got his answering machine (turns out he had gone outside to turn the pool off). Nice voice, sweet and sexy. So, I sent the red lace bra picture. He called right back.

Our conversation was long and wide-ranging. I sipped a large glass of white wine, while we discussed our favorite positions, how we kissed, the cuddle factor and logistics with kids at home. He mentioned his son was away for the weekend. I mournfully advised him I had made plans with girlfriends for Saturday night, and I had never broken a date with girlfriends because of a guy—don't you just hate women who do that? You're only good company until someone with a penis calls. That type of woman has not been on my friend list since junior high school. Anyway, he manned-up and hid his disappointment. After some heated good-byes, he did suggest I drop by on Saturday, wearing very little, for a late evening soak in the hot tub and/or a moonlight swim. I said I would consider it, even though I knew it was unlikely that I would leave my friend's house to make a booty call.

Saturday was hot. My son was making me crazy. Soon-to-be-Ex-boyfriend Bob was being noncommittal about plans for the next day. And it was July 13. I don't remember now what events happened on the 13th of July in 1988, but I was in a mood. As the afternoon waned, Ken's e-mails became sweetly desperate. I could stop by any time that night. He was going to clean the pool, work in the garden, make some sauce, and then relax in the hot tub with some Coronas and lime and a little night music, probably Van Morrison, on the CD player that piped music around the pool. I could just call him when I left my friend's house, and he would talk me down the Northway. I was tempted.

But, no. I was going to a friend's to watch a chick flick and nosh. I would be wearing my *hang out with the yenta's sloppy clothes*, not one of my *I'm meeting a new, potential lover for the first time, and I have to look perfect outfits*. But, it couldn't hurt to shower before I went over; I had been doing chores all day. I should wash my hair because I had been swimming, and I wanted to get the chlorine out. I might as well shave my legs, although I knew *the curse of shaving the legs* all too well. And who said I had to wear shorts and a T-shirt? It was hot, and my friend's house did not have central air. I could just put on a sundress; it was not new, it was practically a schemata! And I didn't even need a bra with it because it was fitted on the top.

So there I was, headed to my girlfriend's house in a hot pink and turquoise sundress. Was it a coincidence that my fingertips and toenails were painted a complementary shade of fuchsia? Of, course my flip-flops matched; I always matched shoes and attire. Just like I always matched underwear. I was a bit OCD like that. Was it my fault the panties that matched the sundress best were thong panties? And my summer fragrance just happened to be "Love Spell," by Victoria's Secret.

I had fun with my friends. I loved them all. All safely and sanely married for many years, all a bit confused about my desire to have sex when most of them were expressing relief their husbands no longer seemed that interested or had taken to sleeping in the guest room because of the snoring. I certainly was not going to confide in them the details of my trysts. They thought I was still in a *better-than-average-later-in-life* relationship with Boyfriend Bob. And I let them think that— better they should maintain their good impression of me, their vaguely charitable feeling of sympathy for my widowed state. I didn't think they could handle the sometimes tawdry adventures of Dina, Warrior Princess.

I feigned exhaustion around 8:50 when the movie ended. I passed on the make-your-own-sundaes and said I was heading home. I had a busy day of yard work on Sunday and needed a good night's sleep. And I had to let the dog out, since my son was probably at his girlfriend's house. A few too many excuses, but my friends were used to my busy days and sleep-deprived nights. I left them in the kitchen. I walked out to my suburban mom minivan and tossed my bag into the passenger seat. I sat down on the edge of the driver's seat and kicked out of my panties, tucking them neatly into the side pocket of my purse. As I backed out of the driveway, I called Ken. He answered on the first ring.

"Hello, Dina."

"Hello, darlin'."

"Where are you?"

"I'm heading down the Northway. Where are you?"

"I'm sitting in the hot tub, waiting for you."

"How did you know I would come?"

"I didn't know, I just hoped. And I hope you haven't come yet."

"Ha. Ha. No, the movie was a chick flick, not porn."

"What are you wearing?"

Why do men always want to know what you are wearing? I do not get excited by the notion that a man is wearing boxers or briefs, though I do prefer boxers. The color of their underwear likewise does nothing to arouse me. But tell a man you are wearing a hot pink lace thong, and he is likely to explode.

We chatted as he directed me to turn here, turn there, once I got off the Northway. Soon, I was pulling into his driveway. Cute house. Driveway along the side to an unattached garage. Marigolds clustered and tomato vines crept up tall stakes on both sides of the path that led along the garage to a pool gate identical to my own.

"I'm here."

"I'll come out to meet you."

"No, stay where you are. I can find my way." The path was visible in the soft glow of solar lights. A really pretty setting.

"The pool gate is rickety...."

"I have one just like it. Do you have a towel for me?"

"I have several."

"Hang up and close your eyes."

I can't say whether it was because it was July or because I had been in a bad mood all day, but I had felt the unhappiness lift as soon as I had heard his voice on the phone. It might have been a vaguely exhibitionist streak brought about by my weight loss of nearly fifty pounds during the previous twelve months. Appreciative comments, lustful stares and, let's be honest, hot, sweaty, satisfying sex, with several men had certainly boosted my self-confidence to the point that I even considered what I was about to do. I still don't know why I shed the sundress and kicked off my sandals as I wandered down his garden path. The cool night air felt marvelous on my damp, bare skin. I felt brave and bold as I unlatched the gate and turned the corner to the left.

And there he was. Sitting in the hot tub, brown hair damp but lifting in the breeze. What I would soon discover were soft brown, sweet eyes, clamped tightly shut, a bottle of Corona, swinging from the hand that draped over the side of the tub. There were beach towels piled next to the two steps up to the tub. I ignored them and climbed the steps. Sitting on the edge of the tub, I swung my legs up and over. The water was a fiery kiss on my feet and ankles as I slid into the hot bubbles, opposite Ken. His eyes flew open before I was fully submerged, so he got a glimpse of my still perky breasts in the moonlight.

"*Damn!*"

"Hey, darlin', have you got one of those beers for me?"

He stuttered, he stammered, but I ascertained his answer was yes. Mutely, he handed me a cold beer from the cooler perched on a lawn chair next to the tub. I smiled my thanks and took a long slow sip. My insides were jittery; I had used up most of my courage during that twenty-step nude saunter to his secluded pool. If he didn't say something coherent soon, I was going to lose my nerve.

"You are without question the most beautiful, sexy woman I have ever seen."

That would do.

As if speaking the words aloud had breached some barrier of shyness, we both burst into laughter. He moved toward me and took me in his arms. The man had not lied; he was an exceptional kisser. Soon, the stars, the swirling currents of fevered water, the cool breeze, the Corona and the kisses had me perched on the edge of the hot tub where he fulfilled all of his urgent promises. There were men before him, and there have been men after him, but there was never a man who gave me the courage to soar like that beneath the star-studded sky.

We laughed and we loved that night and through the summer. Our encounters were playful and passionate but also friendly and affectionate. I took care of his gout; he rescued me from a rough encounter with the dangerous bad boy soon to enter my life. A year later, he moved to Syracuse for business, and I moved on.

MR. LESS IS MORE

Robin Williams. But Robin Williams in *One Hour Photo*. A thinner but scarier looking Robin Williams than in *Mork and Mindy*. *How could a guy who worked in a church be scary?* Not so much scary, but edgy. I could not believe our first date was in a church. *Do you call it a date when it is all about the sex?* When sex is a done deal. It's a date if food, drink and conversation ensue. It's a date if you have a place and time to meet. It's a date if he holds your car door open for you. And then gives you a big hug.

"God, you're gorgeous! You are so much prettier than your photos."

Effusive praise makes me uncomfortable and suspicious. But I was willing to accept it from him.

I met Mr. More, as was my practice, online. I think he was at Match.com or Cupid.com, the only two dating sites I was frequenting. He had an MBA and had been a college professor. A divorce and something else, never really discussed, had led him to his current position as a deacon at a large and prosperous church in the city. He was responsible for the janitorial staff and some administrative duties; I think he also sang in the choir and had some part in the Sunday services. For these tasks, he received a modest remuneration and living quarters. *Uh-huh*, his apartment was in the old and impressive gray stone church, on the same level as the choir loft and with a big stained glass window.

That first night, he led me up the main staircase of the church, past the doors to the sanctuary and up the next flight of granite steps, by gargoyles and posters promoting Bible Study. And there we were, around the corner from the Sunday School Principal's office, at his apartment.

He had done his homework; he knew I was coming from work so he had set out a tray of cheese, crackers and fresh veggies. A frosty cold Corona Light appeared before I could put my purse down; the lime wedge the perfect size to slip easily down the neck of the bottle.

Mr. More was a fairly decent kisser. He had a nice mouth and a pleasant smile. I could tell he had just shaved, he smelled of Palmolive soap, and his skin had that soft sandpaper feel that comes from closely scraped whiskers. He tasted of Colgate and I of Corona, but it was not an unpleasant mix. The kissing was having its desired effect on me, as was half a bottle of beer.

I liked him; I really liked him. We had been e-mailing and talking on the phone for weeks before I could maneuver my schedule around to meet him. My son had just graduated from high school and was not leaving for college until late August. It was early June, and I was exploring my options, having decided Boyfriend Bob was soon to be Ex-boyfriend Bob. He had failed to make the right choices on our trip to Maine just before Memorial Day, and while I was still using him to fill my Friday nights and Sunday mornings, I no longer loved him, if I ever really did. Mr. More was funnier, sexier, and more outrageous than Bob. A good candidate for a lover to replace my lover, I thought, as the kisses deepened.

I realized as his hands drifted over me that I was becoming very adept at duplicity. I was never a liar as a kid, my fair skin burned red every time I offered up a lie. I never felt the need to lie to my husband about anything, not even the cost of a new pair of shoes. I was ever faithful to him; only a few men even earned a second glance from me. I took my vows seriously as did he, but fidelity was no hardship. I subscribed to the Paul Newman theory of faithfulness: why go out for hamburger when you had steak at home? But, I felt no such stricture on my behavior with Boyfriend Bob or any of the others. Mr. More knew I was in the process of removing myself from Boyfriend Bob.

Mr. More led me into the bedroom. The kitchen was just inside the door and the rest of the room was a dining/living room. The double door off the kitchen opened into a huge room, lighted by the stained glass rose-shaped window. His bed, a huge platform bed, was in the middle of the floor. The perimeter of the bedroom held his desk, dresser, an easy chair with a good reading light, the door to the closet, and the door to the bathroom. A floating bed clothed in white dominated the room. The virginal surface served as a canvas for the palette of color streaming through the stained glass window. I could see dancing diamonds of magenta and cobalt and gold on the hardwood floor. I swallowed hard, bemused by the setting, titillated by the bed. It looked like I was going to be seduced on a cloud.

He undressed me and ministered to me. I felt like a much-desired courtesan. He was making me the center of his attentions, but I knew that his turn would soon come. Sometime later, laughing that deep throaty laugh of the sexually satisfied, I raised my sweaty body up on my elbows to smile at him and said, "Your turn!" He was already undressing, praising me and letting me know by his words how excited he was about what was to come. He hung his shirt and trousers neatly on the desk chair and turned, naked, to me.

What was wrong with this picture? He didn't have a great body, but then, neither did I. He was a bit paunchy as middle-aged men can be, but that was not the problem. I had not been to bed with that many Tom Cruise body doubles lately, so I was learning my way around the aging male body. But it seemed to me he was missing something. Something very important. Something I was not sure I could proceed without. *He did not have a penis!*

I was sure of it. But he seemed so unconcerned by his male endowment or lack thereof I knew I must be mistaken. The lighting in the room was dim, and my eyesight is not the greatest, even under the best conditions, but I couldn't see a penis in that shadowed area between his thighs. I mean, he was talking the talk, he seemed excited, he seemed aroused, but where was his damn erection? As he moved closer to me, I caught the glimpse of something, but I could not be sure what it was. *What if he was a transvestite or a transgender or a cross-dresser or a lesbian with a hairy chest and no boobs wearing some fake penis?*

Then I saw it. He definitely had a penis. It was no bigger than my thumb. *I can work with this,* I thought. *I can make this happen.*

And I did. I managed to satisfy him and leave him breathless, sweaty and grinning.

Another conquest. As I left him, I was not sure if I would ever return. I liked him; I was glowing. But it had all been a little strange for me.

When I reported the evening's events to my friend Gerald and my posse of girlfriends at work, Gerald immediately christened him Mr. Less-Is-More. We laughed about my adventure. We were all sure I would never see him again. I mean, why would I?

I returned to him many times that summer. For laughter, for kisses, for care and consideration, for sex. He fell in love with me and left me because I could not make the final break with Boyfriend Bob. I still laugh about Mr. Less-Is-More, but there are times when I really miss him.

I had learned so much from Mr. More. One was the Japanese talent for turning beloved childhood cartoon characters, like Winnie-the-Pooh and Hello Kitty into clever little sex toys. Yes, there were vibrators available in the shape of Mickey Mouse, Pooh Bear and my favorite, Hello Kitty! Mr. More's other piece of information was a new website: Adult Friend Finder. A site for consenting adults who were looking to *hook-up.* A whole candy store of delights that would not rot my teeth but, I feared, would taint my soul.

I suspected Bob, too, had begun to look around, but I knew I would not bump into him on such a site. He required a less-adventurous woman, one who would be cowed by his intelligence and class. I, on the other hand, was looking for escapes and thrills. I had given part of my heart to Bob only to be disappointed by his detachment and depressed by my inability to fully commit to him. So, I kept him in my pocket while I distracted myself with new playmates, men who would not want any more from me than I was prepared to give and who were unlikely to commit the unforgiveable sin of falling in love with me.

PEPSI-CAN KEN

Most men on Adult Friend Finder either post no picture, or they post a picture of their penis. The first time I saw such a picture, I had to enlarge it because I could not believe the thumbnail photo was actually that particular body part. But, there it was, that upright symbol of male pride. Looking at penis pictures then became a giggle-filled adventure for my girlfriends and me during our monthly Friday night get-togethers. I viewed it as both entertainment and education; some of my friends had only ever seen one penis in their lives. For months, we viewed a wide variety of male appendages with much raucous, Margarita-fueled hoots and hollers.

Ken fell into the second category. His picture was a rather impressive looking penis, grasped firmly in one hand. Even from the tiny photograph, I could tell he was well endowed. But, I had already experienced Ten-Inch Tim, so it was going to take more than size to garner my admiration and surrender.

Ken was also tall, dark-haired, and quite good-looking. He was a nuclear physicist who had given up his home in the suburbs to his "crazy" wife; he now lived in an apartment complex near Knolls. Ken was going through a bitter divorce; his wife had sole custody of their two children through some impressive machinations by her lawyer, aided by the still-present prejudice among some Family Court judges in favor of the mother. He was dealing with anger and frustration, a vocal and effective advocate of fathers' rights. It was apparent to me from the start that my legal career held great appeal for him.

He begged me to visit from almost our first communication, promising to delight me with his pride and joy. In the midst of his bragging about the size one evening, I laughingly opined I had only his word to go by.

"You've seen the picture. My fingers hardly fit around it."

"Yes, but you might have very small hands. Pictures can be altered to deceive," I said, thinking of The Midget and Dirty Ears.

"If I prove what I say, will you come to see me?"

"I will. But, you need to give me some perspective, something I will recognize so I can judge by comparison." I was not giving in that easily.

"Are you this tough on the bench, Your Honor?"

"Tougher."

The next day there was an e-mail with an attachment. When I opened it, I almost choked on my Diet Coke. There was the now familiar penis grasped firmly in Ken's left hand. It looked huge. Even more so when compared to the Pepsi can clasped in his right hand. Yes, he was definitely bigger than a can of Pepsi, much bigger. I admit to showing the picture to my girlfriends. There was a communal sucking in of breath and a group sigh.

I had to make good my promise as Ken had fulfilled his end of the bargain. He suggested Friday night, but I had made plans with Boyfriend Bob. I thought I could do Saturday night, but Ken was going away. We decided to compromise on Sunday if he was back in town.

Friday brought a hot summer night. Heat makes me cranky, and Bob was always conservative with the air-conditioning. Instead of dinner and a movie out, he had made a plate of cold munchies and set out chilled white wine, putting a black and white movie in the VCR. I was uncomfortable and fidgety through the film. And I was thinking of Ken.

Bob's lovemaking was uninspired, but I admit I wasn't giving him much to work with. I still enjoyed him, but too much was between us now, and once my head was out of the game, nothing else worked right either. We both ended up, shall I say, unfulfilled. He walked me to my car around nine thirty. I had pled a headache. He kissed me goodnight and waited, as he always did, for me to make the turn at the end of his street before he went inside. He really was a nice guy. Somehow, that increased my irritation. And irritation always kick-started impulse.

I dialed Ken's number. "Hello, handsome."

"Well, hello. I thought you were busy tonight."

"I was. I'm not now."

"Where are you?"

"I'm in Albany."

"You could be here in twenty minutes."

"I could, yes."

"Would you like a cold can of beer and the last few innings of the Yankees game?"

"I would like a cool shower."

"Anything for you, Your Honor."

"I've been with someone."

"I didn't ask."

"Doesn't that bother you?"

"Does it bother you?"

"Yes."

"Are you coming over anyway?"

"Yes."

"Whatever you want to happen will happen. If you want nothing, that's what it will be."

I was there in fifteen minutes. He opened the door. Taller than I had thought, dark and handsome, thinner than I preferred. But a glimmer was in his eye and a smile played around his lips as he pulled me into his arms.

"Hey, you look like you could use a hug."

I fell into him. He just held me. I was shaking.

"I put out clean towels in the bathroom and a cold beer. Take your time; I'm watching television in the bedroom at the end of the hall."

What the hell was I thinking? I did not love Bob. I had probably never really loved him in a way that would sustain a relationship. So I was going from one bed to another. Not really one man to another because Bob had not completed the mission. But, I had to admit as I looked in the mirror, that was just a technicality. And morals should not be measured by a technicality. Still, I had already crossed the line I had never crossed before by cheating on Bob with Hot-Tub Ken and Mr.

Less-Is-More. I shrugged and kicked my clothes out of the way. *Already damned, I might as well enjoy myself.*

I wandered down the hall, beer in one hand, the other clutching the knot of a huge yellow towel between my breasts.

Driving home later, much later, I made myself face some harsh realities. I was not the woman my mother raised me to be. I was not the woman who had married her great love, who was totally faithful to him while he was alive, and who then mourned him for fifteen lonely years. I was some crazy, impulsive, selfish woman, taking what I wanted, when I wanted, to hell with the consequences. On the other hand, I was alive and finally feeling at least passion after too many years in a cocoon of sorrow. And I wanted nothing so much as to *feel*.

And, Ken had certainly made me feel. He was a generous and attentive lover, and he was so much fun in bed. We had laughed and sighed and moaned, and when I left him, I was more relaxed than I had been in months. But the hard truth was he was not the one for me. And I was not the one for him. He was too bitter and too caught up in his custody battle; I did not have it in me to take on one more fight. I was not as adventurous as he liked, even with having just gone from Bob to him. We had left it that we might get together on Sunday when he returned from his weekend away. We both knew he was going to meet another woman.

On Monday, he sent an e-mail that he had met a woman named Debbie in Poughkeepsie, and it was love at first sight. She would be moving in with him by the end of the month. He said I was lovely, sexy, smart and kind, but she was everything. He did ask if I would be interested in a ménage sometime later in the summer. *Yeah, he was way more adventurous than me!* I gently demurred and wished him well. I already had his replacement in mind.

DÉJÀ VU

One of my yenta friends, Megan, had a Rabbit that died. It had led a good long life, over twenty years by Megan's count. She had left it in the bedroom unattended while she took a shower, and when she emerged from the steam twenty minutes later, her two dogs were playing tug of war with the poor Rabbit! It could not be resurrected despite her best efforts. She had tried to find a replacement online after unceremoniously, but regretfully, dumping it in the garbage before her elderly and sometimes ailing husband arrived home from playing Gin with his buddies.

"So," she related to me in a telephone call the morning after the tragic event, "we need to go shopping."

"What do you mean 'we'?" I retorted. "I have no idea where to go for a Rabbit. And why do you need me anyway?"

"I found a shop in Schenectady that might have the Rabbit I want. And you're going with me because there's safety in numbers."

So there we were one weekday afternoon, getting out of Megan's Volvo station wagon, both wearing our conservative dresses, cardigans tied around our shoulders and practical leather flats. We looked for all the world like two suburban matrons on our way to a charity luncheon. I was even wearing my pearls; Megan had picked me up at my office for our lunchtime adventure. She had promised to pay for our meal as a reward for my reluctant cooperation.

"Are you sure this is the place?" I asked, eyeing the nondescript beige cinder block building suspiciously. "Where's the sign?" All I could see were two blacked out windows and a solid metal door between them.

"The sign's in the window," she retorted, forging through the garbage ahead of me on the narrow sidewalk. "C'mon, scaredy-cat."

"I'm not scared. I am just being cautious. What if someone I know, what if some lawyer who knows me, sees me in there?"

"No one will say anything. Do you think they want to admit they were in here?" She laughed derisively over her shoulder as she yanked the heavy door open and stepped inside.

She was right. I gulped and followed her into the dark interior, past the small neon sign I had just noticed blinking in the window: *XXX Adult Store*.

It was dim inside, and it smelled of stale incense. The big, grizzled man sitting behind the counter just inside the door barely offered us a glance. I followed Megan to the left, toward shelves stocked with various boxes and videotapes. We walked past a young, skinny man wearing a filthy Carhartt jacket and a NASCAR baseball cap, while perusing the videos.

The next aisle held an assortment of *toys*. Some I could figure out for myself as I glanced furtively at the Day-Glo colors of various latex creations ranged before my eyes; some I did not ever want to know about, intimidated by their size or color or name. Megan was closely inspecting and rejecting each item along the top shelf.

"I think the vibrators are down here," she called out as she turned the corner into the next aisle.

Choking, I blushed to the roots of my hair and turned the corner right behind her. "Jesus, announce it to the whole store, why don't you?"

"No one cares what we're here for. Look at all this stuff. I just know they have my Rabbit!" She reached out for a rather large box containing a hot pink latex penis the size of my forearm. I think it was called the Intimidator, or it should have been. But it didn't have bunny ears or whatever it was that had made the Rabbit special, so Megan shoved it back on the shelf. Up and down three aisles we trooped, pausing before anything that looked like a penis, well, not like any penis I had ever seen, but with a generally recognizable shape of a man's most prized appendage. However impressive most of them were, none was the Original Rabbit. Megan readied to leave when I stopped her with a hiss.

"We've been in here for over half an hour, we have to buy something or we're going to look like voyeurs!" I still had some sense of Puritan propriety even in a sex shop.

Laughing at me, she pointed to the other side of the store. Black curtains were hung across a narrow doorway, beneath a sign that proclaimed *Private Viewing Area*. She snorted and said, "Voyeurs? What do you think is going on in there?"

I gasped. *Jesus God, gross me out!* I still thought we had best purchase something but Megan was having none of that. I quickly looked up and down the display at the end of the aisle for the cheapest, least offensive thing I could find. *French Ticklers*. $5.99. Three rubbery animal heads with rubbery tongues sticking out and rubbery hair exploding from their round rubbery heads. At the time, I had no idea what a *French Tickler* was, but they would do. I pulled a ten-dollar bill from my wallet, hating to have to accept change from the cashier's grimy paw.

Smiling through gritted teeth, I said, "Thank you," and beat a hasty retreat behind Megan. "Yuck, yuck, yuck!" I spat as I climbed into the car next to her. Then we erupted into gales of laughter that carried us down Central Avenue. Our hilarity intensified when I opened the package of French Ticklers to play finger puppets with them. They were condoms with little animal heads on the tip and some ridges along the length, designed to "increase and enhance female pleasure." I'll never know if that was false advertising. Boyfriend Bob gamely agreed to use one during our next intimate encounter, but my ensuing laughter caused some unexpected *shrinkage* on his part, so I never got to feel the full effect of the little rubber monkey head.

Such was my first exposure to an adult store, a sex shop, an exotic entrepreneurship. But it was not my last.

My next visit was also unplanned. I was looking for one of those Indian bedspreads we all had in college. My daughter needed a large, inexpensive window covering that would go with her great-grandmother's oriental carpet. Boyfriend Bob directed me to Déjà Vu, a *head shop* in a strip mall on Wolf Road. He didn't tell me it was next to a Roman Catholic chapel that had a weekday noontime Mass for the faithful—meaning the over-sixty-five set that popped in for the Holy Sacrament then hurried past Déjà Vu to the Chinese Buffet. What an audience for my first sojourn to the sin site!

The shop looked innocent enough from the parking lot; Indian clothes on display tastefully in the two large front windows. A bell chimed as I opened the glass door, no heavy metal door here, but there was that smell of incense again. A young woman with multiple piercings smiled from the cash register. I wandered down the side of the store toward the Indian bedspreads hanging on the wall. I quickly found a spread that would match my daughter's carpet. After I pulled it down from the display, I pivoted toward the cash register but too quickly. I started to lose my balance and reached out to steady myself. My hand landed on the bulbous head of a black penis, three feet high, as wide as my wrist and attached to a base on the floor.

I shrieked. Then I burst into giggles. The salesgirl rushed over with a concerned, "Can I help you?"

I pointed to the thing poking up from the floor.

"What the hell is that? No, wait, don't answer that. I don't really want to know."

My face the color of my red nail lacquer, I paid for the bedspread, keeping my eyes firmly fixed on the sales clerk. I couldn't wait to get back to the office and grill Gerald, font of all kinky information. Gerald and his partner were very sexually active, so I figured he knew everything about toys. Coffee spurted out of his nose at my question: "What the hell would anyone do with a big, three foot-long penis affixed to the floor?"

After he attempted to answer my question with a straight face, he decided I needed a guided tour of Déjà Vu. We waited a week; I didn't want to appear to be a regular to the pious pushing their way down the sidewalk from the chapel to the Chinese buffet. Once there, Gerald began a nonstop, detailed explanation of all the toys (I didn't need the drug paraphernalia explained to me, I was in college in the 70s, after all). There were dildos of all shapes, sizes and colors; there were as many vibrators with cords or batteries (batteries are best, Gerald explained, because the cords could get in the way, but the vibrators ate the batteries like…well, I can't use the analogy in polite company). I had pretty much figured this stuff out on my own; I wasn't that naïve, although I was a bit taken aback by the variety of shapes and *sizes* they came in. But, the assorted clamps to be used on body parts I couldn't imagine pinching, much less with metal teeth, fascinated me the most! Also, there were many *toys* to be used in parts of the body I had never considered to be sexual parts; but then, I was not a gay man or, at the time, a particularly adventurous woman. And then there were the lubricants, gels, oils, and lotions. As Gerald said, for certain things, "too much lube is just about right."

We laughed and giggled like school kids out on a field trip to a museum, viewing their first painting of a nude. Once again, so as not to appear cheap or voyeuristic, I bought a small tube of green apple jelly. Gerald bought a giant tube of Electro-glide or something like that. I don't even want to think about what happened with that viscous gel.

I related this shopping adventure with much detail to my closest friends (all twenty or so of them). I was amazed and amused that once they discovered I knew the proper etiquette for a sex shop, the requests started flooding in. Some wanted me to take them on a tour to this heretofore forbidden site; some of them had *shopping lists* for me to fill on my next solo trip. It took me awhile to absorb these secret details of my friends' lives.

For the next three years, after Boyfriend Bob became Ex-boyfriend Bob, I was a *regular* at Déjà Vu. I got around the church crowd by taking a late lunch hour. Sometimes I went alone and sometimes with Gerald, who would spring for take-out from the buffet if I would drive the quarter-mile from our office to the store. I was on a first name basis with Judy and Claire, the sales clerks. I brought brown paper bags back to my girlfriends, and occasionally, Gerald. I am slightly embarrassed to admit eventually I earned a preferred customer discount.

And I became the adventurous woman I hadn't known I wanted to be. But, that's another story.

AND SO IT GOES

Breaking up is hard to do. I was never a fan of it, never very good at it. I usually let the guy do the deed. If I was desperate to get out of a relationship and the man was not taking the hints, I acted out. I made it virtually impossible for him to stay with me. In my head, it was better to leave them angry than hurt.

I had not had to resort to such subterfuge very often. There had not been that many boyfriends in my life. There had been only a few in high school and only one who meant anything in college. And I broke up with him just days before he was to put an engagement ring on my finger. The pain from that separation sent me into a tailspin for months. I swore off men. Then I went to law school and met my future husband on the first day. And I know with bone- deep certainty I would never have broken up with him.

I didn't know what to do with Boyfriend Bob. He was not right for me; I was not right for him. We were drifting, and I was cheating. I still liked him enough to be uncomfortable with my actions, but not enough to stop and make another effort with him.

So, I did what I had done in college when there was a guy I liked but was done with, a nice guy who, through no or very little fault of his own, was no longer the *one*. I blamed the fracture in our relationship on myself. Right after the New Year, fifteen months after we had met, I sent Bob the I-am-confused-my-life-is-a-mess-it's-not-you-it's-me note. I cited my precipitous entrance into the dating pool, my son's opposition to my dating and the stress of my job as the causes of my distraction, absences and general lack of enthusiasm. All of that was partially true, but mostly it was Bob and his emotional unavailability.

I was right to do it like that. He sent a lovely note back telling me he understood, that my son had been an issue coming between us, he wished me only the best in the future and he would always love me.

Two weeks later, he was publicly dating an acquaintance of mine with whom he had been communicating since the summer. *Who knew?*

THE PROFESSOR

Write me.

That's all he sent to me in the message: Write me! *What was he thinking?* I didn't respond well to terse instructions. But, his two words caught my attention in the midst of longer, wordier missives.

Write me.

Simple, declarative, proper grammar and spelling. I had to look.

He was the man I had been searching for through page after page of passionate and pornographic pleas, graphic and ungrammatical e-mails and IMs. There he was. A few years older than me, a political scientist, a professor, Irish, a movie buff, a published author.

Then the kicker: he lived in Chicago. Indeed, his profile was seeking a woman my age, average to curvy, intelligent, educated, active libido, living within fifteen minutes of the Inner Loop. I had only been to Chicago once to visit my baby brother and his new wife; but even I knew New York, anywhere in New York, was more than fifteen minutes from Chicago's Inner Loop.

All right. He was geographically challenged. I could work with this.

I wrote back:

Dear professor,

I'm good, but I am not good enough to make it to Chicago's Inner Loop in fifteen minutes. Did you fail to notice that I lived in New York?

Kisses, Judge Dina

He answered immediately. Yes, he knew I was from New York, but my profile had so intrigued him he had to contact me anyway. *Where was I right now?*

I was home with a bad allergy attack. I had taken Benadryl early in the morning. It had gotten rid of the headache and runny nose but had left me loopy and off-balance, so I had stayed home. That would bring more trouble from the boys at the office, so I had fired up the computer to at least write the monthly newsletter. In the midst of summarizing recent decisions, I had received the notification that I had mail.

I sent off a quick missive:
I'm home. In bed.

That should work. Frankly, it was a bit of a stretch, my computer was in the bedroom, though not a laptop. I was, in actuality, sitting on an uncomfortable State reject stenographer's chair.

Call me.

This man loved two word sentences! I could best him at this game: *when?* Within seconds, he responded with his telephone number.

What was it about him? I still don't know, but I started dialing his number. He answered on the second ring: "Hello, Tom O'Leary."

Oh my God! His voice! His voice was James Earl Jones deep, it was Kris Kristofferson raspy, and it had a hint of the Irish, like Gabriel Byrne. It was the quintessential whiskey voice: deep, rough, hot. It was the kind of voice you wanted to have whispering in your ear early in the morning right before its owner turned you into his arms and slid inside you. It was the sexiest voice I had ever heard.

I had always thought my voice was too high when I was nervous or embarrassed. Since I had started dating, I had received compliments on my voice, but I always figured the compliments were given with ulterior motives. Most of those men wanted to get me into bed. So, I deliberately paused, dropped my voice into a deep Lauren Bacall whisper and said:

"Professor? It's the judge."

He sighed. I had him. He stammered hello to me. I responded. He was good at flirtatious banter, as good as me. Better. He teased me about not blocking my telephone number; I pointed out I knew where he worked because he had not only sent me the university's main number, but his extension. He had the grace to give me points for my comeback. He asked me what I was wearing. Sitting there in my rattiest nightshirt, I gave him the lie: black silk nightgown, slit up to there. He laughed. He had me with that laugh, that bad boy chuckle.

We talked for an hour about everything: the law, politics, the *New York Times*, the *Guardian*, the films of John Ford, sex, drugs and rock n' roll. Then his voice deepened, and he began to tell me what he would be doing if he were sitting next to me. Graphically describing to me how he would make love to me. I sighed, I blushed, I was getting aroused. I let him lead the way. I told him what I was feeling; I was honest. Our voices were barely whispers, sighs, groans. *Damn, he was good.*

He had to go; I hated to hang up. He promised to call later in the evening. I was breathless with anticipation. I gave him my cell phone number, he gave me his. I drifted through the rest of the day, high on Tylenol Sinus and his voice. He called late on my cell phone, just to tell me goodnight. I had the sweetest dreams.

The next morning before work, I checked my e-mail. He had written to tell me how wonderful it had been for him, how he had never connected so immediately to another person, how he wanted us to meet and be lovers. How he was married.

Married. *Damn.*

Why are all the good ones married? Because most women married to a good one are too smart to let them get away. But, was he really a good one? He was married, and he was searching a pretty racy online dating site for women within fifteen minutes of his office. He was a dog.

My first reaction was regret. My second one was anger. My third reaction was guilt because I knew I would stay connected to him.

That phone call took place over ten years ago. We have never met, though he has been in New York and I have been in Chicago. Four years ago, we missed each other by five minutes. I had just left Millennium Park when he called to say he was there, looking for a hot blonde.

Trapped with my family, I was almost happy I could not rush back to him; I didn't want to ruin our relationship with reality. But, I wanted him, desperately, hands shaking as I told him "maybe next time."

He sends me his *Slate* column, his op-ed pieces from the *Chicago Tribune*, his scholarly articles. I send him briefs, decisions, chapters from my romance novel. He is the first person I call when I have read a really great book or seen a quirky indie movie; he does the same. He seems to sense when I need some words of support and calls. I write when he has been absent for awhile and ask how his wife or his mother is feeling; both suffer from chronic illnesses, and he is a caregiver. My secretaries used to fight over who would answer the phone when I told them I was expecting a call from him; his voice is that compelling.

He likes to say we are like Ellen Burstyn and Alan Alda in *Same Time, Next Year*. A couple who carry on an affair for twenty years, one weekend a year, though both are married when they meet. Except he was married, I was a widow with men in my life, and we have never had even one night together.

To paraphrase Rosie O'Donnell's character in *Sleepless in Seattle*: he doesn't want to be in love, he wants to be in love in the movies. We are Bogart and Ingrid Bergman in *Casablanca*; we are John Gavin and Susan Hayward in *Back Street*; we are every hero and heroine in every thwarted love affair ever put on film. I wonder sometimes if our relationship survives because it is not played out in the real world but on the written page or computer screen, in whispered telephone conversations late at night. But, it continues.

It is not right. He doesn't see it as being unfaithful, but I know it is. The intimacies we share should only be shared with a spouse or lover, not an interloper. He argues no one is hurt by our friendship, and we are, truly, friends, above all else. Still, our attraction to each other plays an important part in our relationship; we tease, we flirt, we suggest all manner of outrageous things to each other, things I have never anatomically been capable of doing; and with his age and bad heart, things that would probably kill him. But, more often than not, he asks about my book and my kids, and we talk about his daughters and his students.

    I can't imagine my life without him in it.

GEORGIO

Tantric sex. That stumped me. I had been maneuvering my way through several online dating sites for some time, and I could decipher most of the acronyms (BBW, BDSM) and knew many of the references to position (slow and deep, on top), partner (sub, dom, bi) and preferences (oral, kinky, intimate, discreet), but I had not come across tantric as a reference to sex. There it was, as the profile line next to a photo of a tanned, white-haired, laughing man, with Vegas spread out behind him. Intrigued, I opened his message.

He called me *Cara*. He was from Argentina, but his parents were Italian. He worked on the Second Floor at the Capitol, and he taught business courses online. He lived nearby, had several dogs and a huge garden from which he obtained the ingredients for his famous tomato sauce, which he called gravy. He wrote with an accent; that is, he used some idioms incorrectly. His exotic prose and his handsome face immediately charmed me. He was cocky, assertive, and into tantric sex. I had to question him about that. He explained it meant the two partners were incredibly attuned to one another to prolong the experience and heighten the orgasms. The process involved gazing into each other's eyes, continuous kissing and caressing, deep breathing, and certain positions where the partners were joined but not actively engaged in intercourse.

Okay, I was mucho intrigued now.

He insisted on a photograph, and after a few more e-mails, I relented and sent him the red lace bra picture and the one of me in my mink in Lake Placid. I reserved those photos for men on my A-list: they intimated sensuality and affluence. I knew I would need both to ensnare Georgio. Now, he was *mucho* interested, especially once I let him know I had been a judge and had no children living with me but did have a pedigreed Yellow Labrador at home. The man was into status symbols.

We spoke on the phone to set up a meeting. The moment I heard his voice, I knew I had to have him. Think deep and sexy; Antonio Banderas combined with Marcello Mastrioanni.

Think Latin and cosmopolitan and in control. We danced a bit on the phone, trying to determine where we would meet—State Street or Wolf Road—until I tipped my hand by suggesting my house. I rarely invited them to my house; I didn't want that level of intimacy. But, I wanted Georgio. We agreed to the following evening around nine. It was early autumn; my son was off at college, and the Legislature was not in session.

He arrived a few minutes early in a nondescript dark sedan. He was wearing black Ray-Ban sunglasses, a starched white business shirt, faded blue jeans, loafers with no socks. He was gorgeous with his tall, tan physique, perfect white teeth; I watched his sexy saunter up to my front door. I was wearing a starched white shirt, white lace camisole peeking through, faded blue jeans torn at the knee and the ass, bare feet, except for red polish. My blonde hair was spiked, and I cradled a goblet of cold Beune Blanc in my hand. The diamond on my right ring finger matched the ones in my ears. I had carefully chosen my clothes; it was my seduce-older-richer-guy outfit. The shirt was expensive and had come straight from the laundry; tied at the waist, it hid my less than slender middle. The jeans were my daughter's cast-offs and gave that *I really am not out to impress you* vibe and showcased my still halfway decent butt. The diamonds bespoke wealth and conceit, the bare feet a casual attitude, plus no socks to pull off awkwardly. It was a look that worked on the right man, and Georgio was the right man.

Alex, my aging Yellow Lab, sat at my feet, tail wagging in delicious anticipation. In his canine mind, man equaled someone to play fetch with, so he greeted every masculine visitor, delivery man or potential lover, with the same easy affection. I opened the door to this exquisite man. When Georgio stepped inside my foyer, I caught a whiff of cologne or aftershave. I couldn't identify it, but even now, years later, if I smell it on a passing man in the mall or at a restaurant, I have an immediate reaction. His sunglasses came off to reveal dark brown eyes and thick black eyelashes.

To his credit, he first greeted Alex, scrunching his ears and murmuring a mixture of Italian and English. Then his gaze fell on me. His hand reached out to cup my chin. His thumb stroked my lower lip. He whispered *Cara* before he kissed me. *Okay, the man could kiss. He could really kiss.* His lips were a seductive promise on mine, brushing, touching, whispering across my mouth. I didn't move. There in my foyer, the door lamp casting a trail of light out into the encroaching darkness, I stood like a statue, barely breathing, wine glass dangling from the fingers of my right hand, my left clenched on the newel post to keep me from toppling into his arms. In a daze, I realized he was winning the opening salvo of our little battle of the sexes. I gathered my wits and touched my tongue to his lips. *Take that.* In an instant, his arms were around me, pressing me to him, lifting me to his all-encompassing embrace. *Okay, I surrender.*

After several more moments of kissing, we both stepped back at the same moment. We stood almost glaring at each other.

"Would you like a glass of wine?" I did not stammer.

"Yes. White?"

"Yes." I turned and walked down the hall to the kitchen. I knew his eyes were on my tush, partially revealed by the rip in my jeans. "Close the front door, would you, *por favor*?"

He complied.

We shared a glass of wine and more kisses, spread around the kitchen and back deck, with Alex in between us or just the two of us clasped in a tight embrace. It was not too long before we stumbled up the stairs. I had set the stage with candles and perfume on the sheets, *Lolita Lempicka*, the really good stuff. He undressed me down to cami and bikinis; I undressed him down to white briefs (I much prefer boxers, but I was not going to complain). Georgio wore a thick gold chain around his neck from which hung a heavy crucifix. My eyes skittered away, a brief flash of guilt coursing through me at that sign. I wore a thin gold chain, with a chai and my children's baby rings, dangling between my breasts. He was muscular and tall; I was soft and short, but stretched out on my bed, I fit perfectly into his arms.

He was kissing me senseless. I was not in control. So I slid down his body and gained the upper hand. *Literally.* He muttered, "*Oh, Dios mio! Madonna!*" Then his strong arms pulled me up into a sitting position. He plunked me down onto his lap, my legs encircling him, his legs crossed and drawn up. He pulled my cami up and over my head. We sat like that for a long time, chest to chest, lips to lips, his hardness pressed against me. *This must be the tantric part. Cool.*

But that was not it. He slid off my bikinis and removed those ridiculous white briefs. *Oh, my!* He had the most perfect penis I had ever seen, and by then I had seen quite a few. It was perfect in size and shape and status; he was circumcised, hard, and looked to be just a bit bigger than I needed. I couldn't wait to feel it, but he withheld that pleasure for what seemed like forever as he teased me and made me tease him. But, when we finally joined, I fit him like a glove. And he was as a maestro with a fine instrument. If I could have sung the *Hallelujah Chorus*, I would have. *Perfect.* This was what I had been searching for! And I must say, I left him gasping and grinning as I sauntered to the bathroom to fetch a warm washcloth to soothe his fevered brow and other parts.

Now, he was in great physical shape, and I was certainly not. But, I had learned attitude was everything, especially with a supremely confident male like Georgio. Women friends, who heard some of my bedroom tales and were in far better shape than I, were astonished I would walk around naked in front of any man, especially one I had been intimate with. My theory was two-fold: act like you have a great body, and they will see you as having a great body; men only looked at breasts anyway, and mine were still pretty damn good. And, if they had a problem with my voluptuous curves, scars and marks, I didn't want them. With rare exceptions, it worked.

Only a few men, and they were not nearly as perfect as Georgio, had any issue with my age or weight.

As I returned to the bed and ministered to him, all I saw was admiration and desire in his eyes. "Cara, you unman me with a single touch." And I did. Again. And again.

So began our trysts. We met most often early in the morning, before work. I would be in my room and I would hear the front door open and close. "Cara, I bring you tomatoes!" He would call up the stairs as he left them on the kitchen counter and got a treat for Alex. Our tantric lovemaking was saved for the nights when we had more time. We met once or twice a week during the Legislative session, less frequently in the summer when my son was home or Georgio was off to Argentina or Italy. It was all about the sex, so there was no talk of dinners or movies. But he did bring the most flavorful tomatoes and the most delicious sauce.

We also spoke frequently. He became my source for the inside scoop at the Legislature; he would track down bills and amendments for me. I was his legal advisor on leases for the many rental properties he owned or the traffic tickets his son received. Whenever I was lonely or horny, I would summon him and he would come to me. I reciprocated as best I could.

Then...the phone call. "Cara, I am getting married."

"Really? Who?"

"Remember my friend, the one who I have been helping because she is so ill? Well, she is dying, and I must marry her so I can take care of her now and her estate when she dies."

I knew about the friend, who occasionally stayed at Georgio's house with him, his aging mother and his sometimes-errant son. I had to admire his loyalty to her, but I was saddened to end our affair. I wished him well and admitted I would miss him. He admitted he had fallen a little in love with me. The truth was I had fallen a little in love with him, too.

It was six months before I heard from him again. It was a casual inquiry about some legislation, but he also wanted to know if I was with someone. I told him I was not, though there was a man in my life. He wanted to meet me; he told me his wife was at death's door and he needed me. I believed him but was unable and unwilling to acquiesce. He persisted over the next few weeks; and I confess, he was wearing me down. My own love life was uncertain, and I had such fond memories of that perfect penis.

Then the e-mail.

I'm Georgio's wife, and I am not dying. I was quite ill, but I have recovered, and we are quite happy, or so I thought, walking our dogs and puttering in our garden. But, apparently he wants more. I read his e-mails to you, and I do not blame you. You seem like a nice woman, but Georgio wants what he wants when he wants it, and he wants you. I thought you should know. I am not sure what I am going to do about him. Today is our first wedding anniversary.

Well, hell. I was pissed. At him and at myself. *How could he be such a liar? How had I been so gullible?* He wrote and called again and again. She had lied, he said, about her illness, to get him to marry her. Now, he had discovered she was much healthier than he had thought, even though she had no interest in sex. And she was about to be much richer as her father had passed away and left her a large sum of money. I surmised he had not been totally altruistic in marrying her, knowing she was an heiress, but I felt some sympathy that he had been misled as well and had been celibate for a whole year.

I suggested he practice the tantric sex by himself. He was not amused.

Que sera, sera, Cara.

JEWISH MARKS

I'm Jewish, by choice and "by injection," as we *shiksas* who have married Jewish men sometimes say. My Jewish husband was the best man I ever knew, certainly the best man I ever dated.

When I decided to start dating again, I was just looking for an age-appropriate, single man who might want to have sex with me. As I moved through the process, I realized I was a bit pickier than that. My range of acceptable had narrowed with each strange or unsatisfying encounter, but I had not yet been particular about my prospective date's religion. Except I thought Moslems and born-again Christians were probably not going to meet my other dating requirements: interest in a short- or long-term intimate relationship. So when I turned to online dating services, I did not limit myself to JDate, the online dating site ostensibly for Jewish singles; any religion or none was acceptable to me in my quest to find a friend and lover, not a husband. I didn't think it was likely I would hit the *beshert* (soulmate) jackpot twice in a lifetime.

After a couple of years on Cupid and Match, I had found several interesting men. Some I had just met once, some I had dated, and one had been my lover for a year. The Rabbi was Orthodox but immoral; Ex-Boyfriend Bob was Jewish but not particularly observant.

My psychologist kept telling me I was not going to form a lasting relationship with any man until I could refer to him by name, not title. I suppose he had a point because my list of lovers and almost lovers and men who-never-had-a-snowball's-chance-in-hell already included The Midget, Dirty Ears, Shaved Snake,

Mr. Less-Is-More, Pepsi-Can Ken, Hot-Tub Ken, and Pitney-Bowes Ken. None of them were Jewish.

Unlike Cupid and Match, AdultFriendFinder.com is an online dating site for people who want to have sex. The site has many levels and variations, but basically it is for people who are looking for an intimate relationship. Some people really missed the mark, though.

As was my practice, I had checked out women too, on AFF, to see what my competition would be. Ever the editor, I was appalled at the writing skills of most of the women. It was not the grammar or spelling that offended me the most. It was the inconsistency in their ads that frustrated me. One woman had a beautiful photograph of herself, hair pulled back in a Sunday school teacher bow, minimal make-up, pretty white ruffled blouse. Her ad read like an XXX-rated porn novel. She was interested in acts I had never heard of and she described all her various physical attributes in graphic detail. Another woman's photograph was a close-up of a very intimate area of her body, the type of photo I had only seen before in *Our Bodies, Ourselves*, only this one included black leather. I read her profile with trepidation and was stunned to find she was interested in holding hands, long walks on the beach and Piña Coladas. I suspect neither lady was very successful in her quest.

My profile on the site was unadorned; I let my words sell me. No pictures of me until I felt reasonably assured the man I was communicating with was not someone I knew professionally or from my shul or the dad of one of my kid's friends or, worse, one of my friends' husbands. Even without the picture, I received several inquiries daily. After all, I was looking for an intimate relationship, not a marriage proposal.

None of the initial inquiries on AdultFriendFinder came from Jewish men. I was not surprised because I still believed most Jewish men were like my late husband—nice guys, guys who didn't know their way around tools of any kind, guys who thought sex was a gift from God. Guys who would rather read the sports news in the *NY Post* than look at *Playboy*, guys who were considerate and thorough, but not real adventurous, lovers…nice Jewish boys.

One evening, I was proven wrong. I found a note from a very handsome, Jewish man who was passionately interested in communicating with me. His name was Mark and he was from New York City. He had moved upstate after his divorce and his two children only visited on the weekends. Mark was funny and irreverent and he loved to call me "Judge." A sometime musician, he scored music for videos and commercials. Instant messages starting popping up from him all the time—each one made me smile or made me laugh. Some even made me sigh.

After several days of e-mails and telephone calls, we agreed to meet at Applebee's. I came from work, having left all pertinent information about my impending date in a sealed envelope with Georgeann. Enclosed were Mark's name, address and telephone number, along with his screen name and e-mail address. As always, I agreed to call her at ten o'clock that evening to check in and let her know I was okay. These are just some of the precautions I had learned any woman must take when meeting a man for the first time, no matter how harmless he sounds online or on the phone.

I arrived at Applebee's at the appointed hour, and there he was. Very good-looking, even though he had a little less hair than in his photograph. Mark shook my hand and leaned in to give me a kiss on the cheek…my trademark move!

"Gotcha, Judge," he murmured with a laugh.

We ordered drinks and chatted. Mark was the same as he had been on the phone: witty, charming and sexy. We ordered another round of drinks and some appetizers. I felt a little *zing* as he reached over and stroked my fingers. The chemistry was definitely there. Time to make a move.

"Did you feel that, too?" I gazed at him and smiled.

"Yes." He paused and teased, "You're hot."

"I am that, yes." I was flirting outrageously with him. "And a bit naughty, too."

Where had that come from?

"Define 'naughty.'" A lawyer, I could deflect a leading question with the best.

"You do that judicial look with your eyes, but you lick your lower lip, just so, slowly. You know what you're doing."

"Well, darlin', consider where you found me. It's not like we met on JDate."

He took a sip of beer and stroked his finger across the middle of my palm. I felt that touch down in my gut. I looked deep into his brown eyes and sought to regain the upper hand.

Before I could parry his move with one of my own, he asked me, still smiling, still stroking my palm, "Do you like toys?"

So much for me being in control. I wanted to say, "Define toys," but I had already used that line, so I fell back on another of my *put the ball in their court* answers.

"Well, I do have a set of engraved Smith & Wesson handcuffs."

It was his turn to look surprised. His eyebrows flew up and then he chuckled. "I have a cage."

What? He mentioned it so nonchalantly at first I thought I had not heard him correctly. "Really?" I took another sip of wine.

"Really. I think you would like it."

I knew at that moment Jewish Mark and I were going no further. But in the interest of research for my dating memoir and providing pertinent information to my girlfriends, I said, "Tell me about it."

"It's gold and it collapses. I store it in the bedroom closet when my kids come to visit."

Yuck. How do you mention "cage" and "kids" in the same sentence unless you're the witch in Hansel and Gretel?

"What do you do with it when they're not around?" I had withdrawn my hands from the table; they were clasped tightly around my glass of wine.

"I tie up naked women and lock them in it."

Right! "And naked women let you do this?" *Was this guy certifiable?*

"They love it."

"I'll bet they do." This time I gulped the last of the wine. "And are you naked too?"

"Oh, yeah, it's a real turn-on." He was genuinely grinning at me, like the two of us were sharing some really cool secret.

"Well, I can understand how it would be arousing for you to have a naked, bound woman at your disposal, while you, um, enjoy yourself." I think my voice squeaked on that line, but I was trying to maintain my cool. And, even though I thought he was nuts, I really wanted to know how his story would end. "But, does the woman enjoy this too?"

"The woman climaxes like crazy!"

Stop? This made no sense to me. I should have left then because he was really starting to make me uneasy, but I had to ask that last question.

"If you're outside of the cage, how does the woman tied up inside it climax?"

"I poke her with a stick." He grinned, satisfied, as I choked on my wine. *Well, I just had to ask.*

"Okay, Mark, now I have something to tell you." He leaned forward with anticipation.

"Put both your hands on the table in front of you." He quickly complied.

"See that black minivan outside the window? That's my car. See, I've just unlocked it," I said, as I pushed the button on my key ring. He was literally licking his lips.

"I am going to stand up and put on my coat, and then I am going out to my car. You are going to sit here just like this until I get in the car and wave to you." His eyes were gleaming.

"Then I am going to drive away and you are never going to contact me again. And if I ever hear about you from any woman I know, I am going to put *you* in a cage." His mouth dropped open as I slid out of the booth, purse in hand.

Needless to say, my phone call at 7:30 that night to Georgeann left us helpless with laughter, wondering where the nice Jewish boys were.

A few months later I met another Jewish Mark online. I thought it might be Cage Guy, as I now referred to him, but after a few chats with Jewish Mark 2 I knew it wasn't the same guy.

Jewish Mark 2 would never lock a naked woman in a cage for his pleasure. He wanted his satisfaction up close and personal, he wrote to me one night, because punching a woman in the face at the moment of climax really heightened the pleasure for both of them.

Since then I have blocked every man named Mark who has contacted me. Call *me* crazy.

THE WINE CRITIC—FIRST ENCOUNTER

I will never quite forgive Kevin Costner, Pierce Brosnan, Harrison Ford, Michael Douglas and Clint Eastwood. There I was, barely in my fifties, and each one of those luscious men, either my contemporaries or slightly older, had done just what the media said all men in their forties, fifties and sixties should be doing—they had found sex and romance with much younger women; women, in some cases, young enough to be their daughters. Extrapolating data from their case histories led me and many of my single female friends to but one conclusion—we were the trophy wives/lovers of the seventy-to-eighty-year-old set. And I was finding those who were in their sixties. My adventures were becoming more wide-ranging than even I had ever believed they could.

In addition to local lovers, I had also attracted newspapermen—Tony from the *Chicago Tribune*, Evan from the *NY Post*—not much longevity with either. I sent Tony back to his more age-appropriate girlfriend. The *Season* in Saratoga ended after six weeks and so did Evan, though I still get my horse-betting tips from his column. I figured either the *Washington Post* or the *New York Times* was due as my next dating source. And then there he was on AdultFriendFinder. Marshall Hennessey.

My first impression was erudite. My second was a bit full-of-himself. My third was that he was very horny. I was right on all three counts. And he knew all about white burgundies.

I admit, although the site was one for hooking up, I had decided not to dummy up my profile. Just because I didn't want to marry them did not mean I was willing to lower my intellectual standards. Surely, there were bright, funny, experienced men online who just wanted an intimate relationship with a smart, sassy, and sexy fifty-ish woman? And I needed to be able to talk with them. If I only wanted a quick roll in the hay with no conversation, I could drive over to The Rusty Nail and crook my finger. I wanted to be seduced and that meant my mind as well as my body. Not only was my profile full of alliteration, double entendres and tests, it listed my honest-to-goodness obscure favorites. From the operas of Puccini and the songs of Eric Clapton and Garth Brooks to white burgundy as my drink of choice and the Adirondack Mountains as my most favorite place on Earth. One intrepid man attempted to correct me by pointing out all burgundies were red wines. I slapped him down in public and then blocked him from further contact—pompous ass.

Marshall loved Puccini, Clapton and Beaune Blanc. I had to look that up, as the only white burgundy I was familiar with was the spectacular bottle of Pouilly Fuissé that had been a long-ago but well-appreciated wedding gift. Beaune Blanc is a white wine made in the Burgundy region of France, along the Côte du Beaune. Research was required before I even responded to his first message. And he had a wine shop in the Adirondacks and a home on Tupper Lake.

Bingo!

We began communicating immediately. He was a bit too much for me even before I learned he had been the first wine critic at one of the world's largest newspapers and then Senior Managing Editor for a specialty wine magazine. He was enamored with my law degree, my former judicial title and my red lace bra picture. I hooked him within days; he had landed me by the second e-mail.

It was summer 2004. Marshall was becoming more and more anxious to meet. So one hot August morning, as I lazed around by the pool on one of my infrequent days off, I decided it was time to drive up the Northway and explore my past and perhaps my future. I told my son I was going to Tupper Lake to look up some relatives, and I was not lying. My father had been dead for almost eight years, and my old hurts were dissolving into fresh regrets that he had died while we were estranged.

I headed out in the heat of late morning in my deluxe, now almost famous, minivan, AC blasting and leather seats warming my sometimes tricky back. Springsteen, Garth and Faith were blaring from the speakers, and my Diet Coke was cold and refreshing. It was a good omen.

I turned off Route 87 at Exit 29 and looped up through the mountains, passing North Creek and the Hudson River, busy with white water rafting tours, turning sharp left at Long Lake, seaplanes taking off as I passed over the bridge at the inlet in town. Right turn at Blue Mountain Lake, climbing the steep incline past the Adirondack Museum. Straight north for a long stretch.

I eased into the Village of Tupper Lake. The lake makes its appearance first. It's not a discrete-edged lake, like Lake Placid. It is surrounded by wetlands, the shoreline blurred by grass and spots of dark water. My dad frequently told us about the Royal Canadian Air Force plane that crashed into those wetlands early in World War II, mistaking the snow-covered surface as a large field rather than a partially frozen lake. Many brave RCAF men were lost on that wintery night, he said, and I said a prayer as I passed by on my way into the Village. There was the Catholic Church, St. Alphonse's, we attended when visiting relatives for funerals or weddings.

There was the oldest synagogue in the Adirondacks as you turn to go into Faust, a suburb of Tupper Lake. There was the old family home, poor looking even now. I stopped the minivan and stared at the ramshackle house where I think some second or third cousins now reside. I thought of the grinding poverty my father knew as a boy and young man, and I felt some measure of forgiveness enter my heart. Much of what he became had come from his wretched upbringing.

Let the past stay in the past. Forgive and forget.

In much lighter spirits, I turned toward Saranac Lake. One of the prettiest drives in the North Country is the road between Tupper and Saranac, dotted with inlets, ponds and small lakes, interspersed with stands of ancient pine and young birches. I looped around Lake Flower into Saranac Lake's business district.

Marshall's store is in the middle of town. I parked my ride and checked my lip gloss in the mirror. Tan and blonde, eyes outlined in navy blue, lashes thick and black, I was ready. I was going to meet my aristocratic lover in torn blue jeans and a starched white business shirt tied at my waist, bejeweled navy flip-flops on my feet and blood red polish on toes and fingers. I was *so* ready.

Entering the shop, I saw no one. I turned to the left and wandered over to a wall of bins laden with dark green wine bottles, all bearing French labels, most from Chateau Lafitte. Lafitte is a world-renowned vintner. I did not recognize many of the varieties, but did manage to hone in on a bottle of Pouilly Fuissé. The voice behind me startled me, but I did not jump, I did not turn.

"Can I help you find anything in particular?" *Mmmm. As sexy in person as over the phone.*

"I'm not sure. I was led to believe that you carried a rather extensive collection of white burgundies, but I am a little disappointed by the rather paltry selections I see here." My voice was smooth, but my insides were jittery and uncertain.

A pause. A sharp intake of breath. *"Judge?"*

I turned, pulling off my sunglasses as I did. I faced a white-haired, white-mustachioed, red-cheeked man, with the brightest blue eyes I had ever seen. A bit taller than I had thought he would be, definitely older than the fifty-five years he had posted on his profile, the red cheeks probably a result of imbibing large amounts of alcohol frequently. And that air of absolute certainty of self, that assuredness of the well-born, well-educated, well-traveled, well-known, self-made man. Exactly the man I was looking for; exactly the man I needed more than I knew. I stepped into him, wrapped my arms around his neck and kissed him hard and deep. Laughing, I looked into his startled eyes and said,

"*Bonjour*, Monsieur Hennessey. *C'est moi.*"

THE WINE CRITIC—PART DEUX

I took Spanish in high school and college. Insane, given I grew up in a town thirteen miles from the New York border with Quebec. *I should have taken French.* I would think that often during the months I spent with Monsieur Hennessey.

C'est manifique! That was his response, his blue eyes dancing with laughter, his hands rubbing up and down my back. We were alone in the store, surrounded by hundreds of bottles of wine and liquor, thousands of corks strewn across the base of the two front windows in a careless display of just how much wine this man had drunk over the years. He was thrilled I had made the long trek north, thinking I had come here with the sole purpose of seeing him. I did not disabuse him of the notion, especially not after he offered to close the shop early and provide me with dinner at the lake, preceded by a serious bout of lovemaking and followed by a moonlight cruise in one of his antique wood-hulled boats.

"You can stay the night, can't you?"

"Sadly, no, I have to work tomorrow and my son doesn't know where I am." I did not do sleepovers easily.

The first time the complications of my life would interfere with his plans but not the last. He quickly arranged to pick up dinner and for a part-time employee to cover the store. Before we headed out, I announced if he wanted hot and heavy sex that night, we would need some Tequila. Wine would put me in a romantic mood, but for the type of seduction he was expecting, I needed several shots of that fiery, liquid courage. *It is good to know a man with a wine and spirits shop*, I mused, as I lifted a bottle of Sammy Hagar's Cabo Wabo Silver off the shelf.

"I didn't even know I carried that," he muttered, as he marked the $65.00 charge down on a ledger next to the cash register. I snickered.

I followed him and his vintage Cadillac out of town, stopping at the gourmet food store for what looked to be an enormous basket of food. Back along the scenic route from Saranac to Tupper. Waving casually to the guard in the gatehouse at the entrance to the enclave of twenty or so private, waterfront, homes that ringed Big Tupper, I felt positively *aristocratic*.

Marshall's log house, perched high above the waterfront, affording expansive views of islands, mountains and million dollar homes from the wrap-around deck. Inside, it was a natural wood paradise, an antique-laden, Frenchified version of an Adirondack Great Camp, complete with a stuffed boar's head over the fireplace. Turning to him, I promptly announced the long- dead animal would hereafter be called "Rogue," the same nickname I had given him. The desire flaming in his eyes silenced me.

He moved into me with graceful ease, pressing me back against the kitchen counter, his mouth moving greedily over mine. He could kiss, really kiss, and that white handlebar moustache tickled my upper lip with promises of much more erotic adventures to follow. *Damn.* I was already drunk on him, intoxicated by his utterly complete sense of self.

"Mmmm." I licked my lip ever so slowly. Always a good response to that kind of frontal assault. It gave me time to gather my senses and assess my situation. And it had the added effect of focusing my partner's eyes glassily on my mouth. "Let's open up that Cabo, darlin'. I assume you have limes?"

I made quick work of opening the bottle and slicing the limes. When I asked for salt, he produced a tin of Fleur de Sel. Expensive French sea salt, hand-harvested from evaporated seawater along the coast of Brittany. *Incredible!* Or should I say *incroyable? What was I doing with this man?*

Marshall had never done shots of tequila before, he admitted, as I handed him the shot of Sammy Hagar's premium potion. I licked that space at the knuckle of his thumb, on the soft skin, and sprinkled some salt on the dampness I left there. I think his eyes crossed a bit. I know his hand shook in mine. *Score one for me.*

"Okay, lick the salt, toss back the shot and then suck the lime. On my count. One, two, three!"

I was an expert at this, and he was a quick student. In between kisses, we quickly dispatched two more shots of tequila. Then down the long hall to his boudoir.

I was undressed efficiently and exquisitely, with much murmuring about soft skin and perky breasts. He lowered me carefully to the rustic bed, spread with quilts and Hudson Bay blankets, piled with pillows dressed in antique white lace. He stood near me, next to a twig chair and disrobed, tossing each item of clothing, his eyes never leaving mine. Then he was naked. *Oh, yeah, he was older than fifty-five!* Even so, there was an attractiveness about him, an allure, like Michelangelo's sculpture of the dissolute Bacchus.

But, I had come here to seduce and be seduced. I never wavered and soon discovered regardless of the age, penises function in the same way. He was a generous lover though a bit provincial, a bit old-fashioned. Mutually satisfied, I was gasping and he was smiling, as he rose from the bed to don a burgundy dressing gown (no bathrobes for him). He returned with a chilled bottle of Beune Blanc and two lovely wine goblets. We drank most of it and I ravished him again.

Then, on to a dinner lit by candles sputtering in old silver candelabra. Cold poached lobster, asparagus in vinaigrette and a baguette smeared with Brie. And more white burgundy. *Très Français!*

We motored around the lake in one of his wooden boats. I reclined against pillows; facing him and watching the stars wink on in the darkening sky behind him. In a small inlet, loons were beginning their twilight song. I trailed my fingers into the crystal-clear water and mused: *It doesn't get any better than this.* I did not want the evening to end.

Too soon, we docked the boat and climbed the rough-hewn log steps to his house. It was getting late and I had to leave. More passionate kisses, more hugs, more whispered promises. I departed just before nine o'clock, two bottles of Beune Blanc tucked under my arm, a Diet Coke in hand and a smile on my face.

I was looking at a three to four hour drive, accusations from my son and a rough wake-up the next morning. But, I was singing along with Bonnie Raitt at the top of my lungs, still feeling those involuntary shivers, those aftershocks of strenuous and satisfying sex. As I drove south through the hamlets and the wilderness, my cell phone rang in one of the rare areas where there was reception.

"Judge?"

"Hello, Rogue."

"How are you doing?"

"I'm tired, but I'm fine. Thanks for the Diet Coke. It helps. Next time, I'll bring Red Bull."

Damn! Why had I said that? I never let on that I expected a next time.

"Will there be a next time?"

"Will there?" I was uncertain with this man, unsure of his feelings.

"Yes. I adore you." How easily the words spilled from his lips.

My heart leapt. Maybe he would be the one. For a moment, I let the thought careen around my fertile imagination. I could envision us traveling to France, dining out in New York City, spending the cold months at Hilton Head or Amelia Island, summers in the Adirondacks. So I said, "I adore you, too. I'll see you soon."

Then I thought of why I called him "Rogue." Thrice-divorced, the last time caused by his sojourn in the bed of one of his wife's friends. When I queried him as to why he had done that, he answered she had asked him to sleep with her, and he didn't know how to respond without hurting her feelings. When I suggested *No* might have been an appropriate answer, he was astonished because he had not wanted her to tell his wife he had been rude. I laughed at that one, but it started that niggling worry in the pit of my stomach. This might end badly. But, my life had already had some bad endings, so what did I have to fear?

As I drove on through the night, I started to laugh. *"C'est la vie!"*

THE WINE CRITIC—ADIEU

I started saying good-bye as soon as I met him. He was out of my league, and I was out of his reach. My heart was still buried in a grave in Brooklyn; all I had to give was my body, my mind, some of my time and a little of my soul. But certainly, I could stay through the summer and maybe into the fall. Summer in the Adirondacks was too beautiful to resist. His cabin at the lake was too tempting. Days spent on the deck listening to the loons call and watching the hummingbirds in jewel-colored swarms around the feeders were a balm to my bruised spirit.

It had been a rough summer, with my son preparing to depart for college, and it was going to be a tough autumn. I needed a refuge. Camp Loon, as Marshall called his lakeside log home, was the answer.

I would have wanted him without the pedigree and the accoutrements, I told myself. I found him intelligent, attractive and sexy. But he drank too much, he was not used to being monogamous, he lived a three-hour-plus drive on twisty mountain roads away from me, and I didn't believe I was good enough for him.

My choice in men, with the exception of my late husband, has always been suspect. I have always fallen for the man just slightly beyond my reach, usually a bad boy with a tough track record; quirkily attractive, like Alan Rickman: intelligent but not necessarily well-educated; and, almost always, a heavy drinker. And I have always felt somehow they were doing me a favor by dating me because I was unlovable. My insecurity complex may have come from my placement in the family: the third child, the second daughter, the mistake. Or my status among my friends:

not the smartest, but close, not the prettiest, but close, and certainly the poorest. I had always felt somehow less than the others, needing to earn their affection and respect because I had always believed somehow I did not deserve it just by being myself. I had to be something more. This chronic low self-esteem cost me the man I loved in college; I never believed *he* could love *me*. My late husband had given me my first dose of utter self-confidence and became, to use the title of a saccharine but too-true song, the *Wind Beneath My Wings*. And then he was gone, and I was adrift again in my sea of self-doubt. Despite the best efforts of my shrink and years of therapy, I still doubt myself.

And here I was with a famous, aristocratic, wealthy lover. What to do? Brazen it out.

That had been my mantra for most of my adult life. Act like I was just as good—no, better, even though I believed I was not. And it worked. He chased me, casting his lure that summer, and I let him reel me in. I was putting mileage on my minivan at an alarming rate; my son was agitated by the amount of time I was spending in my hometown, which is where he thought I was going on those three-day weekends, and my not-too-robust bank of vacation time was dwindling. But, God, I felt so alive!

Marshall had a sly, dry sense of humor that never failed to elicit a giggle from me. He was so well-read we often lost ourselves in book discussions for hours. He always cooked, and he was a skilled chef. I arrived in the evening to a well-constructed meal and bottles of wine, chilling or breathing, served on the deck or in the dining room, beautiful surroundings either way.

He was obviously enamored with me, in lust and slipping into love, though he never said so. I was a trophy on his arm, introduced to the other lake-site owners as "the Judge." at the end-of-summer winetasting. I stood apart and observed the guests. I felt out of place among this tightknit, elite group. I knew these women; I had gone to college with these women (a small women's college in the 70's). I had mingled with them at my daughter's exclusive girls' high school in the 90's (the cost of which bankrupted me). I knew their Pappagallo shoes and sweater sets, their strings of pearls and gold shell earrings. And I knew the men. I had occasionally seen them appearing before me when I sat on the bench; I knew them from law school reunions. I knew their Brooks Brothers blazers and French-monogrammed shirt cuffs, the flat accents of Phillips Exeter and Harvard. Marshall was amused later that evening by my assessment of his guests. I identified, without error, the philanderers, the nouveau riche, the old money, the heavy drinkers and substance abusers among the partygoers and the polite, nice, genuine men and women scattered through the crowd.

As was becoming our habit of late, I put Marshall to bed around ten o'clock and then read by the bedside light whilst sipping a lovely champagne cognac from France, for which I was developing an addiction. I would quickly drift into a deep sleep. But, I was up at three in the morning to pee and then wander down the hall to the great room, my white Laura Ashley lawn and lace nightgown floating around me, to remove the brandy snifter from Monsieur Hennessey's limp hand and tuck him in on the sofa for a few more hours of sleep. It was his practice to rise in the middle of the night, sip brandy or cognac and read in front of the fire until he drifted into sleep again. Sometimes he awoke me for a middle-of-the-night tryst. I liked those evenings best; his lips warm with strong spirits, his lovemaking silent and urgent and his arms finally pulling me against him as we both tumbled back into our dreams.

I was dreaming about him far too much. The long, early morning drives through the wilderness that is the Adirondack Park from his home to mine gave me a lot of time to think. Sketchy cell phone reception, no radio stations and my music CD's made me drowsy instead of keeping me awake. I played out elaborate scenarios in my head to stay alert. Retired from the State, living in the Adirondacks and Florida and France. Writing romance novels. Married.

Did I just say that? Did I say "married"? Yes, I had begun to think of marriage as an option for me. I, who had entered the dating scene as a totally assured opponent to the notion I would ever have a long-term relationship again, much less marry, had actually begun to think of Marshall as husband material. I was insane, I told myself during those drives. He had been married three times already; he and monogamy were almost total strangers. I was pretty much convinced he was a good bit older than the fifty-five he had posted on his profile, and I was terribly afraid he might be an alcoholic. It would never work.

But then, the lawyer in me argued there was the house on the lake, the shop in my favorite location in the world, the wine cellar, the intelligence, the sexiness, the joie de vivre, the savoir faire and the money. Had I really become that crass? Or was I trying to justify a relationship I knew was going to hurt me emotionally by the material benefits I might gain?

I walked a precarious and narrow line for the rest of the autumn. I wanted to be with him, but I wanted it to be his idea; so I remained a bit elusive and drew him to me. He was utterly charming and furthered my education in the intricacies of red wines as we explored a few restaurants in Saratoga. But, I must admit, he was not as attractive to me when he was out of his natural setting: Camp Loon and the Wine & Spirits Shop.

I brought the posse to him during our pre-Thanksgiving weekend in Lake Placid, and he arranged a wine tasting. I was sure my aristocratic and knowledgeable lover would impress them; their envy would further reassure me my daydreams of marriage might work. Surprisingly to me, they found him snobby, a heavy drinker and old! Shocked by their reaction, I wondered: what did they see that I did not? I shook off my doubts. After their departure, he came to me, and we shared a wonderful evening.

Wonderful until he awakened me in the middle of the night by dropping a brandy snifter on the slate floor in the kitchen. I helped him back to bed, and it was there and then that he drunkenly proposed marriage. I was astonished. It had been my dream, spun totally in my imagination, built upon no foundation of any declarations of love from him. Even in his proposal, he did not mention love. He told me again he adored me, he missed me when I was at home, and he thought I was witty, intelligent and sexy. And I would be totally stunning if I could only drop twenty-five pounds. I was to be the fourth Mrs. Hennessey, and I did not quite fit the image yet. That was when I knew I would never love him, and we had no future together. I made love to him ferociously; I wanted him to miss me terribly when I was gone from his life.

I saw him a few more times in the winter and through the spring, but the time between visits was lengthening. He left for France in March without me, but with promises I would go with him the next time. I knew I would not. As spring became summer, I visited Camp Loon one more time. There were new names in the guestbook on the table by the door; some of them were women's names. He did not mention marriage again though he complimented me on the weight I had lost during our time apart, time I was spending hopping from one bed to the next.

As summer ended, so did we. He mentioned another's name when we spoke occasionally: Judy. He did plan another winetasting for my friends while we were in Lake Placid in late November. It was there Marshall introduced me to Judy and the large diamond ring on her finger I recognized as his mother's. When he took me aside to ask for my help with a speeding ticket, she was eying me with the open distaste of the current lover for her predecessor—and no small amount of condescension—as she spun the diamond on her finger, making sure it caught the light and gleamed like a beacon, announcing a rough road ahead for me if I trespassed on her property. As Marshall and I concluded our discussions about his ticket, and I named my fee, a case of Lafitte wine, he gave me a copy of the ticket. Another one of my doubts proven true: he was sixty-five to my fifty-two. He had, indeed, lied about his age.

I have no regrets. He gave me a refuge when I needed to escape my job, my home and my life. And I now know enough about wine to impress almost every man I have met since. It is almost enough. But, sometimes I think: *What might have been? Ce qui pourrait avoir été?*

SIR E

I was Princess Dina. My posse had given me the nickname shortly after I began my online adventures in honor of what they perceived as my unprecedented success in exploring the dating pool of the Capital District. Dina was the heroine in my favorite novel at the time, *The Red Tent*, and it rhymed with Xena, Warrior Princess. I received bows from them on an almost daily basis as I related my latest tale of conquest.

A knight in slightly tarnished armor, E was a triathlete, legally separated from his wife, father of twin boys with custody to the wife because he traveled a lot. Younger than me by several years, a workaholic with a lopsided grin and a six-pack abdomen, a techno-geek with the heart of a poet, he beseeched me to meet him. He promised a strong sword and a long lance. He would be, in the words of Chaucer, my own *"verry gentil and parfait knight."* Sir E.

He was as brave as a knight, too, agreeing to meet me at The Office, a bar near my own office, where I went for drinks with Georgeann and Maxie after the office holiday party. So we were already a bit raucous when we got to the restaurant; middle-aged women in holiday attire, in the midst of the Happy Hour twenty-something's. *What was I thinking? Meeting a buff forty-ish guy while surrounded by women half my age. Oh well, he knew my age—he had seen my picture. If he walked, he walked.*

We were well into our second glasses of wine when Georgeann said, "I think that's him!" I turned toward the door. And there he was. Tall, buzz-cut brown hair, amazing smile. Very fit physique. I turned back to my friends. I had told E I would be wearing a red dress. *Let's see if he could find me.*

Georgeann was heard to mutter, "Heartless whore," as she raised her glass to me. Maxie, next to me, was clueless about what was going on.

Within minutes, I felt a warm hand on my shoulder and a voice from above inquiring, "My lady?" I clasped his hand in mine as I looked up and murmured, "My knight." He bent to graze my cheek with a kiss. Both Georgeann and Maxie were gaping at him open-mouthed. He pulled up a chair next to me. Almost as soon as he sat down, a waitress appeared with a beer for him and glasses of wine for my ladies-in-waiting and me. He had stopped at the bar and ordered drinks for us before he even sat down. *Oh, yeah, he was good.*

He was friendly and funny. I liked him immediately. I really liked him. He was so easy to be with. But, I wasn't sure if there was an attraction. Then I felt his hand on my knee. At first, just a gentle caress. I almost missed it; it was so casual and fleeting. I glanced at him; he smiled. *Okay, two can play this game.* I leaned into him, so my breast brushed his arm. His eyes widened, and then he grinned. His next caress was from knee to mid-thigh. I felt that. I felt it in my gut. *Yeah, the sizzle was there.*

Four glasses of wine in two hours, and it was time to leave. I wasn't sure about driving on a snowy evening in the dark. Maxie was in better shape, so she was driving Georgeann; E said he would walk me to my car. Both women gave me the *you better behave but if you don't, we want details* look as we hugged in the parking lot. E hugged them too, which made me smile even more. I really, really liked him.

The famous mom black minivan with gray leather seats beckoned. I clicked the keys to open the door. E was behind me. I turned... to do what? Say goodnight? I didn't want to say good night. Apparently, neither did he. I was immediately wrapped in his arms—my back against the vehicle. He was devouring me with his mouth. I was limp in his embrace.

"I could not keep my hands off you in there. You know that?"

"I felt the same."

"Then, when we were leaving, you were walking in front of me, I wanted my hands on your ass so bad that I almost grabbed you right there in the bar."

"Really?" He was so good for my ego.

"Really. I've been as hard as a rock since I sat down next to you."

I could feel the truth of his statement pressed against my abdomen. *What was I going to do with this magnificent piece of manhood?* Invite him home? Nope, son was home. Suggest a motel. No, that didn't seem right. *Wait.* I had a minivan, leather seats, darkened windows, parked in a remote part of the lot. *Jackpot*!

Within seconds, we were clambering into the minivan. It had captain's chairs in the middle, which meant there was space between the seats. We scooted through the space and collapsed into each other on the cold leather of the backseat. I was wrapped in my mink, over a red slinky dress, with black patent pumps. He was in a sports jacket with a jaunty scarf wrapped around his neck. *What to do with all these clothes?*

I got his tie off. The mink was now a blanket wrapped around us; my shoes tossed haphazardly on the middle seats. The windows fogged to opaqueness; the interior was becoming tropical from our heavy breathing. He fumbled with a condom and then his hands were everywhere. *Pantyhose.* What to do with pantyhose? He looked up at me.

"Hurry," I implored him. I was burning for him.

"Wait, get these things off." His hands were fumbling with my pantyhose; men just don't know what to do with them...pull them off from the waist or from the toes? They really have no clue.

Inspiration had me ordering him, "Rip them."

"What?"

"Rip them open."

"Damn." He sank his fingers into the nylon at the juncture of my thighs and pulled.

He grinned, I gasped. Cold air hit blistering hot skin as the hose tore asunder. Then another gasp, a sigh, a potential scream silenced by E's mouth on mine. It did not take us long; our foreplay had been too intense. Then I laughed, great gulping giggles, as he let his weight sag against me, still holding my bottom in his big hands. The air was steamy with sweat and sex and silliness. His shoulders began to shake, and then he joined me with a throaty laugh of his own.

"*Damn!*" An oh-so-satisfied grin split his face.

"Yeah, what you said." I was still gasping for air.

"What just happened here?"

"You tell me."

"I have never done that before."

"Neither have I. But I always wanted to have my clothes ripped off." The destruction of an expensive pair of those really sheer pantyhose that had the panties knit right in was not too high a price to pay for that thrill.

Said hose still encased my legs, the elastic was still around my waist, the rest appeared to have disintegrated. With my dress pulled in place, and my coat back on, I could enter my house with the evening's activities undetected. We rearranged ourselves into some semblance of normalcy, kissing and touching throughout. He called me on the ride home and again later to wish me sweet dreams. I was still smiling as I drifted into sleep.

It started as a torrid love affair, but it was also an easy friendship. We spoke a few times a day. We shared stories of our previous dating adventures. It was E who urged me to write my tales. And he wanted me to write his, too. He told me about the two lesbians who lived across the hall from him. About once a month, they wanted a man. They all got together for sushi, and he made love with each of them. They returned the favor by teaching him all their secrets. As he said, "Who knows better how to satisfy a woman than another woman?" I was not going to disagree, having been the beneficiary of that tutoring.

It was a month before we could meet again, the holidays requiring family time. It was bittersweet for E, his first Christmas not at home with his boys.

We arranged to meet after work one day in January. At Microtel, halfway between my office and his. He got there first. I was a little nervous. Our first time had been in the dark, only partially undressed, under the influence of alcohol. Here I was, knocking on the door of a hotel room that contained a much younger, much more athletic man, and there would be light.

He opened the door wearing a towel. *Yeah, much younger and in fantastic physical condition. And obviously aroused.*

He blushed at my perusal. I laughed. He laughed, too.

"I wasn't sure whether I should greet you naked or clothed, so I decided on halfway. I took a shower. I got some white wine." He was nervous, too.

I kissed him. He took my coat. We bumped each other in the small room. His arms went around me to steady me, and that was the end of my awkwardness.

John Mayer's songs have the best lines. Especially *Your Body is a Wonderland.*

My breath caught as E lowered me to the bed; gently, with his hand cupping the back of my head, his lips crushing mine. I sighed into his open mouth, welcoming his questing tongue—welcoming his weight and him. It was way better than the backseat of my minivan. After, we lay in each other's arms, chatting and sipping wine, like old friends. Once again, when I left him, I was laughing and languid with satisfaction.

Our next tryst was at my house. He had been on the road for over a month and returned to me, begging for an entire night. That Friday night was one of the best I ever had. He brought pizza and beer; I baked oatmeal-raisin cookies. We made love in almost every room of the house. The dog followed us from room to room at first but gave up when we headed upstairs.

Ensconced in my big bed, we cuddled and chatted. E was open and easy about his sexuality and his adventures.

He mentioned one guy who had almost kept him from joining AFF, the site where we had met. Like me, he had perused pictures of members of the same sex to see what his *competition* looked like.

"I have to tell you, Dina, that I was totally stunned when I saw this particular picture."

"Why? What was wrong with it?"

"Nothing was wrong with it, but it made me pause. I mean, I think I'm in pretty good shape, and I also think that I'm pretty well endowed in that area. And I had seen pictures of guys who were bigger, smaller, and about the same as me. But, I think I've got a pretty good-looking, pretty good-sized penis, don't you?"

Men are so sensitive about their penises. It's like all the insecurities we have about our weight, our wrinkles, our cellulite, our breasts, our butts, are all rolled up for men in that one organ: if the penis is good, for them, everything about them pales to insignificance.

"Yes, darlin', your penis is just about perfect," I reassured him, and I was not lying.

"Well, I'm looking through profiles, and all of a sudden here's this penis looking back at me. The guy has a death grip on it, and it's bigger than his fist, like it should be. But, right next to it, in his other hand, like for size comparison, is a frickin' can of Pepsi! Can you believe that shit?"

By this point, I was giggling uncontrollably. He looked at me like I was crazy until, between gasps and snorts, I told him the story. A newfound admiration spread across his handsome face.

"You got him to do that? Damn, girl. You *are* good!"

Not to be outdone, E shared one of his outlandish sex adventures. He had decided to experiment with submission and domination. He found a Dominatrix advertising in Metroland and arranged to meet her. At her house in the country. When she came to the door, she was older and dressed the part in black leather and long black hair. She led him upstairs in her old Victorian home. To the second floor. And then to the third.

"I'm telling you, Dina, I was a little nervous. The house looked like something from a vampire movie."

The third floor was fitted out as her chamber. There were assorted tools and devices, lots of black leather and a hook at the peak of the roof from which was suspended a chain. She instructed E to shed his clothes.

"So, I get naked and she walks all around me, touching me here and there with this little black leather crop. I got a little turned on, but I was also starting to sweat. She tells me nothing will happen that I don't want. All I have to do is say the magic word and she will stop."

"What was the magic word?"

"Stop."

I snorted. He grinned and continued.

"She puts my wrists in padded handcuffs and tells me to raise my arms so she can fasten them to the chain. I'm stretched almost to my tiptoes. Then she blindfolds me."

"Seriously, weren't you scared?" I would have been too timid to even go up the stairs.

"Yeah, because then I hear the door open and close. And I realize that I am all alone in the country, in the attic of this house; no one knows where I am, no one around for miles. I can't see, and I can't move. And all I can think is that I could die hanging from that beam, and no one would ever know. And I'd never see my boys again."

I was scared just listening to him. I didn't need to point out how stupid he had been, but obviously because he was in my bed with me, it had turned out all right.

"She came back after what seemed like hours but was really only like fifteen minutes. She took the blindfold off. I must have looked scared; she could tell because, trust me, my erection had disappeared the minute I heard that door close. She lectured me like I was some kid, told me never to do that again—go to someone's house and let them restrain me and blindfold me— unless I knew them a whole lot better and could trust them. She unhooked me then and asked me if I wanted to continue. I said *no thank you*. She didn't even charge me, just slapped my butt and told me to behave in the future."

"Jesus, you were lucky."

"Tell me about it. I decided then and there that I was not interested in S & D."

"I know what you mean," I said, and told him about Cage Guy. We laughed ourselves to sleep.

We went on like that for many months. Once or twice a month, when he was in town. But, I felt increasingly he was missing his boys so much that he was burying himself in work even more than he had been before his separation. On what was to be our last night together at our old favorite, Microtel, I told him he had to go back to his boys. They would be starting Little League in a few months, and he had to be there for them. He admitted he had been seeing his wife again, and they were trying to work it out. She required more of his time; he required more of her interest.

"Idiot. If you were around more to help her, she wouldn't be so tired, and she would probably be more interested in sex."

"You think?"

"Yeah. But even if she isn't, you have to do what you have to do to be with those boys right now. They need a dad. Trust me, I know. Nothing at your job is as important as they are."

When I kissed him goodnight, I knew it was good-bye. A good deed on my part, but I knew I would miss him. We hadn't been in love, I told myself, but still it hurt to have him gone from my life.

Like John Mayer says, I spent quite some time after dreamin' with a broken heart.

E sent me a little pewter knight, with lance and shield, on a rearing horse. It is still on my desk. My own *verry gentil, parfait knight*.

YALIE

    I fell in love with him when I was just sixteen and again when I was almost twenty. And for the last time when I was fifty-two.
    We grew up in the same small town in northern New York. Henry was the doctor's son; I was the daughter of a contractor. He lived in an old brick house on a tree-lined street; I lived in a small clapboard house on a mixed commercial-residential street. Both raised by strict Catholic parents, he attended parochial school, I was a public school girl. But we both liked to act, and we both excelled at public speaking. We were the featured speakers at the American Legion Memorial Day celebration; I read the Gettysburg Address, he read Logan's General Orders of the Day. State Senator Stafford complimented our efforts; thirty-three years later, Henry would run for Stafford's seat in Albany.
    But in 1970 he was a tall, dark, handsome, trim, confident senior in high school. And he was a bad boy. I was a short, slender, sophomore, growing into self-confidence and totally out of my league. We dated sporadically that spring and summer; his kisses were a sweet seduction but could not give him what he wanted. My refusal to have sex with him was the reason for our split. I still believed what the nuns had taught us: you would get pregnant the first time you had sex.
    And I wanted nothing to tie me to that rural, conservative, poor town I called home. So, I kept my knees together and lost Henry to a girl from the Catholic school who had already learned the nuns frequently lied.
    Four years later, I was a much smarter sophomore in college. Home for the Christmas break, I had grown three inches and gained ten pounds, all in my tits and my ass. My brown hair was

down to my waist and my glasses had been traded in for contact lenses. I had traveled to NYC and DC, worked at the United Nations and the ACLU. I was supremely self-confident. And I was no longer a virgin.

I looked up from the beer I was enjoying with my girlfriends at The Franklin, and there he was. Sitting in the corner, not quite as trim but even more handsome, moustache curling above those arrogant lips. He raised his beer to me; I acknowledged the gesture.

We became lovers that night. He seduced me with kisses and Shakespeare. I have always been a sucker for *Romeo and Juliet*; I had lost my virginity to a British grad student at Cornell who recited the entire balcony scene while undressing me. But, while no longer a virgin, I was not that experienced. It was difficult to gain much experience with college boys. They were so afraid a girl might change her mind they tended to rush through foreplay. I kept waiting to feel that overwhelming passion I had read about in my romance novels. Close, but not close enough. And those boys, Henry included, were, I think, so astounded they were actually having sex, they frequently, shall we say, arrived at the parade a little early. Fortunately, they recharged rapidly. But, it was hell on their technique. Henry was better than average, but I was still waiting for that elusive explosion.

We were both involved with people back at college; we became semester-break lovers. Whoever arrived first at The Franklin would play *The Joker* by Steve Miller on the jukebox and do a turn around the bar until we found each other. We made love under the dining room table at his mother's house, under the Christmas tree, in my dad's Olds while still parked in the garage, in the back of my dad's store, in the park. We were inseparable, much to the consternation of the Catholic school girls who still saw him as their property. But, the summer between my junior and senior year, I was in England. That Christmas Henry was away. We met up again the summer between college and law school. He had started a Community Theatre at a rehabilitated factory in town. He wanted me to postpone law school for a year to stay in Malone and help him. As tempting as he was, I declined. If I did not leave then, I never would. I went off to law school and met my future husband the day before classes started. I did not see Henry again for twenty-seven years.

I heard he had returned to Malone in the late 90s as a community development director. Immersed in my own depression, I paid him no mind. After all, what would he see in me? A few years later, though, I had just started dating again; my self-confidence was returning. And Henry had decided to run for the State Senate. I sent him an e-mail wishing him luck, offering my assistance on certain key issues and promising him dinner after the election.

He lost the election, so we scheduled dinner for Lake Placid, not Albany. I was a nervous wreck. I had seen his campaign picture; he was still gorgeous. The moustache was gone, and the hair had grayed, but the warm brown eyes still held mischievous secrets, and the lopsided grin made the kind of seductive promises I knew he could keep.

I opened the door of my condo to him and immediately slammed it in his face. He knocked again.

Opening the door, I leaned against the doorjamb, knees shaking, as I asked, "Do you have a portrait hiding in your attic or what?"

"No, just clean living, your Honor."

"Right." I snorted.

"When did you get blond hair? I like it!" With a quick kiss on my cheek, he came through the doorway and back into my life.

Almost thirty years apart, and we were back in sync almost at once. We shared a lovely dinner in an almost deserted restaurant on Main Street in Placid, looking out over the freezing lake. Wine flowed and so did memories. Henry had left for New York and Broadway the summer after I departed for law school. He almost made his mark at Shakespeare in the Park, but then opted for Yale Business School. My jaw dropped.

"You went to Yale?"

"Yeah, without ever receiving my Bachelor's Degree. I dazzled them with my interview."

"I'll bet you did, Yalie."

I felt the attraction but was unsure in the face of his gorgeousness and success in the NYC real estate market. He told me he had two kids and was divorced.

"I heard about your husband, Blondie. I'm sorry about that. How did you manage?"

"You know me, I just push ahead."

He smiled and took my hand. It was a moment, but I pulled away. Back at the condo, we shared some of the Wine Critic's cognac and talked comfortably about his plans to stay in Malone and start an alternative energy consultant group now the election was over. Too soon he left, with a tender kiss on my check and one of his famous full-body hugs.

Christmas rolled around, and I was in Malone, facing the holiday with my vicious sister, her useless family and my poor mom. Walking the dog, Christmas Eve, I called Henry on the cell phone. It was bitter cold and my prospects were dim compared to the icy diamonds the stars made against the black velvet sky. I was happily surprised when he answered.

"Yalie, I'm going fucking nuts here."

"I hear you; your sister is a piece of work. Did I tell you she hit on me when I was at the Blind Ladies' group during the campaign? There I am talking to your mom, and you know I love your mom, Blondie, and your sister was hanging all over me."

"She always hated you when we were dating. But the pickings are pretty slim around here, Yalie; she must have been desperate. I hope you weren't that desperate!"

"Blondie, in your family, it has always been only you for me."

"I need a drink or five and some mindless sex. This holiday is endless."

"If my son was not staying with me, I would be happy to help you out."

Whoa. Did I just proposition Henry, and did he just say "yes"?

"I'll be back in town in February."

"I'll be waiting. Try to have a Happy Hanukkah, Blondie."

"Yalie, have a Merry Christmas."

I returned to my mother's house two months later. My sister was being alternately sickeningly sweet and venomously nasty to both Mom and me. Henry and I made plans to have drinks at a local bar.

"I thought you came home to visit Mom," my sister snarled as I got ready.

"I did, but Mom is watching television, and I am going out with Henry."

"You'll be doing more than that if I know you and him."

"Yes, Mary, if I'm lucky, I'll probably be fucking his brains out for most of the night." That shut her up.

When he pulled into the driveway, I kissed my mom goodnight ("Have a good time dear, with that nice Davis boy"), brushed by my sister who was glued to the window, and ran out to meet him.

"Blondie, I would have come in to get you," he began as I slid in beside him.

"Shut up and kiss me like you mean it. She's watching."

He did just that. The man could still kiss. At the risk of being disloyal to my late husband, Henry probably ties him in the kissing department. If he had a moustache still, he might have had a shot at first place.

We laughed and held hands over drinks. I bemoaned my mother's fate at the hands of my sister, he detailed his father's slow slide into dementia—one of the reasons he had moved home a few years before, to help his sisters and brothers with his father's care.

Then he did it. In a perfect Scots brogue with a twinkle in his eye, he recited Robbie Burns, *To a Mouse, On Turning Her Up in Her Nest With a Plough*, finishing with his typical cocky smile:

But Mousie, thou are no thy-lane, In proving foresight may be vain:

The best laid schemes o' Mice an' Men, Gang aft agley,

An' lea'e us nought but grief an' pain, For promis'd joy!

Still, thou art blest, compar'd wi' me! The present only toucheth thee:

But Och! I backward cast my e'e, On prospects drear!

An' forward, tho' I canna see, I guess an' fear!

How many women are seduced by Robbie Burns and a dislocated mouse? We drove in freezing silence to his apartment on the top floor of an old house on Park Street. *Still living in the good neighborhood.* Messy apartment, strewn with blueprints, topographical maps, bees' nests and seashells, black and white photographs of the Adirondacks and pressed flowers (he had a passion for landscape architecture), and mismatched wineglasses.

The kissing continued and escalated. We tumbled into an unmade bed with a white down comforter and incompatible sheets, books piled around and on it. I started unbuttoning his shirt and stopped.

"Yalie! You've got chest hair!"

"Yes. I don't know where it came from, but I started getting hairier and grayer at the same time."

"I like it." I kissed him in the middle of his chest, unfamiliar but still like coming home. To my delight, other things had changed as well over the years of our separation. He had learned patience and new techniques. It was I who got my brains fucked out. I was still smiling when I stumbled into my mother's house well after three in the morning, my only regret that my sister was not still up to see me.

We became, over the next several years, *friends with benefits.* If I was in town, I ended up at his apartment for at least one evening. He visited Albany a few times a year and frequently stayed with me. But we spoke or e-mailed weekly. He was my sounding board for the drama developing in my mother's house; I listened to him rail against the powers in our hometown who believed just one more prison would rescue them from financial ruin. The added bonus was it made my sister crazy that I was with Henry on any level. We both saw others, I was involved in relationships and so was he. But when I was in Malone, it was just the two of us: Blondie and Yalie.

He also allowed me to explore any kinky notion I came up with in the safety of his arms. Whatever I wanted to try, he was game. His services were invaluable. Spanking, for example. It seemed to me there was a lot of patter online and in erotic romances about spanking being a major turn-on. I couldn't see it; spanking brought to mind my father's belt on my bottom—embarrassment, pain and fury. But Yalie had attended an erotic spanking class while he lived in NYC, and he offered to teach me the basics. Let me just say: I still don't get it. But, we had a good laugh, and the intimacy that followed more than made up for my slightly smarting tush.

We moved on to my engraved handcuffs during one of his visits to my house. A word of caution here: when you are playing with restraints it is best one or both of you has not had too much to drink. Suffice to say I awoke at three in the morning, my wrists chafing against the metal cuffs, Henry snoring softly beside me. My arms were almost numb, and the key was nowhere to be found. After several attempts, I awakened Henry and set him to searching for the key. He eventually found it tangled in the sheets. Thereafter, whenever we played *Cops and Robbers* we taped the key securely to the palm of my hand!

One Friday night in late summer, I arrived at my mother's house after dinner. I planned to visit with Mom briefly, shower and change, meeting Henry while she watched the Yankees. My sister breezed by me as I entered the house.

"I have to go to the church." She worked at the time as the secretary at the Methodist Church.

"I'm going out at nine."

"I'll be back by then; Mom will be fine even if I'm not." She was already out the door when she tossed over her shoulder, "Oh, and Mom needs an enema." Then she was gone. *What the hell?*

I found my mother in the living room, glued to the television, the Yankees' game blaring. "Hey, Moms, how are you? Are we winning?" I bent and kissed her wrinkled cheek.

"My girl, we are ahead, but it's close. Did you talk to Mary?"

"Yeah, what's up? Aren't you eating your prunes?"

Apologetically, she told me she hadn't *gone* in days but assured me she would be fine. I silently cursed the bitch who was my sister. I told Mom we would take care of her in no time.

"Remember when my son was a month old, and you made me give him an enema on the kitchen table? And the mess! What were we thinking?" I had her laughing as we headed for the bathroom. I found the enema, but I couldn't find any lubricant.

"Mom, where's the Vaseline? I can only see Vicks VapoRub in the cabinet." There were half dozen jars of Vicks but no petroleum jelly.

"Oh, well, dear, I don't know. Just use the Vicks."

I nearly choked, cringing at the thought. *No way was that going to happen.*

"I don't think Mary uses anything when she helps me with this."

I hope she burns in Hell for that alone.

"Mom, wait, I think I have something." I went to my tote and pulled out the *goodie bag* I always brought for my visits with Henry. There it was: Green Apple Gel.

"I have some lotion, Mom, I think will work."

The process took only a few minutes, me joking with Mom to keep her relaxed and unembarrassed. She mentioned it didn't hurt at all, unlike when my sister helped her. *Fuck the bitch.*

An hour later, Mom comfortably ensconced with the Yankees, my sister nowhere to be found and me showered and changed, I left my mother with her phone beside her.

"You call me when the game is over if Mary hasn't come back yet. Or if you need anything."

"Yes, sweetie. You have a good time with that nice Davis boy." Mom had always liked Henry.

Yalie was waiting for me with a large goblet of chilled white wine. He let me rant and rave, call my sister every name I could think of and get the hate out of me. But when I came to the part about the Green Apple Gel, he cut me off.

"Blondie, I think we better retire that item from the goodie bag. After what you just told me, I am never going to be able to use it again. And damn your sister for that because that flavor was my favorite." We made do with the Mandarin Melon Gel that night. And many nights thereafter.

In June 2006, I was in town to see my sister-in-law, visiting from Kentucky. By then, my sister had gained total control over Mom's affairs, and I had not seen Mom for a few months.

After lunch with my sister-in-law, I went to Henry's apartment. We passed the afternoon in each other's arms. As I was leaving, he asked me if I was stopping to see my mother. I said I was not. As much as I was worried about my mom, I no longer had any legal control over her affairs, and I could not deal with my sister. And, my mom had not recognized me the last time I visited her.

"Blondie, suck it up and go. Your mom is eighty-six; how many more chances do you think you're going to have?"

He was right, so I went. My sister was cool as I walked into the living room where the Yankees' game was blasting from the TV. But my mom's face lit up when I bent to kiss her and said, "Hey, Margaret, it's me. Are we winning?" That she was not sure of the score was further proof of how fast she was slipping away, but she seemed to rally for a bit. We had a nice visit, though shadowed constantly by my sister and her daughter. Mom walked me to the door and cradled my face in her gnarled hands as she kissed me good-bye. "I love you, Morgan."

"I love you too, Mom."

It was the last time she would call me by name. Five months later, she was hospitalized and died the day after Thanksgiving.

Henry came to the wake. My brothers greeted him warmly; my daughter and son told him his campaign signs were still in our garage. He put his arm around me as my sister sidled up to him with one of her *friends* and introduced us as "My sister and her old boyfriend, Henry."

He smiled at her, with that Henry cocksure smile, and responded, "Always her friend, Mary, always her friend."

And he still is.

MEN

What is it about men? Is it the chromosomes? Testosterone? Testicles? I'm not sure what it is about men that make them voyeurs.

Ask any man his fantasy and, unless he is gay, he will tell you "two women." Two women in bed with him. Or two women kissing and fondling each other. Or, the ultimate: two naked women rolling around in the mud in mock battle, hair pulling a bonus.

I don't get it. I love to look at handsome guys. I'll buy a calendar I don't need to be able to look at a bunch of handsome, built, partially naked firefighters. I'd pay ten bucks to watch Kevin Costner, George Clooney, or Daniel Craig just read a phone book on screen for two hours, and I would be happy with the eye candy. But two men kissing each other? Two men naked together? Doesn't do a thing for me. I've even done an informal poll, and I have yet to meet a woman who is turned on by watching men kissing or being naked together. Proof men and women are inherently different. And I have more.

I was a redhead as a kid. A carrot top. I still have the freckles to prove it. Though my "natural" hair color became medium brown, laced heavily with gray, it is now an unnatural pale blond. But I still have a redhead's complexion, so I do not tan naturally. Even in the long ago days of baby oil mixed with iodine, I burned, blistered and peeled. I was left with a pale beige cast to my otherwise pink skin. Now, after a bout with skin cancer, I arrive at the shore with my beach umbrella, a floppy hat and sunscreen.

But, I still subscribe to the notion that tan fat looks better than white fat; so for the last half dozen years, before I depart for the Jersey Shore, or before I get naked with a new lover, I go into the salon for a spray tan. I don't use the spray tan booth; I go to the salon I've gone to for almost twenty years. The salon where I get my hair cut and colored, where my eyebrows and bikini line are waxed, where I can always trust Denise to tweeze one of those horrible I'm-over-fifty-and-postmenopausal chin hairs. Where I can get spray tanned in the privacy of the basement tanning room, curtains drawn, music playing. Just me. And Denise.

A trip to Vegas with my kids in 2004 prompted me to schedule my first spray tan. I did not want to be lying by the pool at the Luxor like a great white whale. I thought bronzed barracuda was a better look, and twenty-five bucks was a bargain for a boost in self-confidence. But I was bringing two swimsuits to Vegas, one with a halter top and one with a tank top.

Downstairs, in the basement, I stripped off my jeans, and was pulling my T-shirt off when I asked Denise what to do about the swimsuits.

"Either way, I'm gonna have tan lines showing and I hate that." I was standing in my rattiest bikini briefs (sometimes the tanning solution can stain) and an old white bra.

"Well, you could tuck the straps into your bra, and then you won't have any strap marks." Denise suggested. "But you still might have marks on your back."

"What do you think if we unhook the back of the bra, and I'll just hold it in front? Then I'd have a nice smooth tan on my back."

Denise considered. "That would work, or you could just lose the bra." I looked at her and snickered.

She continued, "Lots of women do that. Some women just have me tan them naked so they don't have any lines."

We both smirked at each other and then laughed. *What the hell.* After you've given birth, you have no modesty.

I pulled off the bra and stepped onto the sheet while she loaded up the airbrush with tanning solution and bronzer. The bronzer would give me immediate color and show her where she still needed to spray. I covered my initial embarrassment over being almost naked with another woman by launching into a nonstop monologue about my recent dating adventures. As Denise told me to turn, lift an arm, turn my leg out in a variety of semi-balletic poses, I told her about the Professor and the Wine Critic and Critter. Critter was still one of my favorite beaux, he was tough, funny, incredibly bright and an imaginative and energetic lover. The airbrushing completed, I had to stand with legs and arms akimbo, belly sucked in as best I could, in front of a fan and a heater, so I wouldn't smear the tan or my clothes when I got dressed. My cell phone rang. I answered it with two fingers. A dark sexy voice purred in my ear.

"Hello, Critter."

I loved that voice. "Hello, Critter. What's up?" I always called him Critter back.

"I'm driving home from a job in Fultonville. What are you doing?"

"I'm standing almost naked in front of a fan at the salon." *Might as well ratchet it up.*

"What?"

"I'm at the salon drying my new spray-on tan before I get dressed. Didn't I tell you that I was going to get tan before I went to Vegas?"

"Yes, but I thought you were going to go to a tanning booth."

"I can't take the chance that I would burn, so I decided to get a spray tan."

"So, you're in a spraying booth not a tanning booth?"

"No. I came to the salon, and Denise airbrushed the tan on me, so I could be sure there wouldn't be any streaks or missed areas."

"Get the fuck out of here." He squeaked. "You got naked with another woman while she painted a tan on you?"

"Well, I've still got my panties on, and she had all her clothes on; but, yeah." I was grinning.

"You *are* a little animal. And I bet you're just loving this."

"Yeah, the tan looks great." I was laughing outright.

"That too. I gotta pull over. Tell me all about it."

Giggling, I detailed the story of losing the bra, the transformation of me from fish belly white into a sleek shimmery bronze and the improbable poses I had to maintain during the process and afterward. The man was truly turned on by my recitation; by the images I created in his mind with my words. He made me promise I would show him my tan lines when I returned from Vegas, and that I would call him whenever I was going for another tanning session.

"Why do you want me to call you before I go in for the tan?" I'd already described the process to him.

"So I can think about you naked with another woman while it's happening. Major turn-on, babe." *Who knew?*

So, over the years, I have continued to call Critter as I am on my way to the salon for a tan. It makes his day. Enthralled by my tan lines, another erstwhile lover, The Lawyer, once offered to pay for my tans, if I would let him come and watch the process.

Men. I rest my case.

THE FELON—WHAT WAS I THINKING?

There are some things you just know you shouldn't do—run between parked cars to fetch a ball that rolled into the street, touch your tongue to the flag pole in below-zero weather, dive into a pond when you don't know the depth and date a much younger, and much-better-looking-than-you, man.

In the fifteen years after my husband died, I did not do any of those things. I was ultra- careful; I wrapped my children and myself in as many layers of protection as I could. Nothing was going to breach the security net I wove around us. Nothing. Still, life often intervened, and danger sometimes slipped into our lives, uninvited but present nonetheless.

During my foray into online dating, I had maintained a separation between my home and family, my job, and my lovers. Most of the time. Very few men had gotten through the carefully constructed borders around my family and my job. A few had met some of my friends; even fewer had met my children or even been to my house. A few pushed but most were willing to accept my boundaries.

After all, what red-blooded American or Canadian man in his right mind is going to say no to no-strings-attached sex? Even with a slightly matronly, somewhat out-of-practice, too blond, fifty-plus-year-old? Not too many. In fact, there were a lot of men who responded to my online profiles. I had decided about three months into the adventure there were some men who were not going to be right for me, but with whom I would correspond and maybe meet anyway. I fancied myself as doing research for my single friends and for women like me everywhere, who thought they were destined to be alone, save for a cat, a dog, an unemployed adult male child or another single woman friend. I just knew there was a book hiding in all those profiles, phone calls, and margaritas at Fiesta's.

So, when I received Nathan's first message on AFF and read he was almost fifteen years younger than me, I did not immediately delete him. And he was Jewish—there had not been any really good Jewish guys since ex-Boyfriend Bob, so I was ripe for the taking by a nice Jewish boy. Despite my encounters with the Rabbi and the Jewish Marks, I still had the notion in my mind that if he was Jewish, he had to be a good guy, like my late husband. And Nathan was gorgeous! Dark hair, blue eyes, a bad-boy grin, and a body to die for. It couldn't hurt to just look, could it?

What was I thinking? I asked myself as I read his next message, imploring me to call him.

So I declined his invite, citing our age difference. He responded he had always liked older women, and besides, what were a few years anyway? If our roles were reversed, no one would even raise an eyebrow at the fifteen years that separated us. Good argument. He was articulate. He had traveled extensively and had recently returned to the area because of his mother's health. His father was a Rabbi at a local synagogue and his uncle's books had helped me through my period of grief and mourning. And he was so damn good-looking!

We spoke on the phone, and the voice sealed the deal. His voice was deep, slow, and full of unspoken promises. Dark promises. We agreed to meet at a wine shop on Central Avenue after work. I was unusually nervous as I freshened up in the ladies' room at the office, using the goodies from my Booty Bag. I had taken to keeping a small tote bag in my office, which the Posse had christened "The Booty Bag." It containing the items I might need to prepare for or clean up after a before-work tryst, a nooner, or drinks and whatever after work. The bag was well-stocked with extra panty hose and underwear, deodorant, cologne, make-up, toothbrush and toothpaste, wipes and lotion. And Tylenol. Getting ready for Nathan. I used most of my goodies, cleaning, spraying, creaming, layering foundation, shadow, mascara and lip gloss in the unforgiving fluorescent light, trying to conceal one, two, five years from my face. *What was I thinking?*

In all my suburban mom/lawyer splendor, I waited in front of the liquor store, wearing the mink and a buttoned-up black silk top and pants, freezing in my luxury minivan despite the heated leather seats. There he was—black wool coat, black turtleneck, faded jeans the exact shade of his piercing blue eyes. Then he smiled, and I knew I was in all kinds of trouble. Perfect white teeth. He hopped in the front seat and leaned in for that first kiss. That tell-all first kiss, because if it isn't there for the first kiss, it isn't going to be there for anything else. I felt the sizzle in every nerve ending in my body. He had a bottle of white burgundy, my favorite, and an easy excuse—expired inspection—for his Volvo being at home.

We drove to his rented townhouse, and I noticed the Volvo—and a Porsche—in the driveway. But I was more impressed by the exquisite silver *mezuzah* (a tiny piece of parchment contained in a small case holding verses from the Torah) on his front door jamb. *Such a nice Jewish boy!* The interior was both masculine and religious—leather sofa and a collection of antique *Kiddush* cups (a small goblet, usually silver, used for wine on the Sabbath when a blessing is recited), big screen TV and a *mezuzah* in every doorway. I was hooked. And more superlative kissing. Long, slow, deep kisses punctuated by sips of the excellent white wine and mixed with interesting conversation about his travels in the Pacific Northwest. I knew we would be lovers before the evening was over. *What was I thinking?*

Upstairs, past his office, down the corridor to a large bedroom filled with a huge sleigh bed, covered in deep garnet and forest green tapestry bedding, Oriental carpets strewn over the hardwood floor. Candles on all surfaces were quickly lit, soft music played from the small stereo on the table by the full-length mirror. Catching a glimpse of my reflection, I looked fragile and fey in the candlelight; my blond hair like a halo around my face, my lips rosy and full from the hour of kisses. I was seductive in the black silk that clung where it should and concealed where it must. He came up behind me, all dark and dangerous. A faint warning sounded in my muddled brain: *what are you thinking?*

Ever heedless to my good angel, I turned into his embrace. He was as skilled at undressing me as I was at being undressed; as talented a lover as I was at being seduced. His body was hard and lean and lovely; he spoke words of endearment and encouragement; poetic words and coarse words intermingled in a tantalizing love song. I was swept away, not in control as usual, but controlled by him; my body and mind held in thrall by his touches, movements, positions, demands. We made love for hours. I was consumed by him, only managing the upper hand at the very last, turning him into the supplicant. As we were dressing, he abashedly confessed his license had been suspended recently due to an old DWI charge from his youth. He assured me his lawyer was handling it, but that was why he wasn't driving. Although I recognized that faint buzz of alarm from my lawyer brain, I heard myself tell him, "I understand, these things happen."

Later, as I drove up the Northway, I looked into the starry sky and the frozen moonlight and thought: *It doesn't get any better than this. If tonight is all I have with him, it has been an experience I will never forget and never regret.* I fully expected that to be my only night with him—he was too young, too handsome, too talented a lover to be with a woman old enough, at least in Malone and some Third World countries, to be his mother.

The next morning, as I was regaling my girlfriends at work with some of the details of the evening, he called to tell me how great it had been, how much he liked me, how much he wanted to see me that night. Even though my brain was telling me to end it now, on a high note, my lips were agreeing to meet him at Popeye's for fried chicken and biscuits. That led to hours of laughter in the greasy fast-food restaurant, renting a movie, drinking Budweiser, and having sex on both the leather sofa and the loveseat. The next night he was packing for a business trip to Florida. I brought him a pocket-sized copy of the *Kama Sutra* to read on the plane, and he took me bent over piles of neatly folded laundry in the middle of his huge bed.

I was already missing him the next day, when a gorgeous arrangement of white lilies and blue irises arrived at my office to wish me a Happy Hanukkah and to thank me for *everything*.

My coworkers walked by more often than necessary to admire the scent, the colors and the sheer extravagance of the bouquet. I was in my glory. *I'll end it when he comes home*, I told myself, even as I looked forward to his daily calls, full of his travels and his lusty plans for me upon his return.

So there I was, at midnight on New Year's Day, in the arrivals area of the Albany International Airport, waiting to take him to his townhouse. Dressed in the mink, black boots, faded jeans and a black turtleneck, hair and make-up perfect even at that absurd hour. I was learning that when you are the older woman, you work harder at looking good enough. As I waited in the almost empty terminal, I thought, *This is it. I'll bring him home, and that will be the end of it. It can't last. Better to get out now.*

Then he was there, striding down the hall toward me. Skin bronzed after a week in the sun, long and lean in jeans and a turtleneck, the light blue cap making his eyes pop like Paul Newman's, and the tan turning his teeth to blinding white. He smiled broadly when he saw me; his arms were reaching out to me twenty feet away. A woman my age, standing near me, was watching him with real appreciation. She turned, looking for the object of his interest. Her eyes widened, I thought, at the sight of me—a woman who was obviously also in her fifties. She stared as I walked into his embrace. His arms were tight around me, he was kissing my face, nuzzling my hair, murmuring how much he had missed me, how good I looked, how happy he was to be home with me. I hugged him back, kissed his neck and turned as the woman walked by me. Her face was wreathed in a smile, she was giving me a *thumbs-up* and she mouthed the words, "You go, girl!"

Nathan was holding my arm and steering me down the escalator. I was lost in a haze of delight at his return and my victory in the older woman competition. And despair. There was no way I could end this now. I would have to wait for him to end it, as I was sure he would. *What was I thinking?*

THE FELON—THIS IS NOT GOING TO WORK, IS IT?

One of my favorite movies is *Love Actually*. It is one of those great British ensemble pieces, funny and moving, with at least a dozen interwoven stories and all my favorite actors and actresses—Alan Rickman, Liam Neeson, Colin Firth, Emma Thompson and Laura Linney. Laura Linney plays a slightly frumpy woman who works with a gorgeous Italian man with whom she has always been secretly in love. Then, a miracle! He takes her home after the company holiday party, they pause at the door to her apartment, their good-byes are awkward, and then he sweeps her into his arms for a passionate kiss. He makes a move to come into the apartment, and she asks him to wait a moment. She steps away from the open door, out of his sight. You then see her doing the *Happy Dance*, hopping up and down, fists clenched, elbows bent, eyes closed, and a look of pure ecstasy on her face. Composing herself, she invites him in. Her Dream Man, her Prince Charming, the answer to her prayers. I always smile and then sigh at that part of movie— it's my favorite scene. *You just know it is* not *going to work out.* I was experiencing the same feelings of doom about my own situation.

It was a cold night, a week or so after New Year's. We had gone out for dinner and returned to dive under the covers to warm up by making love. A few hours later, Nathan got out of bed to take a shower. I lingered, hating the late night drive up the frozen Northway that was awaiting me; but I had an old dog at home, and it was too early in our relationship for me to be spending the night. *Relationship? When had I begun thinking of this as a relationship?*

Somewhere between picking him up at the airport on New Year's night and meeting him at his apartment occasionally for lunch and what my girlfriends called a *nooner*.

I shrugged and slid out of bed, clutching one of the throws around my naked body. My naked, aging, overweight and scarred body. The light was bright from the hallway, and as enamored as he seemed to be with me, I was not exposing my curves and inadequacies in the harsh fluorescent glare to my handsome young lover. I turned to look out into the hallway to make sure he was otherwise occupied before I dropped the blanket to slip into the clothes strewn about the floor. I froze. At the end of the hall, in full view, I saw him standing in front of the bathroom sink, brushing his teeth or shaving; I can't say which because all my attention was focused on that body. That very naked, very beautiful body. My breath caught in my throat; I felt the flush creep up my torso to flame my cheeks and glisten on my forehead. *God, he was gorgeous!* And he was mine. I turned back into the room, away from the open doorway. And did Laura Linney's happy dance. I thought as I had on that first night that if this were the most perfect moment I had, the best moment I remembered from our *relationship*, it would be enough. *Because I knew it was not going to work out.*

Caught up in the thrill of a romance with a gorgeous younger man, I was afraid of becoming a caricature of myself. By day, responsible mother of two adult children, model widow of a long-dead husband, and assistant counsel at a state agency—I was the least-likely candidate for a May-December love affair. Or was I? My shrink had warned me my venture into the world of online dating and my quest for intimate but not lasting relationships was my rebellion against my near-perfect behavior to that point, an *acting out* after years of circumspection. What more dramatic assertion of self than to allow myself to be pursued by an inappropriate man? A very attractive, alluring, aggressively sexual, much younger man. I was the center of attention with both the Posse and the yentas; my brothers were shaking their heads in wonder, and my sister was green with envy. I was smug and satisfied.

When did I start trying to convince myself it might work out? Probably from the beginning, though I still deny it. Maybe when he came back from Florida to me, even though I knew there was a woman in Florida. There was one in Seattle, too, and an ex-wife. But, I had baggage, too. There was the tail end of the Wine Critic, the two Assistant Superintendents and, always, the Professor. By now, I was used to juggling dates with two or three men in the same week, and, once or twice, in the same day. But, I was getting tired of it.

And I was enthralled by Nathan. His knowledge of Judaism was superior to my own; his Hebrew was fluent. I lit candles on Friday night at his house using his grandmother's silver candlesticks before we sat down to the roast chicken dinner he always made. Sure, he drank Budweiser with dinner, but there was kosher wine for me. We made love to Puccini's *Turandot*, fast becoming my favorite opera. And he was a master at making love and all its coarser variations. His tastes were a bit more avant-garde than mine had been up to that point, but I chalked it up to his fewer years and greater experience.

And, I reasoned, these new experiences added to my growing research file. Not to mention my skill level. He often wore me out, and that pleased me. Having been accused of being sexually intimidating by a previous lover, I had learned to rein in my desires until I was sure of the response. It was always *yes* with Nathan. We talked and laughed into the night several times a week, always at his apartment. Sometimes he fell asleep, and I could not waken him to walk me to my car in the wee hours of the morning. But, I figured, I wore him out and smiled to myself. *I began hoping it would work out.*

All was not perfect, though. One Sunday afternoon, I drove us to his father's synagogue to drop off some computers for the Hebrew School. I was made-up and coiffed, dressed in the mink and jeans, my now regular uniform with him. As we were leaving, an older woman approached us and greeted Nathan with some familiarity. She told him how good it was to see him back in town and how wonderful he looked. She then turned to me and said, "You must be so proud of your son." Before I could sputter a response, he hustled me through the doors and into my car. He explained she was the other Rabbi's elderly mother, at least eighty-five, and she had terrible eyesight. He spent the afternoon making it up to me. But her comments had confirmed the thought that was always lurking in the back of my mind: *This was never going to work out.*

The next Friday night, we were having dinner at his apartment. He was being particularly attentive as we retired to the living room. Rather than put on a movie, he turned on the stereo.

The haunting refrains of *Turandot* filled the small room. Nathan sat on the coffee table, facing me and took both my hands in his. His blues eyes were dark and earnest. I knew in the pit of my stomach I was not going to like what he had to say.

"You know how you keep telling me not to worry about the DWI ticket?" he softly asked me.

"Has something happened with that?"

"No, I am still set to appear next month. Louis is hopeful that I will get off with an extension of probation."

The police had stopped him while he was driving to the local convenience store. He had a suspended license, he had told me, due to an old DWI charge. Nathan had expressed his concerns to me that he might go to jail for the offense. I constantly reassured him he would not get jail time, just a stiff fine and an extension of the suspension, possibly a revocation of his license. After all, he was represented by an experienced criminal lawyer.

"So, what is the problem? Is there something else?"

"Yes." He paused, squeezed my hands, and looked away. My unease was growing; something was terribly wrong, but I couldn't imagine what. He turned back to me. Swallowed.

"I spent ten years in prison in Arizona." Ridiculously, my first reaction was math-based.

Ten years in prison? He was only thirty-five! When the hell had he had ten years to spend there?

"When?"

"From the time I was eighteen to when I turned twenty-eight."

"What did you do?" I was scared. *Please, God, don't let it be rape.*

"You know how bad things were at home for me then, how cruel my father was, how demanding my mom had become? I ran away from home when I was eighteen with my girlfriend and a buddy. We drove cross-country. We worked when and where we could. But, we got to Arizona and couldn't find work, so I wrote some bad checks. My friends got away, but I was caught and took the whole rap."

Ten years for bad checks? That is a hell of a lot of bad checks or a few for large sums of money. I wasn't a lawyer for nothing. I was shaking; I felt betrayed, I felt scared, I felt angry.

Nathan's head was bent over our still-clasped hands.

He looked up at me. Those marvelous blue eyes were brimming with tears and regret. My heart shifted in my chest. My anger at him dissolved to be replaced with anger toward his parents and toward the system that would put an eighteen-year-old kid away for ten years for a few bounced checks. And toward the friends who had let him hang for them.

I reached out for him. We clung to each other, weeping for all those lost years. Then making love for hours, his words of devotion and love falling like a balm on my aching heart. God help me, I believed every word. How deeply had I fallen, how neatly I was ensnared. How enamored I had become with my handsome young lover. *How could this ever work out?*

Driving home in the early dawn hours, a new question formed in the back of my brain, in the depths of my soul, one I could not bring myself to speak aloud. *How was I going to get out of this?*

THE FELON—WILL THIS EVER BE OVER?

Life is sometimes like a car wreck: horrific yet irresistible. You don't want to look, but you can't look away; you don't want to look into someone's life; but then there you are, right in the middle of it, watching it crumble all around you, helpless to do anything but powerless to walk away. So, you stand, head bowed, and let the pieces of a life tumble around you. You'll pick your way through the debris when it's over. *If it is ever over.*

There was no way to end it, no way to extricate myself from the mess my relationship with Nathan had become. That is what I told my friends, my shrink, myself. But, also, in the deepest, darkest corners of my soul, I did not want to end it. *I could save him.* I think from the moment I had learned about his felonious past, the neglect of his parents, the failures of the criminal justice system, the betrayals of the other women he had loved, I became something of a Jewish Mother Teresa. I thought the love of a good woman, the affection of an older friend, the experience of a lawyer, would set him on the right path. Then I would magnanimously let him go, a credit to my efforts, a slap in the face of everyone who said I was a fool.

My life became incorporated into his. Because his license was suspended, I did the marketing, and I took him to his appointments at Probation during my lunch hour. I came over in the evenings to review contracts for his web manager business, fold laundry and make love.

Except on the evenings his other light of love, Alexis, was around. Then I was home, alone, with my dog and my recriminations. Or, I was trying to form a normal relationship with the suburban assistant superintendent of schools who was emotionally unavailable or the upstate assistant superintendent who was a bit too bitter about his recent divorce to move forward. Nathan called me to tell me goodnight, and I looked forward to those whispered words of love, even though I knew he called me when Alexis was in the bathroom. I knew this from my nights with him, because he called her when I was in the kitchen or the basement.

He was convinced he was going to receive a jail sentence, and I did my best to disabuse him of the notion. I spoke to his attorney, a friend of his father's, who thought he had a fifty-fifty chance. I knew there was something I was not being told: jail time was not the usual sentence for a violation of probation on an old DWI, the criminal classes I took in law school had taught me that. Because Nathan was so sure he was going to jail for at least six months, as the court date approached, he became more and more focused on showing me how to manage his business, how to alter websites at the client's whim, and how to administer the websites he had created.

And how to generate billable hours, *creatively.*

"No one has ever loved me the way you do," he would murmur in my ear. "You are my best friend, my favorite lover, the most wonderful woman I know." He usually said this when asking a favor or telling me he was working late that night; not to come over after work, just go home and get some rest; he would see me tomorrow. *Another Alexis night*, I would think, both disappointed and relieved. *It would never be over.*

Evenings with him were becoming a frenetic jumble of work and sex, long talks, and long nights holding him while he slept fitfully. The pattern suggested to me he was bipolar; he had more energy than a toddler on a sugar high sometimes. Other times, he slept for a whole day. I was adapting to these patterns myself, days when I accomplished more than three lawyers combined at work; days when I dragged myself through only one decision and almost fell asleep on the drive home. I was losing weight, losing my mind, losing my confidence that I had made the right decision in staying with him. *I'll stay until the hearing at the end of February. If he goes to jail, that would be the end of it. If he doesn't, I'll just leave him.* I knew in my heart the chances were excellent that if he avoided jail, he would soon begin to avoid me. I was his crutch during this time of temporary disability. Once restored to his normal circumstances, he would no longer need me.

I did try to distance myself, tried avoiding a phone call, making an excuse as to why I could not see him that night or the next. My flimsy efforts ended the night he told me I was his *beshert*, his soul mate. I pulled back from his embrace. *How could he say such a thing to me?* He knew my long-dead husband was my true *beshert*; there could be no other man for whom I was such a perfect match, such a perfect completion of one whole entity.

"You know, your husband died when he was thirty-five. I'm thirty-five now. I believe God sent me to make it up to you for taking your thirty-five-year-old husband, to give you back what you lost." I sat there stunned. I should have slapped him for his sheer effrontery. Instead, I began to cry. There had never been any answers for me as to why God would have taken such a lovely man from me, such a wonderful father from his children, such a valued friend from all in our circle, such a conscientious advocate from all he served. Perhaps Nathan *was* my consolation prize—payment for all the lost years of love and passion. Even now, years later, I am amazed at how perfectly he played me and how easily I was played. Even now, I am amazed I still believe it in some small, secret space in my heart.

Events began to move swiftly. Nathan's court date was approaching; and then the day was here. We drove there together, meeting his father and his lawyer outside the courtroom. His father confided to me he and his wife were so disappointed in him. I was astonished to hear this man of God tell me about *his* problems on the day his son was going to court and maybe to jail. *No wonder he turned out so screwed up* was all I could think, as I sat across the aisle from him in the courtroom. Judge McNamara is a hanging judge; he hands out harsh sentences, and he has no patience for excuses. We assumed the worse when Nathan was called before him, and he began to read the charges. He fortunately and surprisingly seemed unaware of Nathan's time in the Arizona penal system. *Bonus.*

The lecture the judge delivered was brief and unsympathetic; he told Nathan to get his affairs in order over the next two weeks, as it was likely he would be sentenced when he next appeared before him. The judge wanted to know what he would do to turn his life around in the time he had left. Nathan was despondent; his lawyer and I were overjoyed. If Nathan were going to jail, the judge would have spared him the lecture. We explained to him the judge was giving him a second chance. If he could show he was keeping his probation appointments, gainfully employed and had a plan for his future, the judge might just extend his probation, maybe revoke his license, but no jail time. I dropped Nathan off at his apartment and headed back to my office. It was hard to leave him; he was so gorgeous in his navy Armani suit, so sweet with the hopeful look in his eyes. *See,* I told myself, *all he needed was some direction from someone who believed in him.*

I stayed late to catch up at the office. Around eight that evening, my cell phone rang. I didn't recognize the number, but something told me to take the call. It was Nathan. He was in jail in Cambridge for driving without a license and refusing to take a breathalyzer test. I almost hung up on him. *I should have hung up on him,* I repeated to myself over and over as I drove through the icy February night, five hundred dollars from his home safe in my purse and desolation in my heart. They arraigned him in the firehouse, the judge in suspenders and a wool hunting cap, the town cops standing on either side of my handcuffed lover, still handsome in his rumpled Armani. I guaranteed his appearance for his trial in one month, knowing he was now certainly going to be incarcerated in Albany County Correctional Facility, and the deputy sheriffs would transport him to Cambridge. We drove home silently; I couldn't look at him; I wouldn't let him speak after his initial lame explanation: a client had called just after I left him with a computer emergency. He had driven to Cambridge and was on his way home when the Cambridge police stopped him for erratic driving. He had the temerity to be insulted by what he felt was an unjustified stop. I knew Alexis lived near Cambridge. He had traveled from my encouraging hug, to her demanding embrace, to the arms of the law in the space of a few hours.

That was my breaking point. I should have done it before. I should have done it when he explained why he couldn't drive. But, I was too caught up in his lies. He played me. And I let him. The lure of a handsome, sexy, clever Jewish lover was too strong for me.

And I paid the price for my foolishness, for my sexual greed. Extricating myself from him and his hold over me took days and days. He was not pleased. There were threats. There were pleas for forgiveness. There were promises of love. I wavered, I admit.

But, in the end, though it broke my heart, I left him to his fate. Judge MacNamara sentenced Nathan to nine months in the county correctional facility, with the possibility of getting three months taken off his sentence for good behavior. Nathan was also compelled to serve one month in the Washington County Correctional Facility for his foolish jaunt to Cambridge. He lost Alexis at about the same time he lost me.

I was shaken to my core by the loss I felt, by the betrayal, by my stupidity at having believed any of his lies. It would take me some time to recover my equilibrium and move on. My hard-won confidence had taken a permanent hit, and I have still not fully recovered.

JAMIE—FACT OR FICTION

There were Chinese sampans in the background of his photograph. I noticed the boats before I noticed the man. That should have been some kind of warning to me; over the years, I would frequently focus on something in the background and miss what Jamie was up to. Jamie was, from the beginning, a sensory overload. And I was due for some sensory stimulation; most of my feelings had died during the long goodbye with my last ill-chosen lover. So I was ready for a new man and a new adventure.

Jamie was wearing a green polo shirt, a tan baseball cap, and aviator sunglasses in his profile picture. A sweet but tight-lipped smile. Not the handsomest man I had received a wink from on AdultFriendFinder, but I was intrigued by his profile: big-boned, loves to dance, world traveler, former VP of a Fortune 500 company, restorer of old houses, government employee, eighty percent separated, wants a full-figured woman, loves vintage wines. *Well, okay.*

Everything I wanted: big guy, dancer, wine connoisseur, loves to travel, public servant like me. Again, focusing on the good stuff, the extras, I missed the big one: eighty percent separated.

His missives to me were well-written, grammatically correct and told of travels to Sicily, Thailand, South Africa, and France. The photos showed him in these exotic locales, always wearing a hat and sunglasses, always that shy smile but with a devilish tilt to his chin. Our political spats online told me he was obviously a Republican and way too conservative for me, but he respected my arguments, so it made for even more stimulating conversation. He said he was fifty-five years old and his name was James. I have a history with men of that name, so I set about devising a nickname for him. He didn't seem like a Jim or Jimmy to me, so in the beginning, I called him *darlin'*.

He sent me his phone numbers: cell, home and office. I thus surmised he had nothing to hide. Late one afternoon in the autumn of 2004, I read an e-mail from him at work while taking a break from decision-writing, and I was compelled to call him. When his soft, patrician voice answered, I was taken aback. He was pretty assertive in his e-mails, but he seemed so shy on the phone. I introduced myself as "the judge" which is what he liked to call me. He was so sweet on the phone, thanking me for making his afternoon, I melted even more. Once again, I failed to notice where I was calling; he had just said it was his "work" number. When I checked it later, I realized he worked for the Power Authority...as a consultant. Not a regular State employee like me, but an appointee.

After that, we spoke several times a day. Because our conversations were heating up, we used our cell phones almost exclusively. The flirting became seduction, the seduction became completion; we drifted off to sleep to the sounds of each other's sighs. I was still looking just for the next good time, someone to take the bad taste of the felon out of my mouth and out of my soul.

I soon learned he had a military background; he had joined the Army at eighteen, serving in Vietnam, most of Southeast Asia and the Pacific, and at a number of bases in Florida, Texas, and the West. He spoke casually of exotic locales, spinning tales of a playboy bachelor officer careening around Singapore and Hong Kong on a Harley, or Miami and Key West in a Shelby convertible, usually with a woman, always under the influence. But there were a few stories of intrigue and espionage, back alleys and money drops. And poison snakes, eels and alligators, both amphibian and human. One of his stories of combat and camaraderie, made my decision on his nickname: Jamie. My favorite hero of my favorite book at the time, *Outlander* by Diana Gabaldon, was a Scots warrior—big, redhaired, fierce and loyal, sensual and tender, and called Jamie. It was as though my dream lover, Jamie, had walked out of the book and into my life.

Little did I know how prophetic my choice of this name would be.

Our schedules had prevented us from meeting in October and early November. As Thanksgiving approached, and I told him of my plans for my annual trek to Lake Placid for Thanksgiving with family, preceded by a weekend of partying with my posse of girlfriends, he became quietly insistent we meet before I leave. The only time I had free was on Thursday night after nine.

"Perfect, love, I'm flying into Albany County Airport that evening from Niagara Falls. I can meet you at the Desmond for drinks."

"Just for drinks, Jamie, don't be booking a room. I haven't the time for it before my trip." The Desmond had a great bar, but it also had lovely Colonial-influenced rooms—the perfect spot for a seduction.

"Are you always so sure of yourself?" Jamie laughed.

"Sure that you will want me or sure that I won't succumb to your charms?"

"Both."

"Yes."

Laughing again, he agreed to my terms.

I almost canceled. The night before we were to meet, he sent me a photo at three o'clock in the morning. He was still up working on a project, and his near exhaustion was evident in the droop of his eyes and the sag of his cheek. What hair he had, and it was less than I had thought, was standing up in spikes. He looked like a tired old man. I thought, as I gazed at his picture, I could not do it. He was nothing like his other photos. *What had I been thinking?* But it had been his words and his voice and his experiences and his stories that had wormed their way under my skin, into my head, not his face or frame. I realized then it mattered very little to me what he looked like.

But, it might matter to him what I looked like; so an hour before we were to meet, I was showering, lotioning, perfuming, spraying and slipping into dark jeans, black sweater, black tasseled loafers, and my ubiquitous mahogany mink. Down the Northway in my brand new, deluxe SUV, onto Wolf Road, my heart stuttering as it still does at the sight of the sign for the

Albany County Correctional Facility. The Desmond was a softly illuminated bulk ahead of me. And there he was.

Leaning against the pale red brick, Jamie looked like Indiana Jones. Tall, wearing a tan baseball cap, brown leather bomber jacket, creased khakis and deck shoes, a beautiful silk scarf at his neck, his hands tucked into the jacket's pockets; he walked toward me. He was smiling that close-lipped shy smile. He approached my side of the SUV, and as I lowered the window, he tipped his cap and said, "Good evening, judge."

"Hello, soldier."

He leaned in to kiss me. His lips were cold and thin, but the kiss warmed me immediately. I looked up at him as he straightened and said, "Get in the car."

"What?" His expression was perplexed.

"Get in the car." I arched a brow in challenge. Challenging him to defy my request.

"Where are we going?"

"I'm abducting you."

"You are not." His voice was full of disbelief.

"Yes, I am. I want whammy kisses."

He grinned at that, came round the front of the Santa Fe and climbed into the passenger seat. I took off for the far corner of the parking lot, away from the bright lights and the busy traffic on Albany Shaker Road.

Jamie had confided in me that in his early years as a professor at a large university in New York City, he had a graduate assistant who, upon obtaining her degree, had set out to seduce him. He succumbed to her charms (once again I failed to note this fact as important, so enthralled was I by his story), but she was disappointed by his kisses. A sometimes bisexual, she taught him how women liked to be kissed. I have to say, she was not only an adventurous student but a helluva instructor, because the kisses, which she called *whammy kisses*, were enough to have me gasping with pleasure behind the steam-covered windows of the Santa Fe.

We sauntered into the Desmond a short while later, me flushed, Jamie grinning. His grace of movement—the gentle pressure of his hand on my back as we were escorted to a loveseat by the fireplace, the ease with which he divested me of the mink, folding it carefully on a nearby chair—and his slight pause to wait for me to sit first were all insistent tugs on the heart I had hardened during the final weeks of Nathan. Vodka martinis were our drinks of choice. We sat by the fire, already holding hands, chatting and laughing as comfortably as if we had known each other for years rather than for an evening. Midnight came too soon; I had work in the morning, and he faced an hour drive to his home in Columbia County. But I did not want to leave him.

Jamie walked me to my ride, my hand tucked in his elbow, his hand covering mine. He opened the door for me, but turned me to him for one more kiss. I was a perfect fit in his arms. Perfect. The embrace, the kiss, the man. Perfect.

We lingered at the car for another thirty minutes. I wanted to ensure he would not forget me in the week I would be away. He was already that important to me. I laughed at his protestations as I brought him to completion in the empty parking lot, next to the nearly deserted road. He looked as stunned as I felt when I finally let go of him.

"Good thing you're a judge. What if the cops came by?"

"I wasn't that kind of judge."

He laughed and hugged me again. "Good thing we didn't get caught, then, although that would have been worth a night in jail."

"You've been in jail before?"

"Not that kind of jail." He kissed me again before I could make further inquiry.

"I'll be heading up to the Seaway on Monday. I could take you to dinner in Lake Placid."

Perfect, I thought. The Posse would be gone and my kids would be a day away.

"If you don't have to be at the Power Plant until Tuesday morning, you could stay in Placid with me, if you'd like." *Where had that come from?*

"I'd like that very much, Your Honor. I'll bring some wine if you bring the mink."

"The mink always goes to Lake Placid. I need something to keep me warm."

"I don't think there will be a problem with that."

I was still smiling the next day as the girls and I headed north after work, and it wasn't because we had a great weekend planned; it was because of Jamie.

JAMIE—LAKE PLACID & KINDERHOOK

I met him at the front door of my condo wearing almost nothing but my mink, a red ribbon around my neck and a smile. His eyes lit up when he saw me, then he glanced down and saw my bare toes and a wicked grin spread across his face. He stepped through the door and wrapped me in his arms, his lips cold but demanding on mine.

Moments later, we were old friends. Despite my nerves at having him come to Lake Placid, my sanctuary, I was almost immediately comfortable with Jamie. He was a man of such innate grace, such self-assuredness, tinged with a bit of shyness. He plunked his wine carrier on the kitchen counter and said, "I brought a bottle of 1987 Chateau Talbot that I dug out of my wine cellar. Either we are going to have a really good time with it, or we are going to be making salad for dinner." He uncorked the bottle with ease and sniffed. "Oh yeah, we are going to have a really good time!"

I produced two new wine goblets bought for the occasion and licked my lips as the ruby liquid swirled around the crystal like a garnet river. I toasted us with "L'chaim."

He smiled. We stood in the kitchen/dining area, sipping the gorgeous wine and chatting about his drive up through the mountains.

"I'm glad you invited me for a number of reasons, Dina, not the least of which is saving me from making this drive tomorrow at three in the morning."

"What are the other reasons, Jamie?"

"Your blond hair, that mink and this..." His fingers trailed around my neck, tracing the red satin that encircled it.

"I thought since you were bringing me wine, I would make sure I had a gift for you, too."

"And what is my gift?"

"This," I said as I opened my fur coat to reveal the red lace bra and matching panties. My wine glass dangling from my fingers, I stepped into him. Once again, the perfection of our fit caused a warm feeling to spread through me. And we should not have fit because he was easily six feet tall, while I was just a bit over five feet; he was big-boned, and I was curvy. But being in his arms—almost from our first embrace—felt like coming home.

Bottle tucked in his arm, he took my hand and let me lead him upstairs. The mink fell across the bed, with me on top of it. His sweater and shirt, trousers and shoes were strewn around the room. We were a tangle of limbs and lips in the late afternoon light, peeking through the closed blinds on the window. After Nathan's physical perfection, I should have been looking for more than an aging man with thinning hair and a paunch. And I found that man in the shadows of my bedroom in Lake Placid. Jamie was strong; he easily lifted me here and there. He was gentle; the brush of his fingertips was like a sigh on my skin. He had stamina beyond his years as we made love a second time and a third. Jamie was as adventurous as I, pushing my limits as I pushed his, leading and then following me from one position to the next, from one satisfaction to another. I had met my match.

We left for dinner with me still not completely satisfied. I wanted even more of him.

Jamie parked on Main Street, got out of his Jeep and came around to my side to open the door. Holding my hand, he helped me step across the icy divide between the vehicle and the curb.

"That's a nice man you have there," a lady passing by called out. "I wish my husband still opened the door for me."

"She's worth it," Jamie replied, hugging me close. I *kvelled* (felt proud and warm inside). Through dinner, in the warm glow of the candles and several Cosmopolitans, we chatted, we flirted and we held hands. Back at the condo, Jamie introduced me to his favorite libation: Magic Drinks. He filled two tumblers with ice and then stirred two shots of Crown Royal and one shot of Sweet Vermouth, a little water, a little angostura bitters, a squeeze of orange and half a packet of Splenda into each glass. Garnished with an orange slice and three maraschino cherries, it was Jamie's version of a Manhattan, a drink I hated in my younger years. Sipping cautiously, I fell under the spell of the drink's magic. And potency. It was not to be the last night I tumbled almost drunk into bed with Jamie.

Jamie was a cuddler. Bemoaning the crumbling of his marriage, he complained he had not been touched with affection in seven years. He pulled me close to his side, my head resting on his shoulder. Heaven for me. When his back, broken by the Chinese Army in the early 1960s, became uncomfortable, he turned on his side, back to me. But, he pulled my arm up and over him, his arm reaching back so his hand could rest on my hip; my face nuzzling his back, we drifted into sleep.

Awake before dawn, we made love again in the dark. Jamie dressed quickly and efficiently, a veteran of many early mornings in bedrooms not his own. I dragged my heavy red satin robe around me and shuffled down the stairs to fill his thermos with hot coffee and pack pumpkin cookies for the road. Then, with a long kiss and an all-encompassing hug, he was gone.

"I'll call you later, sweetheart."

"You better, soldier."

I went back up to my bedroom and fell asleep with his pillow cradled in my arms, my tears muffled by the softness. I missed him too much already.

After a joyous Thanksgiving, tainted only by my longing for Jamie, I returned to Albany.

Back in my office on Sunday, to get a jump on the work piled on my desk after an absence of five days. Jamie's number lit up my cell phone screen. We had been chatting and texting several times a day since our first meeting. Had it really only been ten days?

"Hello, sweetheart. Where are you?"

"I'm in my office, digging through briefs that came in while I was gone."

"How much more do you have to do?" Jamie was very supportive of my professional obligations.

"I'm just about done here. I can't read another word. How is it that someone can graduate from law school and still not write a simple sentence?"

"They don't teach you how to write in law school, you know that." Jamie had a healthy disrespect for lawyers.

"What are you up to this afternoon, soldier?"

"I'm next door at the Lone Star, waiting for you. Can I buy you a drink?"

Hell, yeah!

I was out the door and across the parking lot in minutes. There he was, at a booth in the corner of the nearly deserted restaurant, two frozen margaritas on the table before him. Jamie rose as I approached and gathered me into his arms. God, I loved the way the man hugged. Then he tucked my head under his chin, my arms pulled up against his chest. Just like my husband had hugged me—like I was the most precious person in the world, and he wouldn't have let anything hurt me. Like no one had hugged me since.

It was the first time in fifteen years any man had touched me in precisely the same way my husband had touched me. For an instant, it was as though I was back in his arms—back in the arms of my lost love. My heart cracked open at the realization. The pain was immense, but only for an instant. Then I felt my heart move within me, and I realized the last chain had finally fallen off my carefully guarded capacity to love again. In that one hug, Jamie had reawakened me, allowing me to relish this reminder of my husband in the midst of feeling tenderness for the man who was holding me.

I slid into the booth after Jamie helped me out of my coat. I was grateful for the margarita because my head was spinning from five hours of legal wordplay, and my hands were shaking from the feelings Jamie had made me experience. Cold, tart, salty liquid courage gave me some time and some perspective. But, I was still on edge. I was already needing him too much, and the need was slipping into caring. As soon as the waitress left with our appetizer order, I plunged in: "So, explain exactly to me what you mean by 'eighty percent separated'." He gulped. Not a good sign. "And, don't ask me to explain what I mean by 'explain'."

"Well, your honor, I am eighty percent separated from my wife."

"You're playing games with me, soldier. Does that mean you are eighty percent through the statutory one year of legal separation ending in divorce?"

"Not exactly." He was waffling...not a good sign.

"Well, why don't you just spell it out, so I don't have to continue this charade of cross- examining you?"

"Listen, it's complicated."

Oh, brother, if I had a hundred bucks for every time some man had said that to me, especially in the past year with Nathan, I would be paying off my son's school loans a lot faster.

"I'm a lawyer, I can understand 'complicated'. What I can't understand is why you are dancing around this."

He looked me straight in the eye before he spoke. "Because I already care way too much for you, and you are not going to like my answer."

"Try me." But, I already knew I was in trouble. Because I had started to care way too much for him, too.

"My wife and I haven't lived together in years. We haven't touched each other in even longer. She mostly lives in New York City, and I mostly live in Kinderhook."

"Define 'mostly'." I was still a lawyer and I wanted answers. I just didn't want the answer I knew was coming.

"Well, we have social obligations from time to time, so I might stay at our duplex in Manhattan, or she might be up here in Kinderhook."

"So, have you filed any papers?"

"We are waiting until we can sell the place in Kinderhook. It's getting too expensive to maintain."

"Let me get this straight: you have been married to this woman for several years, you attend social events together, you don't fuck her, and you haven't filed for divorce...yet?"

"Yes."

Well, hell. What was I supposed to do now? *Duh*, the voice in my head said, my mother's voice, my best friend's voice, my shrink's voice. *Walk, no,* run *away.*

I looked down at my drink. I looked at his long fingers stroking my hand. His elegant wrist, wrapped in an exquisite antique gold Rolex watch. I looked into his eyes. And I stayed. Despite my promises to myself there would be no more married men, I let myself believe this would be different, and I stayed.

Jamie said all the right words. As soon as his house was sold, they could divide the property finally, and he would be free. We could be together then. He cared about me, but we were not going to fall in love with each other...yet. We would enjoy each other, see where it led. No one would be hurt. He wanted me. I was brilliant and beautiful. Sexy and funny. His words were a balm on my troubled soul; his fingers were a caress on my needy body. He was the supreme challenge and the ultimate prize.

Much later, when he walked me to my car, we held hands, stopping to kiss every few feet. We talked on our cell phones all the way home. And again at bedtime. And again as dawn broke in the morning sky.

The next night, after work, I took my first drive east out Interstate 90 to Exit 12. He talked me along the way through Columbia County. I found his house easily enough. Standard four-bedroom Colonial, down a long drive, huge flagpole on the left, spotlighted American flag waving in the cold November air. There was a boat in the driveway and Jamie's ancient green Jeep. And there he was, balancing martini glasses in his hands at the end of the driveway. We hugged as soon as I stepped out of the car, vodka sloshing on the driveway and me.

I had assumed his house was roughly like mine. He worked for the State, he drove an old Jeep, and he favored plaid shirts and khakis. But, there had been the Talbot, the Rolex, the "social obligations" and the duplex in Manhattan. As I stepped into his house, I realized how totally out of my element I was. While the kitchen needed an update, the rest of the house was like something out of *Town and Country*. The pocket doors off the dining room opened into a two-story high library, with a sliding ladder affixed to the bookcases, a coat of arms on the wall and the bust of some dead Roman looking down from a high ledge. The library opened into a hexagonal atrium with a copper roof and a black and white marble floor. As we meandered back through the dining room, he pointed out gold-encrusted Louis XIV porcelain serving pieces. And the Marquis de Lafayette's portable wine cabinet. *Damn.*

Dinner was delightful at his favorite local restaurant. As was becoming our habit, a great deal of alcohol was consumed. Once back at his house, Magic Drinks were the order of the evening. While he made our drinks, I wandered around the family room. Framed letters in Martin Van Buren's hand lined one wall. Tucked in the corner, on the wall by the fireplace, were a framed certificate and a black sword. It looked old. It was. The certificate attested it had belonged to Major George Washington during the French and Indian War. I am a history buff. I am a Revolutionary War buff. *Double damn.*

"Do you want to hold it?" His voice was right behind me.

"Yes." *God, yes.*

The sword was removed from the wall and placed in my hands, still in its scabbard. It was cool to the touch, heavier than I imagined it would be. I was transfixed. I was on sensory overload. And it did not end there.

Jamie hung the sword back on the wall, and we made our way upstairs. What was a nice master bedroom in my house was a full suite in his. Cathedral ceilings, fireplace, eclectic collection of art on the walls, bay window looking out over the back acreage, huge bathroom.

But the bed was full-size, not queen or king as I expected. Dark wood spindles comprised the head and footboards, a nice folk pattern quilt covered its surface, pretty lace-trimmed pillowcases and dust ruffle completed the look. As he undressed me, Jamie told me the bed was from the Revolutionary War.

"Tell me George Washington slept here," I managed with a drunken giggle.

"No." He deadpanned. "At least I don't think so."

Whoever's bed it was, it was not terribly comfortable with its horsehair mattress, but we made good use of it. First, Jamie took me. We gathered our strength and imbibed more Magic. Then, I proceeded to take him. Laughing down into his face, our hands clasped together on the bed, my knees gripping him, I was in charge and reveling in it. Here, at least, we were equals. For now, at least, this man belonged to me. Then, a creak and a crash. The bed seemed to tilt in the corner behind me. I froze.

"What was that?" I squeaked.

"I think a bolt came loose and the bed springs fell."

Jesus, I had broken George Washington's, or some other historical figure's, bed! It was probably worth more than my biweekly paycheck. He was going to be so pissed by my over-the- top bed sport. Embarrassed, I started to climb off him.

"What are you doing?"

"Jamie, I broke the bed."

"Stopping won't fix it." He moved deeper into me and grinned. I fell in love with him at that moment.

I grinned back, my movements now accompanied by the creaking bed frame.

JAMIE—BOUDOIR GYMNASTIQUE

The tag tied to the bedpost read, "No more *boudoir gymnastique*." The repairman had a clever sense of humor, I thought, and tucked the note into my purse. Jamie had blithely told him he and his latest paramour had broken the bed during a night of vigorous sex. So it was in Jamie's world. Even though Jamie was legally married, the housekeeper, the yard guy, the repairman, the maître d' at his favorite local restaurant, and the bartender at the neighborhood bar all knew me by name, or at least by title, "The Judge." I kept telling Jamie I had not been a judge since I became Assistant Counsel in 1993, but he insisted on using the appellation whenever he introduced me and frequently when making love.

The early days of our romance were heady with excitement and discovery. I escaped from my office in Albany to his home in Kinderhook two or three nights a week for drinks, dinner, and romance. And refuge. Sometimes, he would come to Albany to take me to lunch. Jamie was a pleasant distraction in the days at work that were becoming increasingly difficult with political wrangling, budget woes and constant undercutting from some of my male colleagues.

Jamie often traveled during the week as a consultant for the Power Authority. Two of his five advanced degrees being in Electrical Engineering and Organizational Psychology, his input into streamlining the State workforce at the power plants was invaluable. Our involvement in labor law was one more thing we had in common, among so many disparities in our lives. And it seemed as if each week I discovered more that separated us and more that bound us together.

Jamie doled out his secrets like candy on Christmas morning or like venial sins told with reluctance to the priest in the confessional. Some secrets were just interesting bits of information, like his listing in the Social Register or his season tickets at the Metropolitan Opera. Others were painful little pricks in the fragile fantasy world of our relationship, like his earlier marriages and older children and grandchildren. But, every day and every night with him was just so damn interesting I kept coming back for more.

Well-read, well-educated and well-traveled, Jamie had more stories than any man I had ever met. While preparing drinks, getting dressed or undressed or simply chatting on the telephone, our conversations ranged from domestic politics to world economy to opera to favorite recipes. Dining out, he might order in Mandarin, Japanese, Vietnamese or French. Late at night, he would regale me with tales of his adventures in Mexico, Vietnam, Miami, China, Manhattan, Spain, South Africa and Myrtle Beach.

He was everything, but he was not mine. I was constantly reminded of that fact when I went to his house. His soon-to-be-ex-wife, as I thought of her, was present in every room. There were portraits of her everywhere, and what was odd was they were all the same damn picture. It always struck me as strange and a bit vain the woman needed numerous pictures of herself in the same pose in every room, in every hallway. I have pictures of myself in my house, but each is different, and in some rooms there are no pictures of me at all. She also had hung dozens of photographs of her parents, her father especially, and various accolades offered to him. He had been knighted for service to the Crown in World War II; Jamie always referred to him as "Sir." He sounded like a right son-of-a-bitch to me, after Jamie told me stories of his many affairs, with both men and women. His daughter was cut from a similar cloth; her affairs were sometimes the subject of Jamie's late-night drunken rants. It seemed she had married a man similar to her father, as tales of Jamie's affairs sometimes slipped out at inopportune moments. Ironically, Jamie's wife shared the same name as the unloved wife of Jamie Fraser in *Outlander*, the hero for whom I had named my present-day Scots warrior.

As the weeks passed, I learned more and more about Jamie's checkered past. There had been three wives, and there were five children. He wasn't sure how many grandchildren he had because he was estranged from his two oldest sons. He sometimes saw his oldest daughter and, only occasionally spent time with his youngest daughter and son, from the second marriage to a woman he had met in China at the end of his military service. His current wife had lured him away from his second wife, with her title, her wealth and her desire to have more children. After five years of marriage, she had told Jamie she had not wanted to ever have children. That was his permission slip to embark on a series of affairs.

"Why didn't you divorce her?" I asked, bewildered by his response to her lie.

"Too expensive. I lost $4.5 million divorcing Josie to marry her. I can't afford to lose that much again. I'm only worth about $11 million now." *Apparently*, I bitterly realized, *she was worth $4.5 million, but I was not.*

Money was a large part of Jamie's persona. He had been kicked out of his family at eighteen for getting a girl pregnant. The girl became Wife Number One. Three children later and numerous deployments to the Far East, and she decided to become Ex-wife Number One. His revenge on his family was to become wealthier than they were. He did so, the hard way: he earned it. He rose through the ranks of academia and then finance to become the Vice President of a Fortune 500 company. His real estate in Kinderhook and Manhattan, Myrtle Beach and Rhode Island had not been inherited. He worked hard, invested wisely, and shopped for groceries and supplies at the warehouse stores. And he never gave gifts.

His failure to give me a present for Hanukkah or Christmas, one month after we began seeing each other, was a sore point between us. I had made him a thoughtful gift basket of home-baked goodies. He accepted it with enthusiasm. But there was nothing for me. When I finally told him how hurt I had been by his failure to make even a small gesture, a dozen red roses were delivered the next day. It was a serious crack in the glorious image I had begun constructing of him in my mind.

I was floundering and I knew it. The affair with Nathan had challenged me to my core. I had fallen foolishly, dangerously, in love with a felon. My self-confidence was badly damaged, my belief in my inherent good judgment soundly shaken, and my heart, which I had thought could not feel enough again to ever be damaged, was broken. Then Jamie appeared. Strong, successful, wise, romantic; he offered protection from the uncertainties in my life. I ran to him when the boys at work were mean, when my son was difficult, when my family was demanding and when I was hurt, lonely or horny.

I had forgotten how important human touch was to me. My late husband was an openly affectionate man; he rarely passed by me without patting my tush, caressing my cheek or planting a quick kiss on my forehead, neck or shoulder. My children were little when he died, and it was years before they stopped crawling into my lap or my bed; there were kisses from them every morning and every night. But they grew up and grew away. Days and weeks might pass without the touch of a human hand, without a hug or a kiss. I think sometimes if it had not been for the dogs, first Alex and then Marley, I might have gone mad from touch deprivation.

Jamie loved to be touched, anytime, anywhere. He would pull me into his arms for a giant hug, he would caress my arm or my breast as he brushed by, or he would back me against the kitchen counter and take me in the midst of preparing dinner. At night, in bed, he was wrapped around me or me around him. In the middle of the night, he would reach for me. I craved his touch, like a dieter craves her hidden stash of chocolate.

I could not stand to be apart from him, so I got into the habit of visiting him when he was at various power plants in Schoharie, Massena and Niagara Falls. We hunkered down at his hotel, took meals at local pubs and restaurants and made love into the wee hours. He rose before dawn to get to the power plants, and I sometimes lingered for a few hours before dressing and heading to my office in Albany. My son was attending college close to home, so he could be relied upon to care for our new Chocolate Lab puppy, Marley. Jamie was my safe harbor from my job, my children and my ghosts.

As Mardi Gras approached, more cracks appeared. Jamie was a member of the Crewe of Orpheus. He had not missed a Mardi Gras parade in years; he bought boxes of colored beads and trinkets to throw at women from Orpheus's float. He would be attending most of the balls during the week. And he would be accompanied by his wife. It was one of the few social occasions for which she demanded her husband's presence, which was crucial to her image as a major fundraiser for an international medical charity. Jamie promised to take me the next year, and he made mad, passionate love to me after I sulked through an evening of him packing his tuxedos and his masks. He left me in the cold Northeast. He called daily and nightly, but the crack was there when he returned.

I was falling in love with him. I was not going to say it first. I waited for words of love to fall from his lips. He was not going to say them first, either. But he showed his feelings in dozens of ways that meant more to me than the words, at least that is what I told myself. A nasty bout of skin cancer found him nursing me through the painful first night of stitches and bandages. A load of firewood was often packed in the back of my SUV when I left early on Saturday mornings to join my friends for bagels. I ignored the fact that sometimes he was also leaving to pick his wife up at the train station. As I put on make-up and dried my hair in the mornings, I sipped tea and nibbled on biscuits he always had waiting for me when I emerged from the shower. I rubbed his feet at night when we cuddled on the sofa; he rubbed my shoulders. And almost anytime I called, he answered.

My birthday approached in April, and I worried how he would behave. He met me in Albany for a lovely dinner. Then I followed him home to spend the night. I went upstairs to change while he made cocktails. He handed me a Magic Drink and plopped down on the bed. I was saddened by what I presumed would be his disregard of my important day. As I cuddled next to him, my hand drifted across his middle. There was definitely a bulge under his belt buckle.

"What's this?" It felt like a box.

"I'm always hard for you, love."

"Doesn't feel quite right, soldier."

"You better check it then; see if I need medical attention."

I unzipped his fly to reveal a white leather box. I removed it from its resting place and opened it. A gold link bracelet rested on the white velvet. I knew immediately it would be too small for my Irish peasant girl wrist. He fastened the clasp, just barely.

"There was another one I was going to get you. I'll bring this back tomorrow and get the other one."

"No, I really like it. I'll just take it to my jeweler and get a link added."

He insisted on taking the bracelet back; I never saw it again. Another crack, as I began to wonder if he had taken it from his wife's collection, knowing I would sulk that evening if there was no gift; knowing it was unlikely to fit me, and I would not be keeping it. It was the only birthday gift he ever gave me. More cracks.

JAMIE—BATTLE LINES

Spring segued into summer. I spent Memorial Day with my mom in Malone; Jamie stayed at his condo in Bristol, Rhode Island, for his favorite Memorial Day parade. I was alone in the North Country, my children were both still in school. I didn't know if Jamie was alone, and it tore at me. I stayed faithful, though, through the long weekend, despite the nearby presence of Henry. Jamie continued to promise me there was nothing left between him and the soon-to-be-ex-wife except legalities and anger. But still, I wondered. And worried.

"I love you," is the easiest phrase in the world. And the most terrifyingly difficult. I had said it and meant it to a handful of men in my life. It was the most important thing I ever said to only one man. Until Jamie. Despite the cracks, despite my doubts, I had fallen in love with him. Easy for me to do given his sexuality, intelligence, humor, grace and experience. I worried about him when he was away; his opinion had become increasingly important to me, his was the voice that woke me in the morning and gave me sweet dreams at night whether we were lying next to each other or hundreds of miles apart. But, I still had not said the words.

Our reunion after the long holiday weekend apart was marked by drinks, dinner out, more drinks and a tumbled explosion into the now-reinforced colonial bed. We couldn't seem to get enough of each other, and I wanted to ensure he would never feel he'd had his fill of me.

Gasping and laughing after the third round of aggressively satisfying sex, we cuddled and whispered sweet nothings to each other. My head on his shoulder, he brushed my hair with sweet kisses, his thumb making lazy circles on my naked shoulder. I reached across him and felt the beginning of an erection graze my arm. When my hand began to drift south, he grabbed it and stopped me.

"God, you really are insatiable, aren't you?"

I froze. It was like a scalpel slicing my gut open. I pulled away from him, almost leapt from the bed and stomped across the sitting area into the bathroom. Slamming the door behind me, I sagged into the vanity chair and shook. *How could he say that to me?*

I had confided in Jamie a few months into our relationship a story about a man I had met online—not on AdultFriendFinder but Cupid. He was fit, divorced, childless and after our first date, presented me with a collection of clamps. I gamely agreed to try some of them, with mixed degrees of success. Then he dumped me for being too sexually aggressive. Unjustified, but it stung. And it caused me to doubt myself: my motives, my libido, my craving for the physical rather than the emotional.

Now, here was Jamie, the man I was in love with, throwing virtually the same epithet in my face! I poked around the bathroom, looking for my lingerie, bumping into the vanity. *Damn.* It was after two in the morning, but I was still inebriated. I would not be leaving. So much for my dramatic exit. Easing out of the bathroom, I slunk back to the bed. I climbed in and huddled as close to the edge as possible. I was not going to make the mistake of touching Jamie again!

He reached out and pulled me to him. I was stiff in his embrace. "We're not going to do it like this, love."

"Like what?"

"We are going to talk to each other when we're angry or hurt; no sulking."

"Yeah, well, I'm angry and hurt, and you're a jerk."

"I'm sorry, but I was just not up for another round with you tonight."

"I was not the one kissing you. You were kissing *me*!" I retorted. "And I was just putting my arm around you, when I felt Mr. Happy poking me. I was just going to give your cock a little pat 'good night'. I was not looking to fuck you."

"Well, I'm sorry. I thought you wanted more."

"Even if I had, you didn't need to call me names. You could have just said you were tired."

"I'm almost fourteen years older than you; I wouldn't dare suggest to you that I'm too tired for sex." This was the first time he had actually admitted to his age.

"Well, I'm trying to get you to leave your wife; I'm not going to hesitate when I think that you want to have sex with me." The *other woman* isn't going to be the *other woman* for long if she starts saying "no" to the lover who still has a wife to go home to, or so I thought.

Silence. Then a chuckle from him and a sigh from me. "I didn't mean it as an insult, just an observation."

"You sounded just like that guy who called me 'sexually aggressive'. You know how bad that made me feel!"

He had no response but to tighten his embrace.

We kissed and made up, the questions of ability and insatiability put aside as we made sweet love in the dark, drifting to sleep while still entangled. We did not speak of it again for weeks.

After all, it was summer, a time for craziness and maybe, just maybe, love.

As did so many men of my generation, Jamie fought in Vietnam. He had joined the Army at eighteen. It was 1958. Few Americans had heard of Vietnam, much less knew where it was or what was going on there. Jamie entered through the backdoor of secret missions in Laos and Cambodia. By the age of twenty, he had become the youngest noncommissioned officer in the Army. That earned him a dinner at the White House and the handshake of a grateful President Kennedy. It also earned him a return ticket to Vietnam, where American advisors were soon to be revealed as American military and intelligence forces. Jamie was both.

He served four tours in Southeast Asia, rising through the ranks to become a Captain. He was a Major on and off but kept getting demoted because of conduct unbecoming an officer. He was a bad boy who followed his own rules, often to the dismay of his commanding officers. But he was also given wide latitude by those same officers because of the assignments he undertook, as I discovered one hot summer night.

Jamie's house in the foothills of the Catskill Mountains is nestled close to apple orchards and historic landmarks. It sits on a large acreage, facing a country road, in a bowl created by a gently sloping rise of land that surrounds it on three sides. At some distance from the back of the house, the Olympic-sized pool sits at the foot of the hill, below a ridge of tall pines. It is completely isolated, with its own cabana and fireplace.

Jamie drinks a lot. It is generous to say he is a heavy drinker. But I was coming to believe he was an alcoholic. Highly functioning, but an alcoholic nonetheless. His favorite summer evening activity was to crank up the pool's heater to 90°, start a fire in the fireplace, place a pitcher of Magic Drinks by the pool's edge, and stay in the pool for hours, hurling battle cries at the moon.

Fourth of July had arrived, and he was mine for the night. We met at his house just as dusk was creeping over the ridge. A long day apart, I was just happy to be with him. The temperatures were still high enough, even with the approach of night, to make me grateful for the pool. It had been a busy day, so my aching muscles did not mind the water that was almost too hot for the balmy evening. We headed down the lawn, glasses and a pitcher of Magic Drinks in hand. Jamie lit the fire while I fetched beach towels from the cabana. Our icy drinks on the edge of the pool, terry robes in a heap by the pool's step, fire shooting sparks into the darkening sky, the warm water beckoned.

Bliss. The air was balmy, the water hot, the drinks cold and strong. We swam laps for a few minutes, kissing as our paths crossed, nuzzling between sips of Magic Drinks in the shallow end. *Perfect.* Or almost perfect. Perfection arrived around nine o'clock with the start of the fireworks at the Empire State Plaza. We could see the really large fireworks displays as they shot high into the sky over Albany. Just above the pine-covered ridge, red, blue, white, purple and gold burst into dazzling light.

"Look, oh, look!" I pointed excitedly to the bright colors competing with the starlight against the black velvet sky.

Jamie smiled, amused by my childlike display of joy at the simple pleasures of fireworks on the Fourth of July. He pulled me to him, wrapped my arms around his neck and began towing me back and forth across the pool. We both had drinks in our hands, the whiskey and vermouth lending a nice buzz to our relaxed meanderings. Then, a boom from the fireworks startled us. His hand shook, the ice cubes rattled against the glass and the brown liquid spilled into the chlorinated water, swirling for a moment and then disappearing. His other hand pressed more tightly against my wrists, clasped at the base of his throat.

"Are you okay?"

"Yeah, the noise surprised me. It's usually so quiet here at night."

"It's the fireworks; sometimes there's a boom if it's a big one."

"Yeah, I know...."

But he jumped again at the next cannon-like sound. Then he began to talk. His voice had changed. It was a bit higher, a bit softer. It was somehow disembodied from the man I clung to.

"Sometimes at night, the shelling would come out of nowhere. You were supposed to know, but communications were sketchy, and sometimes things just happened. The sky was so dark at night *there*; the stars were so bright when it wasn't raining. When a firefight started, the sky lit up. But it was always the sound that bothered me." He jerked at the next blast.

He had not spoken to me in any detail about Vietnam in the nine months we had been seeing each other. He had told me soldier tales of Okinawa and China, Key West and Utah, but not about Vietnam. I knew about Air America money drops, missile silos, nuclear launch codes and fast motorcycles, duplicitous women, and hard-drinking, risk-taking men. But, I did not know about the endless nights *there*. He never called it Vietnam; he never referred to being "in country." That small country in Southeast Asia was just *there*.

Now he could not stop talking about Vietnam. He held onto my hands, striding back and forth through the shallow end of the pool, with me floating behind him like Superman's cape, while the firework's booms punched holes in him like his own personal Kryptonite.

"The worst was when we were deep in the jungles. The paths were just muddy slices of dirt through all the undergrowth. Single file was the only way to go. I went near the end with my radioman. You know how young some of the guys were, they were as young as I was when I joined, but they had been drafted. They were babies. Some of them were not soldiers, would never be soldiers, would never be able to fight, would never be able to kill. They were jumpy and nervous and made mistakes, dangerous mistakes. Some of them had been into drugs before, and some got into drugs *there*. Some guys were high or strung out all the time. They were useless to the unit. There was only one thing they were good for."

He stopped by the side of the pool and poured another drink, his third or fourth. I could see his face in the firelight, it was drawn and tight around his mouth, his eyes were vacant, focused on a distant land.

"I put them in front of the line. I put the junkies there. The land mines were buried, they were placed so you could never see them, never see the trip lines, not even the really experienced guys found them all the time. Someone was going to step on one; it was inevitable; it was a crapshoot. So I used the most expendable. I used them up. I let them die to save the ones who had a chance; the ones who would fight and maybe survive.

"At night, when we dug in, we laid out the perimeter of the camp. Someone had to take night duty in a foxhole on the outer perimeter. Then some were stationed nearer to camp. I staked them out like goats on the perimeter. I knew the Cong might get them, but there could be some small noise that the better guys, closer in, might hear; might get a shot at the enemy and keep them away from the rest of the men. They died in those foxholes with their throats cut or their bellies emptied out on the ground around them. I'd find them in the morning. I'd find them with their eyes open. I'd find the men I let die."

What does a woman say to the man who tells those stories? *It's okay. You did what you had to do; you saved lives. It was a horrible time in hell, and you survived as best you could.* How do you take away those memories, those nightmares? Alcohol? Sex? Cuddling and coddling?

He didn't remember in the morning. And I didn't mention his confession. Another layer peeled away, another crack in his perfect façade. And, God help me, I loved him even more. But I still did not say the words.

July melted into August. The heat brought the soon-to-be-ex-wife from the stale air-conditioned air of their townhouse in Chelsea to the cool breezes of Kinderhook. With her came "Sir" and his lady wife. Jamie became bartender, cook and chauffeur to his in-laws. And a more ardent, if less available, lover to me. We met for long lunches on Wolf Road or in motel rooms for a few hours after work; truncated trysts that were sometimes interrupted by the vibrations of his cell phone. I became whiny and fractious. It was one thing to know he was married, eighty percent separated, when he answered my calls right away, and we saw each other three or four times a week. It was quite another when he was unable to take my calls, when his time was doled out in small portions to me, when I knew she was eating, drinking and sleeping in *my* home with Jamie.

"I'm heading to Myrtle Beach tonight; I can't stand this anymore."

I was momentarily speechless. I had been packing my daughter for her trip to Indianapolis to start graduate school when he called.

"I thought we were going together when I got back from Indy," I protested.

"I'll take you some other time. I'm leaving tonight. I have to get away from them."

I started to cry. I never cried around Jamie; he never cried around me. The only tears we almost shed were during sad movies.

"I don't understand. You can go to Indy with us, and then we can go to Myrtle Beach together. You promised."

"I'm leaving tonight. I'll call you later." He hung up.

Trying to hold a crumbling love affair together while driving a child to graduate school in a new city almost one thousand miles from home is a feat better left to a greater woman than I. But I tried. In phone calls from the road, when I could get away from my daughter, Jamie and I argued about sex, his wife, my need for sharing, his need for solitude.

I arrived home around midnight five days later. I had not spoken to Jamie for two days, so I checked my e-mail. There were two from him. I read the last one first.

What is it with you? It's not just about sex, but you keep arguing about it. We need to talk.

The longer one, sent the day before the one I had just read, was a farewell. He was in Myrtle Beach, alone as he needed to be when his life became too much for him. Like a sick or hurt wild animal, he said he needed to hide and lick his wounds to heal. He hated the crying. We were adults; we both knew what we were getting into. The sex was a problem, too. He had a hard time keeping up with me and could not, would not, continue to try. He was facing some tough choices, and maybe I could not be part of them.

Then, there it was: *But I have fallen in love with you. I do love you. That makes all this even harder. Good-bye.*

It was the end of August, but I sat before my computer shivering. I felt relief that it was over, that I was no longer caught up in the unholy triangle of Jamie, his wife and their money. I could move on; I could find someone else. *Someone else.* I almost doubled over in pain at the thought of Jamie with someone else. I rocked as I held my sides and gulped down my sobs, lest I awaken my son, slumbering down the hall. I could not let him go.

So like Kennedy with Khrushchev during the Cuban Missile Crisis, I responded to the part of his message I wanted to and ignored the rest. I suggested a meeting where we would discuss terms. He wrote back almost immediately though it was the middle of the night. We would meet at the Macaroni Grill for lunch the next day.

As he walked to the table where I waited, I knew I would not leave him. He smiled and took my hand, and I listened to his lies. We would be together, soon. He would take me to Bristol, Myrtle Beach and Paris. He loved me. It was, perhaps, the only time he would ever say the words so easily. I listened and I believed him.

It was only a few weeks later when the words came back to haunt us both. We had been drinking a lot, careening around the kitchen, making even more Magic Drinks after a late evening swim in the pool. Freed by his declaration of love for me, I used the words frequently with him. He was then, as always, uncomfortable with such statements.

He taunted me. "You can't love me. You don't know what I am."

"Yes, I do."

"You don't know what I've done."

"I know some of it."

"I'm no better than an assassin."

"I know about that."

"How do you know?"

"You told me, during the fireworks; you told me about the men in the foxholes, the men at the front of the line."

"I *told* you?"

"Yes." I laughed a humorless laugh. "I hope you didn't drink as much then, Jamie; because if you did, you probably spilled most of our national security secrets to the Chinese. Your mouth just runs when you've been drinking."

It brought him up short. That someone knew his demons and could still speak to him of love.

"How can you love me?"

"Did you kill anyone for revenge? For personal gain? Did you enjoy it?"

"No," was his tortured response.

"Then how can I not love you? You stayed alive and kept your men alive the only way you could." He shook his head in wonder at my unyielding devotion.

It did not last. One more canceled Friday night date because of a social obligation with Sir and Lady Anne in the early autumn had me deciding I would end it. I was finally coming to the realization he would never leave his wife; or if he did, it would be years down the road; too late for any hope of a marriage between us.

I'll tell him the next time he calls. We're over, I'll say, call me when you get your divorce papers, or don't call me.

But I didn't. Jamie's next call was to tell me he was on his way to Mass General for tests.

There was a lump in his testicles, probably cancer. There would be a biopsy. His doctor was damn sure of the initial diagnosis so there would be chemotherapy and radiation in his future.

How could I say good-bye to a man who was fighting for his life? To a man who had told me only a few months before it would take more than my bout with skin cancer to scare him off? To the man I loved? I couldn't.

I had negotiated the terms of our cease-fire at the Macaroni Grill. Now it was for me to face the unconditional surrender of my unruly heart to the vagaries of Fate. And to that war that had destroyed so many lives decades before and was still claiming victims thousands of miles away from the jungles where Jamie had fought.

The Agent Orange that was supposed to help save him *there* was killing him here. We learned later his cancer was caused by that chemical; and, because of it, traditional treatments would not work. He lives on borrowed time, drinking even more heavily than before, this brave warrior of so many battles, terrified of the moment he must once again face the empty eyes of the men he killed.

Jamie went to San Antonio. He needed experimental treatments to nullify the effects of Agent Orange on his immune system. The chemo for his testicular cancer was not working, and the Army oncologists theorized the Agent Orange exposure that caused the cancer was also thwarting the otherwise highly effective chemotherapy used to treat it.

I would have remained faithful to him during those long six months of treatment had he not lied to me about a basic element in our all-too-precarious relationship. In a panic of preparation for his trip to Texas and fearful he would not return or the treatment would not be successful, Jamie had traded his house in Kinderhook with his father-in-law and had taken possession of Sir's condominium in Rhode Island. It was part of a contained community that would provide aides, then assisted living, and then hospice, to residents as the need arose. Jamie had also made arrangements to be buried in Texas.

Despite his promises he was coming back to me and we would finally be together, he had made plans that did not include me. It is unlikely Jamie would have told me had I not gone to his house for one more good-bye only to find the security codes changed and his personal belongings missing from the almost sterile interior I viewed by peeking through the patio windows.

As always, he had reverted to his wounded animal persona, going off alone to lick his wounds, cutting himself off from the outside world, shutting me out.

My response to his lies was to find someone else to ease my hurt, one betrayal met with another.

JACOB

Jacob. There he was on Cupid. Tall, white-haired, looked handsome in the small photo attached to his profile. Divorced, retired from the Attorney General's office, living in Delmar, interested in wine, first editions, antique glass and firewood. *Okay, eclectic interests.*

And Jewish! Bingo! It had been awhile since I had tried my luck with Jewish guys (the Rabbi and the Jewish Marks had put me off and the Felon had made me despair there were any nice Jewish boys left). He had *winked* at me to express his interest, so I didn't even have to make the first move. Apparently, in the P.J. (pre-Jamie) era, we had flirted online, but nothing had come of it. Now I was ready for more than flirting, and he was eager. Maybe a little overeager, as his opening line when I called him was, "I got the house in the divorce. It has a slate roof and two fireplaces in Old Delmar." *Okay, not that I really cared, I didn't want to move in with him, but it was better than visiting him in a basement apartment on Lark Street.*

We agreed to meet for dinner in Saratoga; he didn't want me to have to drive too far after a long Friday at work. He was fascinated with my job. I was at that time the Acting Deputy Chair of my agency; given the political atmosphere, I was practically running the agency.

The Ripe Tomato is a good restaurant just south of Saratoga Springs. We were to meet in the bar. I arrived first and went through the bar looking for a slender, white-haired gentlemen in a sports coat. No luck. I stood by the door and peered out into the front lot for five, maybe ten minutes; my maximum wait time for a lawyer or other professional was fifteen minutes. I was buttoning my coat when I spied a man walking towards me in the rain. *It couldn't be him.* This man wore a topcoat like my Dad had worn to church; not a trench coat, but a topcoat. And a fedora. Not a ball cap or a flat sports cap, a regular fedora. *What was he, like seventy-five years old?* It was my dad's coat and hat that were coming to buy me a drink!

He pushed through the door, removing the hat as he entered. *Good manners and really lovely thick silver white hair.* He looked at me and smiled, and I was struck by his even white teeth and beautiful blue eyes. Paul Newman blue eyes. In fact, he resembled the actor so much my breath caught in my throat. Paul Newman in *Nobody's Fool*, older, wiser and still sexy as hell. I blushed as we greeted each other, then his hand was firm on my back as he led me to a booth in the corner of the bar. The waitress arrived for our order. He smiled at me and said, "I really love a good cognac before a meal, don't you?"

"I'll have a Remy Martin, neat," he told the waitress.

I had not dated a world-renowned former wine critic for nothing. One did not have cognac before the meal, but after. And Remy Martin was good but not as good as what I was accustomed to, not when I had cut my teeth on the delightful champagne cognacs from Maison Surrenne. I condescendingly asked for a white burgundy. His eyebrows flew up. Sadly, but as I suspected, they did not have it by the glass so I ordered Chateau Ste. Michelle Riesling.

"You know your wines," he said, almost accusingly.

"Yes. Yes, I do. I studied with Marshall Hennessey."

"You studied with him? I didn't know he was taking students."

"Well, actually, while we were dating, I made a point to ask a lot of questions."

"You dated Marshall Hennessey? What happened?"

"He asked me to marry him. But, sadly, before I could make up my mind, he asked someone else who said yes. Just as well, he is undisciplined when it comes to women." Jacob almost choked on his damn cognac.

The conversation moved to books. Once again, he was impressed I had a first edition of Marshall's book on wine. He was open-mouthed when I admitted that it had been a gift *and* it was personally inscribed. At least he did not offer to buy it from me. *Move on from past lovers*, I told myself.

In his way, Jacob was charming, intelligent, and funny. We ordered dinner, he deferred to me for the wine selection. We chatted throughout the meal, mostly about our legal careers with New York State. After the waitress cleared the table, he excused himself to use the men's room. I was thinking it was going quite well and he had definite possibilities as a lover to dally with while I was sulking about Jamie.

Jacob returned to the table, but not to his seat across from me; he slid into the booth next to me. When I turned to him with a look of surprise, he put an arm around my shoulder, drew me close, and kissed me. This wasn't a slight brushing of lips that said, "I'm really enjoying myself this evening," but a "tongue down my throat I'm going to have sex with you in the parking lot" kiss. I pulled back. He was grinning. I shook my head in a negative way and said, "I'm not going to fuck you tonight."

He frowned. "Why not?"

"I like you too much. I don't want to screw it up."

He was still arguing with me after he had paid the bill and walked me to the car. He got in the passenger side and attempted to kiss me again.

"No means no. I am not having sex with you tonight in any form or in any location." He finally agreed with me. As I drove away, I was starting to have misgivings.

Saturday and Sunday were full of phone calls and messages from Jacob. I ignored many of them. He tracked me down late Sunday afternoon at the office. It had been a long day, and I was tired; I needed alcohol and some sympathetic company. His offer of drinks, a fire, and a quiet bistro in Bethlehem was all it took to send me down Route 85 rather than up Route 87.

The bar he had directed me to turned out to be his house. *Oh, well, I'm here.* He greeted me at the door with a snifter of cognac and a big wet kiss. We ambled through his very charming house, admiring the antique glass, the cherry wood from his own backyard that was piled by the fireplace, and the dusty first editions on some really impressive bookshelves. The cognac and the fire had the desired effect, and eventually we meandered up the stairs to a cozy bedroom overlooking the cherry trees in the yard.

He undressed first. *Whoa! He was older than sixty-two!* Old man skin. I knew the signs.

Monsieur Hennessey had maintained the fiction he was ten years younger than his sixty-five years until he took off his shirt! And Jamie was even older, though in far better shape. But, Jacob still looked a lot like Paul Newman. And, I was not the image of a Victoria's Secret model, I reminded myself as I undressed, so I cut him some slack.

We fell on the bed together and engaged in some serious kissing. He was a good kisser and an attentive lover. We tangled and touched, and he moved over me like a warm blanket, draping me in soft caresses and wet kisses. His hands and mouth *there* had the desired effect, and I was moaning his name as he brought me to completion.

I was smiling that Cheshire cat smile of a woman who has been completely satisfied. I stretched and reached for him. "Tit for tat" was always my motto. I was a generous lover and gave as good as I got, and I had just gotten it very, very good. Jacob stopped my hand. I looked up at him with a question on my face.

"Just watch."

Just watch what?

He was stroking himself, his eyes half-closed, a whimsical smile on his face.

What was I supposed to watch? I wasn't going to look at his penis clasped delicately between thumb and forefinger, so I looked at his shoulder. *This was probably not going to work.*

It didn't take him long, I'll give him that. Soon, he was snoring quietly.

What the hell, I thought. *Wait, maybe he didn't have condoms. That's why we used "alternative" methods; he wanted to be safe. Okay, more points for him.*

Jacob awoke. I asked him about my condoms theory. "No, that's just the way I like it."

This was not going to work.

I demurred at his invitation to dinner, citing my responsibilities to make dinner for my son. He launched into a lecture about cutting the apron strings as he had done with his daughters. *Oh, this was so not going to work!*

My friends had been hopeful a nice Jewish lawyer would break Jamie's long-distance hold on me. I knew they would be disappointed when I told them Jacob was no longer on my list of potential *better than average, later in life* relationships. However, I wasn't prepared for the coffee that spurted from Maureen's nose when I told her about "watch this." We laughed so hard we were almost kicked out of Bruegger's. But we couldn't decide if Jacob was just *quirky* or was truly *squirrelly*.

I let Dr. A, my longtime psychologist, resolve our dilemma. The coffee spurting out of his nose as I related my story was answer enough.

Squirrelly. Definitely squirrelly.

SURRENDER

He was the only man I had danced with since my husband died. Jamie would waltz with me around the sitting area in his bedroom, tango with me in the kitchen while we were making Magic Drinks and sometimes meet me when I was out with the Posse to twirl me around the dance floor, after pretending to pick me up at the bar.

He was the only man I knew who had read the books of Frank Yerby, a historical romance writer of the 30's through the 60's, and my mother's favorite author. In our youth, we had both read and fallen in love with *The Saracen Blade*; I with the dashing and dark hero, Pietro di Donati, and Jamie with the battles of the Second Crusade and the political intrigue of the Holy Roman Empire.

He was the only man I had introduced to my mother and all of my brothers. My brothers liked Jamie immediately; my mother had thought he was nice-looking and tall, though a bit too old for me, the only time she met him before the beginning of her rapid decline. Jamie came with my brother and me to do battle with my sister when my mother was on her deathbed in the hospital. A week and a half later, he was back, after driving all night, to be by my side at her funeral.

He was the only man I loved. So, when he returned from San Antonio, weak after a successful round of treatments to counteract the Agent Orange in his system, I took Jamie back into my life. I stopped harassing him about a divorce. I knew it was not going to happen, at least not anytime soon. I stopped expecting him to call. When he did, I was thrilled; and when he asked me out, I went. I did not go back to any of the dating sites to look for a new distraction; Jacob had cured me of my curiosity for a time, at least. But when Critter or Biff or Zoomie were available, I took advantage of their willingness and their desire. I adopted a *don't ask, don't tell* attitude with Jamie.

He was the only man I loved. I couldn't keep Jamie, but I couldn't let him go. So, I left us in the hands of fate. I surrendered and tried to make peace with my world.

MARRIED MEN

I am a good person. I never tell a lie, except the occasional white lie so as not to hurt someone's feelings. I am honest with my tax return, though sometimes I value my old clothes slightly higher than the IRS might on my list of charitable contributions. I don't abuse animals or small children, despite my kids' complaint I treat the dog better than I treat them. And I never date a man one of my girlfriends has dated before. But, I have had affairs with married men.

As naïve as I was, I initially drew the line solidly in the sand: no married men, no men who were not at least legally separated, no men who had a girlfriend/lover/housemate. And there were dozens beating at my virtual door every week. They wandered through the online dating sites in droves; especially the sites devoted more to *intimate relationships* than those devoted to *long-term relationships*, although I found them in both. I disdainfully refused their advances, sometimes chastising them about their infidelity, sometimes offering marriage advice, but never getting involved.

Then there was the rabbi, who lured me to New Jersey with his lies of separation and sanctity. Then Richard, my online lover and good friend from San Francisco, who categorized his marriage as over except for the legalities. And, the Professor—erudite and erotic—who I'd never met in person, fearing consummation of our affair. Mere cracks in my solid wall of resolve to stay away, far away, from married men.

I cannot say the same about the others.

There have been men throughout the last eight years with whom I have been intimate, even though I knew they were married or involved at the time. My psychologist would say that it's because I was acting-out, breaking all or most of the rules I had so carefully adhered to for most of my life under the misbegotten notion bad things do not happen to good people. Maybe that is true. Maybe I wanted the thrill of the forbidden. But, I think, as he also suggested, perhaps I wanted intimacy without any fears of a long-term relationship. Most married men do not leave their wives for their lovers, however much they might want to. So they are safe. Grateful. Passionate. Careful. And they were all I wanted for a while.

There was Pitney-Bowes Ken, who professed to have an open marriage. He was a real bad boy, tons of disposable income, infectious laugh, seductive grin. We met for drinks and dinner at Ravenswood or the Rusty Nail or for noontime trysts with room service on Wolf Road. He'd been married three times and was a lusty and generous lover. He told me I was beautiful and the sexiest woman he had ever been with; better than any of his wives. And I believed him. He was available anytime I was feeling lonely and unloved, horny and reckless, or when the Yankees were playing the Red Sox (he was from Boston). Our trysts often revolved around baseball bets…if the Red Sox win, you have to…but I always left him laughing and satisfied, with a smile on my face. Especially the time I realized as soon as I got in my car after waving good-bye to him, that my watch was still in the room. Having left the key on the nightstand and not knowing what name he had used to register, I had to call him back to the hotel to get into the room. He emerged from the lobby, laughing, my watch dangling from his finger, asking me what I was willing to do to get it back. A sizzling kiss later and the watch was mine. I saw him out with his wife last year. He blushed as I walked by his table; she was a harsh-looking bottle brunette. I wondered if she knew just how *open* her marriage really was. He texted me later that evening, once again telling me how beautiful I was and asking to meet *for old times*. I did not respond.

The two construction giants followed not long after I started meeting Ken. Dale was a general contractor in Utica, ten years my junior, and Dwight was a construction manager at a huge building site in Colonie. One wild autumn day, I met Dale at

Turning Stone Casino for four hours of vigorous lovemaking with a well-muscled man. It was a unique experience for me, overweight and just coming out of my shell, to be greeted at the door of our hotel room by a dark-haired, laughing man who swept me up into his arms and carried me to the bed. I would have done anything for him just for that fleeting feeling of weightlessness, not to mention the gymnastics that left the mattress half on the floor and me gasping for breath in a tangle of sheets. That I won a hundred dollars in the slot machines a few hours later was icing on the cake. I lectured him about romancing his wife when he walked me to my car. I was rewarded with an e- mail two weeks later telling me they had reunited, cementing their new intimate relationship at the Turning Stone Casino, but not in the same room. Then Dwight, blond and blue-eyed, needy and willing to be my knight in tarnished armor. One hour-long meeting at the construction site on a warm Indian summer afternoon was enough for both of us, though. I could sense his marriage was not in as bad shape as he had led me to believe, and he was not nearly as energetic or inventive as his younger counterpart.

The next year I stumbled into lust with Sam the transcendental investor, and Todd, the traveling sales manager. Mystical Sam's wife traveled extensively with their movie star daughter and was not into kinky sex, which she defined as anything other than the missionary position. He produced a permission slip from her the first time we were together. It read "Sam has my permission to have sex with any woman he wants, as long as he uses protection and does it in one of his kinky positions." *Okay.* Sam, with his black hair and moustache and chocolate eyes, was not all that kinky and really just wanted sex to last longer than fifteen minutes. Alas, once he told his wife he had found a woman who was not put-off by his sexual visions, she revoked his license to screw around. He still sends an e-mail greeting at the Summer Solstice.

And then there was Todd, another bad boy, in his second marriage and on the road two hundred nights a year. He came through Albany every six weeks or so, stayed at the Marriott and dined at The Barnsider. I was a willing hors d'oeuvres and dessert to accompany his stops on Wolf Road. Our last date involved me arriving at the Marriott at seven o'clock one morning for a breakfast meeting with him in his suite. I sauntered across the lobby in my trench coat and navy Calvin Klein heels, my bulging briefcase hanging from my shoulder. Two old guys, sweaty in tennis whites, ogled me in the elevator to the top floor. I knocked on Todd's door, and it immediately swung open to a middle-aged man in black silk boxer shorts. He was laughing at his sexy overture, expecting me to be shocked. His laughter strangled in his throat when I dropped my briefcase on the bed and opened my trench coat to reveal even less black silk than he was wearing. Breakfast lasted one hour and fifteen minutes, leaving me with just enough time to don the suit stuffed in my briefcase and drive down the street to my office. I couldn't wipe the smile off my face until well into the afternoon.

A few years later, Lawyer Arthur and Steve the Russian would be my summertime revenge on my absent and lying lover. Poor Arthur was unloved by his strictly religious wife and ignored by his four teenaged daughters. Engaged in a solo appellate practice, he was isolated and alone most of the time. But he was funny, brilliant and arrived at my house for our first meeting to bring me chicken soup when I was home with a bad cold. I was too sick and he was too guilty for more than a back rub and some kissing. Arthur remains one of my best sources for legal advice to this day, though we have not seen each other in years.

Steve, the Russian, was struggling with a son on drugs, a traveling wife and two recently married daughters who had left him alone at home much of the time. An architect who had been a Russian interpreter for American forces in Vietnam, he was another hard-drinking veteran with ghosts peering over his shoulder. But his bright blue eyes and riotous brown and gray curls were just what I needed. And my easy approach to sex and willingness to cuddle after seemed to soothe his troubled soul. And it was only for the summer.

I am not proud of these affairs. I wish they had never happened. I don't believe in open marriages, weekend passes, or infidelity. I respect boundaries, laws, ethics. I would hate to think any woman had been hurt by my impulses; I would be devastated if children were harmed by my follies. But deep in my heart, I am jealous of these women who still have their husbands. Husbands who are not really bad men, but men who have forgotten what it is to love and be loved. Even to the point that they would lie to be intimate with another woman.

Deep in my soul, I feel the loss of my own husband. I was ever faithful to him, as he was to me. I loved him every day we were together, even when I didn't like him, and I know he loved me. Why was he ripped from my arms, when all we wanted was to grow old together? Why are these men I have seduced, and the women who let me, still with each other, and I am alone?

There are times I have felt like the avenging angel, intent on teaching them all a lesson about lost love and empty years. In the end, I have no real excuses and many wrongs to amend. I wanted them, and I took them. But I gave all of them back, knowing I had no right to possess them even for an hour.

TOM—EVERYTHING OLD IS NEW AGAIN

As much as I loved Yahoo chat rooms and Match and Cupid, when I discovered Facebook, I truly lost my heart. Quick notes to keep up with distant acquaintances, photos immediately available of nieces and nephews and their children, check-ins with friends about dinner plans and book club news. And finding and reconnecting with friends of my youth.

Peter was the catalyst as he had always been, given his creative mind and wry sense of humor. We had been friends since kindergarten. He had launched a successful career in advertising in New York City, married, fathered two sons and divorced. Now, semiretired, he was living on Cape Cod and had way too much time on his hands. So daily, hourly, every few minutes, there was a post from Peter, commenting on a book, a movie, or the foibles of some errant politician. Almost every post compelled a response from me and everyone else on Peter's growing list of friends. There was Jenny, the doctor's daughter and one of my best friends from elementary school. There was David, quiet boy also from elementary school, now an organic farmer. Tracey emerged from years in Texas, still beautiful, still sweet, and a talented artist. We all reconnected on Peter's loop, filling in the lost years with pictures of our kids and anecdotes about our lives. We drifted back to Flanders School and Franklin Academy, resurrecting black and white photographs of scrubbed boys with brush-cuts and girls with pigtails, stories about Miss Cook, Mr. Maguire, Mr. Beard and go-home drills, Glazier's hot dogs, and the Franklin County Fair.

Then, a few days before my birthday in April 2009, there he was. On Peter's loop, commenting on another of his rants: Tom

Becker. The appearance of his name after thirty-eight years had me lifting my fingers from the keyboard, slumping back in my chair, the air in my little home office becoming cloudy with memories. Tommy Becker. *Damn.*

We had known each other forever. He grew up in the same neighborhood as Peter, Jenny, and Henry. The tree-lined streets of doctors, lawyers, and businessmen. The middle of three sons of a widowed mom, living with her and his grandmother. Tom was blond, blue-eyed and compact. And all boy. There were years he and the Park Street boys terrorized me and Jenny and Vicky and Leslie. Then we started to grow up and he terrorized only me. Not in a bad way. I had a terrible crush on him from about the sixth grade on. He was a talented musician and a good athlete. And funny. And sweet.

I think our mothers arranged for us to go together to the Epsilon Ball, the winter gala of the honor society, when I was a freshman and he was a junior in high school. I still cringe at the photos from that event. I was resplendent in Ben Franklin glasses and a short brown bob, topping a white dress festooned with green velvet bows! Tommy and I drifted back and forth with each other. I became hopelessly enamored with Jimmie Sullivan; Tom had an on-and-off-again relationship with Carol, a tiny dark-haired senior. But, from time to time, we were together.

Comfortable. Testing the waters of romance with stolen kisses and furtive touches, never consummating our attraction for each other. He didn't take me to his prom and didn't sign my yearbook at the end of his senior year. Carol was back in; I was out.

He went off to community college; I emerged from my shy cocoon those last two years in high school by learning public speaking and dating Henry. Tommy came home once in a while, and we would hang out, listening to music, sharing beer and kisses in the rec room in the finished basement of my parents' house. Then I went off to college, and he married Carol, and I never spoke to him again. Until Facebook.

After seeing his comment to Peter, I sent him a message: "Hi. Do you remember me?" He responded, "Hell, yes."

Then a longer missive about his two divorces and three daughters, his move to Virginia, and his careers as a fishing guide/manager of a fly-fishing shop and whistle-player in an Irish band. I wrote back of college, law school, marriage, career, children, and tragedy.

I also mentioned I had always wanted to learn to fly-fish, and he invited me to Virginia for fishing lessons. *Whoa.* He said Virginia was lovely in the spring, but I demurred, citing deadlines and hearing dates. I hoped to be free in the fall. He wrote back: "I've waited this long for you...I can wait a few more months, I hope."

What? As I remembered it, he had left me to run off to community college with Carol, as he had so often run when she beckoned. Tommy had been waiting for me for thirty-eight years? Since I graduated from high school? I did not believe it. He had sent his phone number, so I called him that night. He was shocked to hear my voice. I was shocked he sounded exactly the same. Within minutes, we were back to our old routine, the cadence of youth infecting our voices. Within days, we were exploring the whys and why nots of our relationship in high school. I remembered him loving me and me deriding him because he was always there for me. He remembered me loving him and him breaking my heart with his continual reconciliations with Carol. He said he had written to me in college, one last attempt to win me back. When he received nothing from me but silence, he had turned that last time to Carol. *He was not going to put that mess on me!* Determined to prove my case, I pulled out my college diary from the depths of my nightstand drawer and found the proof. But not what I thought it would prove. Tom had written to me...the lyrics for *Propinquity* by the Nitty Gritty Dirt Band, talking about knowing the kind of girl I was, how I hid my tears with easy smiles and thought with my heart and not my head. And how, despite all the years we had known each other, he had just realized the depth of his feelings for me.

Consigned to the back of my diary for decades, in a red envelope addressed to Tom, I found my response:

And I know now that I loved you, as you loved me.

And sometimes late at night, I wish that I could have a second chance. And someone would take me back five years, and let me live in peace.

Stunned into silence, I hung up the phone. I *had* loved and lost him. *What was I getting myself into now? Would I fall in love with him again?* When I called him back a while later, it was to elicit one more promise from him: promise you will not break my heart again. Tom gave me his word.

We moved rapidly to numerous phone calls every day, and then to phone sex, which left us gasping and giggling. I rescheduled my planned trip to Virginia from October to June; I would travel from a wedding on Long Island to shorten the trip.

I was in the car for ten hours, having made the mistake of driving through Maryland and around DC. It was almost eight at night when I pulled into his apartment complex. I had stopped just outside Lynchburg to brush my teeth, spike my hair, spritz on some cologne. There were butterflies in my stomach.

And there he was. Tom had a beer belly and much less hair, but the blue eyes were still bright, and the moustache still bushy. He smiled, and there was his endearing gap-toothed grin. I stepped awkwardly from the car, and he came to hug me. Just hug me. It had been a long time; it had been decades; it had only been minutes. His gentle kiss, his moustache grazing my cheek brought the jitters in my stomach back to life.

We trundled my gear into his apartment; such a guy's place, with fishing rods and guitar cases, empty beer bottles and half-filled ashtrays. I was cold from the air-conditioning and nerves; he was talking nonstop, showing me around, even the closets. Back in the kitchen, we shared a beer. We had agreed before I sojourned south if the spark was gone, there would be no hard feelings, no disappointment; we would proceed as just good friends; we would play Trivial Pursuit, and that would be it.

I took a deep slug of Corona and faced him. "So, I think you'd better kiss me again."

"Yeah, you think so?"

He leaned into me and fastened his lips on mine. Tom had always been a great kisser, and the moustache was definitely a bonus. My jitters were replaced by small flickers warming my belly. We stepped apart. A simultaneous sip of beer.

Intrepid me, I went first: "I felt that."

He smiled and said, "We could play Trivial Pursuit…" My heart dropped. "Tomorrow night."

Asshole.

He wrapped his arms around me and kissed me again. I let him have the full benefit of my expertise, and this time he looked stunned.

"Where did you learn to kiss like that?"

"Henry."

He looked taken aback. *Fair enough, for the Trivial Pursuit remark.* I snickered. He laughed. We were back.

When we made love, he touched me with wonder in his eyes. We had never gotten beyond first base in high school, scared little virgin I had been. I opened to him, and he took all I offered. At the end, he whispered, "I can't believe I'm inside you. I'm making love to you." I fell asleep with a smile on my face.

The next morning, there was a quiet and slightly standoffish Tom. I expected more lovemaking; after all, we had waited thirty-eight years. I was only fifty-six and he was fifty-seven. But, he said he needed recovery time and went into work. Later he soothed my hurt by calling and inviting me to lunch. That night, he cooked for me; we drank a huge amount of wine and started our Trivial Pursuit tournament. Tumbling into bed, he was a tender and generous lover.

I left two days later, and it was one of the hardest things I have ever done. I had fallen into a routine with him already. We complemented each other; his quietness, my assertiveness; his cleverness, my intelligence. And the memories. Tommy was giving me back my youth. His recollection of the events of our childhood and adolescence was limitless. I did not want to go home.

I promised to meet him again as soon as possible. Maybe he could drive part way, and we could meet in between. Maybe in Pennsylvania.

TOM—FOURTH OF JULY 2009

Route 88 is an almost forgotten highway. It cuts across New York State on a diagonal, from just outside Schenectady to Binghamton. No services along this route, subject to flooding and sudden death, it is still a beautiful ride. Farms climb up the sides of the gently sloping hills bracketing the road. In places it stretches out seemingly forever, then dips and turns, bringing another scenic vista into view.

Late afternoon, Fourth of July. Hot and humid, but no thunderstorms predicted. I drove to meet Tom, on the Pennsylvania border, five-and-a-half hours for me, four and a half hours for him. The sun was bright overhead but produced no glare because the floating clouds drifted through the harsh rays, shadowing the afternoon.

Leaving my son on his twenty-fourth birthday was causing me some guilt, but not enough to cancel this trip. After all, he had arisen at one in the afternoon after a night out with friends in Lake George, sated on the fried chicken and macaroni salad dinner I had provided. His favorite sausage bread was waiting for him when he awoke. A birthday card full of money, his requested gift, sat on the kitchen counter, next to a Black Satin cake from J&S Watkins bakery, the family birthday cake of choice. His plans to watch the Yankees, nap, and head out to Saratoga to complete his birthday celebration did not require my presence. He sulked and pouted a bit but graciously told me to have a good time with my friend, Rachel. The lie had slipped easily from my lips; even at twenty-four, he was unable to accept his mother had resumed dating. Not telling him where I was really going had become my defense mechanism; understanding friends providing me with alibis across county and state lines. Someday, I hoped to be able to stop the lies and subterfuge with him, but not now, not today.

Diet Coke, trail mix and a book on CD; I could drive anywhere. No GPS yet, I still relied on MapQuest to get me to unknown destinations. Reading glasses hung around my neck; my new contacts were meant for distance only. I switched off the book about an hour into the trip and put on the CD of Tom's Celtic band. Irish whistle filled the car, hot fiddle licks and the lead singer's voice, singing of wild mountain thyme. My heart clenched at the sound of Tom's voice in the background and then the haunting melody from his whistles. He was back in my life after thirty- eight years, but his music had always touched me.

My mother's family came from Ireland in the late 1800s. Settled in New England, some made their way to northern New York, carving out a comfortable life on the railroad. Irish mysticism and faith run deep in my veins, tempered by questions from my practical mind and my chosen Judaism. But still, Ireland and its immigrants are part of me, and the songs from the car speakers had me singing out loud, something I never do anyplace else. I can't sing.

The road dipped and curved around a long slow rise. Ahead, on the small peak rising before me, was a huge American flag. Quite possibly, the largest flag I had ever seen, it snapped briskly in the wind. I don't know who put it there or its purpose, but my heart swelled at the sight of it. Child of our first immigrants, my father's family arrived on these shores from England, seeking religious freedom in 1634, and of the more recent Irish rabble who begat my mother, I was raised on love of our country. Fourth of July was a day for remembering and giving thanks. For years—and this year was no different—the movie, *1776*, provided the backdrop for breakfast and preparation for my son's birthday. Eleven o'clock in the morning brought us outside to listen to the *1812 Overture* blasting from the neighbor's windows across the street. Never fireworks, though. My son was afraid of fireworks as a child, so we watched from our house, looking in the distant sky for the flashes from the Commons, five miles away. It was enough. I would be missing fireworks tonight, and I felt the loss of it.

I kept the flag in my sight as long as I could, searching for it in the sideview mirror as the hill dropped away around the next curve. Binghamton was not too much farther; the trip was almost half over. I switched back to the book on CD and then stopped at the Pennsylvania Visitor's Center to stretch my aching legs and use the restroom. As I emerged, a church group offered me a hotdog and lemonade. Free, or I could make a donation; they had just four more dogs to give away before they could leave after what had been a ten-hour day of volunteering to feed holiday travelers. It was a horrible hotdog, but I ate it and made a small donation, grateful for the lemonade and the happy conversation of these Protestants passing out food, drink, and heartfelt wishes for a Happy Fourth.

Pennsylvania. Route 81 south. I had driven this route from my college in the Finger Lakes to my then boyfriend's law school in Baltimore, thirty-one, thirty-two, thirty-three years ago. Mountainous, curvy, crammed with tractor-trailers and always under construction, the road meanders through small, industrial cities and farmland all the way to Virginia. I had been on the road weeks earlier, returning from my initial meeting with Tom. I wondered then whether I would be seeing him again and when; our reunion after all those years apart had gone surprisingly well. The old attraction for him had resurfaced, stronger with the consummation of all those adolescent longings. Could this really be the right time for us? I had heard so many stories of high school romances rekindled twenty-five, forty, even fifty years later that I found myself daring to dream.

Dusk was coming on, fading the light from the sun into the glare from the headlights of the double trailers that screamed by me. I was stiff, and I was getting tired. I switched back to Tom's CD to break the monotony and to remind me why I had set out late in the afternoon of the birthday of my country and my son to be with my old high school sweetheart and see if love was still possible after nearly forty years.

Tommy was already in Pennsylvania. He left Virginia early on the morning of the Fourth to drive to Carlisle and meet his daughter. They had had a nice dinner: dad, daughter, boyfriend, boyfriend's daughter (Tom has an interesting and complicated family life). Tom was now headed back to the hotel room he had booked for us. Cell phone reception was spotty, so I was pretty much on my own for this leg of the trip.

Night was rushing in from the hills around me. I could see streetlights blinking on in the towns I passed. Down in the valleys, the lights looked like a regiment of drunken fireflies, lined up in rows, but with an errant beam flashing off on its own. Then I saw it. A flash of green and gold off to the right. Though it was not yet dark, not quite eight thirty, fireworks were starting to flare. Two more bursts, one pure white light, flashing then dropping in strands like strings of diamonds, and another, red, white, and blue, exploding like a crazy flag.

Cool. How cool is this? I thought as I headed around another curve. Off to my left, a small city nestled in a valley. More bursts of light streaked across the sky, thin trails of white, arcing higher and higher then curving back to Earth, and just after the peak, a fiery cascade of color. Purple this time, then a green and blue mix, followed by several yellow streaks and small bursts. *Beautiful, just beautiful.*

For the rest of my journey, fireworks accompanied me. Every town and city along the way providing me with color and light, bringing back recent memories of fireworks displays in the distance viewed as a parent from my front yard. Older memories followed of childhood Fourth of July fireworks in my hometown, set off at the Rec Park, all of us gathered on blankets on the damp grass. Families together, kids in their pajamas and sneakers, eating ice cream cones and exclaiming in wonder at each new display.

As I pulled off the highway, Tommy was waiting for me in the hotel parking lot—his voice on the Bluetooth in my ear, telling me where to turn. But in my heart were the memories of my youth and adolescence, many brought back by this man I had traveled thirty-eight years and five and half hours to see again. The bright lights in my eyes were not just reflections of the fireworks I had just witnessed, but were also the lights of recognition and remembrance. And anticipation. Lovers and friends, we were remembering together our youth and the joy and pain of first love and first heartbreak.

And in my heart, in my heart, old questions answered, new questions asked, and hope renewed.

TOM—MARIPOSAS

Virginia is for lovers, they say. I think it's true, at least for me. I traveled again to Virginia in August to see Tommy. I stayed for a week. It was our third encounter with each other and was to be our longest visit.

I wondered from time to time during the week whether I had made the right decision to come to Tom. I wanted to put him in a box, categorize our relationship, make a plan for the next month, year, lifetime. He was impossible to analyze—one moment funny and tender, the next quiet and almost distant. I was uncomfortable with my inability to read him. The lawyer in me wanted to label him and our relationship. The woman wanted commitments and declarations of love. The person I was becoming with him recognized neither the lawyer nor the woman was being reasonable, but still I struggled. There was nothing wrong, but nothing was completely right, either.

Friday, we drove up into the Blue Ridge Mountains, early. Having had too much to drink the night before, a regular occurrence, Tom had to be roused vigorously by me for us to make our planned departure time. We had to meet a telephone repairman at the fishing lodge on the Piney River owned by his company. He packed fishing equipment and wine; I packed Diet Coke and guacamole.

The ride was quiet; he is not a morning person. The mountains were beautiful, misted by low-lying clouds, verdant green below the white, almost blue above. The lodge is off-road, up and down hills, a gravel road with sudden drops where the shoulder should be. We arrived just before the repairman, ate our McDonald's breakfast sandwiches standing up. I was skittish, remembering Tom's story that in June a tenant had found a copperhead snake curled in the corner of the kitchen. In July, Tom had spotted a rattlesnake in the tall grass while guiding. I hate snakes, but I loved the lodge. The whisper of the rapids, the buzz of the insects, and the light breeze blowing through the ancient trees was peaceful and calming.

It started to rain—drizzle, really—just when the repairman left. Tom's work was done for the day, so we crashed on the king-sized bed upstairs, the windows flung open to the damp breeze and the sound of the river. Around one o'clock, refreshed after our three-hour nap, we packed up the chilled Pinot Grigio, plastic wineglasses, and Tom's fishing gear and made our way down to the pond; the river was running too low to be good for fishing. I had to follow behind him, exactly, so I stepped where he stepped, as he pushed through the tall grass, swinging his rod to scare any lurking snakes.

It was a beautiful afternoon, sipping wine and trying to catch the elusive rainbow trout that leapt just beyond the line he cast so skillfully into the still water. We tried a variety of flies, all tied by Tom during the cold winter months. He carefully explained each one to me. He fastened first the little dun-colored one, then the black and blue one, then one that was a dull brown, to the thin nylon strand. The fish weren't biting, but I reveled in our time at the pond. I cast a few times myself, first with Tom's hands on mine, his body pressed into my back as he patiently instructed me not to flick my wrist; to cast at ten and two, ten and two, then let the line go. I loved the feel of the light rod in my hand, the cork handle dry to my touch, the line flying over my head and to the right, plopping in the water like a bug landing. The fish were not as impressed with the flies as I was, and we caught nothing.

Leaving entailed locking behind us the three gates that crossed the road. One was at the edge of the river; low from lack of rain, it was more like a stream. As Tom got out at the water's edge, I hopped out too, wanting to walk across the road where the stream flowed over it. Tom stopped to identify for me all the life in the water: nymphs, crawfish, water bugs. His knowledge was extensive, and he explained carefully and clearly. Even a science idiot like me could understand. I was impressed with the breadth of information he imparted to me.

He got back in the truck, and I turned toward the water. My right knee, due soon for replacement, was aching and uncertain, so I was watching where I was stepping as the cold stream splashed against and through my Crocs. The feel was delightful, cool and fresh on my tired feet. Just as I reached the other side of the stream, what I thought were a cluster of pre- autumn leaves moved. I felt my heart rise into my throat, the urge to scream clawing its way up from my gut. *Snakes?* The leaves then fluttered, rose. *Butterflies.* At least twenty-five of them. As big as the palm of my hand, pale butter yellow with distinctive black marks.

I turned to Tom to stop the truck. "Don't run over the butterflies!" I called.

"Don't worry, take your time." He grinned at me. That gap-toothed grin that always made me sigh.

Turning back to the butterflies, still settled along the edge of the water, I began shooing them to move them out of the way of the truck. I was wading in butterflies. They rose one by one, dipped toward me then away, swirled around my head and shoulders. One rested briefly on my hand. I was entranced, enthralled, exhilarated by them. Giggling and dancing, I waved Tommy across the stream. He was still grinning at me and the picture I had made.

"Where's the camera?" he asked as I climbed into the truck. "I wanted to take a picture of you herding butterflies." He was smiling broadly.

The camera was in my pocket, but I didn't need to digitalize the mental photographs I had made as I moved through the cascade of butterflies. I will never forget the sight or the feel of them.

How do you categorize a man who gives you that moment?

TOM—THE IRISH IN ME

My mother's grandparents came from Ireland; from Dublin, County Cavan and County Cork, it is said. The Irish are in me. My father's family was English and French Canadian; and, even though he was a redhead, my mother insisted that my childhood red hair and freckles were from my Irish ancestors. As far as my mother was concerned, it was our Irish heritage that defined us.

No one in my family had ever set foot in Ireland, not since my mother's paternal grandmother, Mary Berry, left County Cork to travel with her sea captain husband and land on the shores of Connecticut about one hundred years ago. So in the summer of 1974, when I was all of twenty-one, I set off for England to work for three months in the offices of the Vice Chairman of the Conservative Party. The first of my immediate family to take flight over the Atlantic Ocean, I boarded British Airways in Montreal late on a May evening with two classmates from college. One was a hearty Irish lass of the clan of Halloran from Massachusetts, the other was a stick-up-her-ass daughter of WASP patricians; but we were the sum total of the college's political science majors, so off we went to study parliamentarian politics.

A red-eye transatlantic flight in those days brought you up toward the North Pole and down again just off the coast of Ireland. Ireland seen through a small round airplane window just as dawn is breaking on the western cliffs is like looking through the peephole of a kaleidoscope of green. "This isle, this emerald isle, this Ireland," I murmured, the phrase playing through my mind as we crossed over Ireland, the Irish Sea and Wales, to arrive in the misty fog of a spring morning in England.

After settling into our lodging and our jobs, we began our weekend jaunts around Great Britain. Out to Stratford-on-Avon, round to Salisbury and the great Stonehenge, down to Dover's white cliffs. A train ride to Edinburgh and two damp days traversing the Royal Mile and climbing Arthur's Seat to gaze down on wet grey stone and green, so green it should have been a color all its own.

Then, on to Ireland. Too poor to fly to Dublin from London, almost penniless students working for the privilege and not the coin, we opted for a train to Wales in the late afternoon and an overnight cruise over the Irish Sea on a merchant ship. With only our backpacks to cushion us, we huddled on the deck, just the midnight blue sky to cover us—a million stars to light our way. Gathered out in the open with us, a group of sons of the Olde Sod pulled up boxes and barrels and broke out their instruments—accordions, harmonicas, mouth harps and guitars. And spoons. Through the night, their Irish voices serenaded us with the songs of Ireland we had never heard at home on St. Patrick's Day, except perhaps for *Molly Malone* and *By the Rising of the Moon*.

I sat in stunned silence, transfixed by the music as I had never been before. I could play no instrument and dared not raise my voice in song; so paltry a voice as mine had no place among these musicians. So, I sat, I listened, I hummed, I tapped my foot, I laughed, and I wept. To this day, over three decades later, I can still feel the salt spray on my face, taste on my lips the dark Irish whiskey they passed around, hear the music ringing in my ears, playing in my soul. I never thought to feel the like again. Until a Sunday in June 2010.

We drove up from Lynchburg into the Blue Ridge Mountains in a light mist. Low clouds hung midway up the sides of the mountains, their pale gray a stark contrast to the vivid green of early summer in Virginia. I was back in Virginia again, the latest of several trips over the year I had been seeing Tommy. He had come to me after my knee was replaced the past September and again at Christmas.

It was at Christmas with his daughters in our hometown that he told me he loved me.

Curled up in the hard bed in a rundown motel at the edge of town, the best our old town had to offer, we had both had a lot to drink celebrating the holiday. He turned off the lights after I tumbled quickly under the covers to get warm.

Putting his arm around me, he pulled me to him and with a kiss on the forehead, he murmured, "I love you, Malone."

It gave me pause, I loved him—I had always loved him on some level, but I was not sure I was in love with him. I always felt he was holding something back. So I held back for a moment. I could say it, I reasoned to myself, I could tell him I loved him because it was true.

But, before I could speak, as happened on too many evenings, he was asleep, snoring softly. He did not hear me as I whispered, "I love you too, Becker."

We left for my house the next day and as my son was home from school, Tom slept in the guest room. He drove back to Virginia the next morning.

As soon as I was able to drive again in February, I began making the long trek to Virginia, often with my brown Labrador Retriever, Marley, to stay for four or five days at a time. We became entangled in each other's lives, in each other's work and with each other's children; our daughters seemed to like that we were a couple. I had become friends with his friends.

So it was on that sunny summer afternoon, Tom and I were on our way to a house concert at the home of his friend, Jim, and Jim's wife, Wendy. Jim is, in Tom's estimation, one of the finest musicians in America. Tom is no slouch himself in this department, playing guitar, banjo, mandolin and, my personal favorite, Irish whistles. We were off to hear Paddy Keenan and John Walsh play for a group of thirty or so Irish music aficionados and musicians. A house concert, so the price of admission was food and drink, instruments and a few dollars for the musicians.

Jim and Wendy's house sits on the side of a hill, with an unimpeded vista of the Blue Ridge Mountains spread out like a feast from their back deck. The walls of the simple concrete block house are covered with photographs of Jim in various bands, his Irish and Southern ancestors and musical instruments. The living room had been largely stripped of furniture and was filled with folding chairs in rows before the fireplace, an amplifier and a bass. The voices were softly Southern, and the hospitality warm. Excitement was a low buzz in the air as we awaited the arrival of the two Irish lads, making their way through the hills from Roanoke after a whirlwind weekend that brought Paddy from Boston to a concert with John in NYC on Friday and another concert in Roanoke on Saturday.

Thirty minutes late, they arrived in the light rain. John was introduced by Jim as one of the finest guitarists in the world, one for whom a guitar company is naming a set of guitar strings. He resembles any collegiate American guy from any midsize town in America, until he opens his mouth and County Kenny spills out. Paddy has the look of the performer, slouched under a black leather hat, a black leather cord tied round his neck from which hangs a huge sculpted piece of silver, loose grey shirt, and soft jeans. With dark eyes and a graying moustache, he wears the years of touring, drinking and playing sad songs on his face. Paddy may be the premier *uilleann* piper in the world.

The *uilleann* pipes, originally known as the Union pipes, are the characteristic national bagpipe of Ireland. Some pipers can converse or sing while playing. Paddy doesn't sing, but he does tell tales.

Laughing at Jim's introduction, Paddy kicked off his shoes, asked for a beer and thanked us all for coming along, from places near and far. It was pointed out then, that I had come all the way from New York. A look of surprised amusement in his eyes, Paddy stared at me and asked in his Dublin drawl, "Now, really, darlin'? And why would you be traveling so far when we've just come from New York?"

"It was no great feat, as I was headed here for other purposes as well." I blushed at the attention. "But, I believe I win the prize."

"Ah, well, that's it then. We'll have a bit of music for you and make sure the trip was worth it."

They began with a trio of jigs, then some reels. *Uilleann* pipes sound to me like Irish whistles but with more range and depth, a hint of the roughness of bagpipes echoing in the background. Difficult to describe, but delicious to hear. I did not know any of the songs, though Paddy and John talked about each set in their gentle lyrical voices, touched with humor and real affection for each other and for the music. They seemed as much in awe of their attentive audience as we were of them. Paddy played a song he had written for his daughter, Sabrina, to teach her to play by ear; John played a waltz he had written as a Christmas gift for his daughter, and together they gave us the ballad of Lord Franklin, lost at sea, exploring the Northwest Passage.

After two hours, they called for the other musicians to join in. Almost everyone began unpacking fiddles, banjos, guitars, and whistles. They gathered around Jim and Paddy and John and began to play. The music filled the small house. It floated in the air, enveloping me in a camaraderie that should have excluded me; but instead, drew me in. I was back on the freighter to Dublin, once again on a journey to Ireland. Jigs and reels brought out spoons and a *bodhr`an*, the Irish frame drum. Tom began on his mandolin but then gently eased into whistle playing.

Jerry started to play the *dobro*, a resonator guitar played across the lap, which prompted everyone to urge Warren to sing *Maggie*, as he strummed a gorgeous acoustic guitar. Tears came to my eyes. John was heard to say, "That was fucking beautiful." Paddy agreed. "Lovely, just lovely."

The music was magic, worth a trip from anywhere. The concert was an experience like none I had ever had before, like so many of the experiences I had been sharing with Tommy. These shared adventures strengthened my resolve to work out the difficulties with the time and distance apart. And with the increasing difficulties in our physical relationship, or rather, our lack of a physical relationship.

We were among the last to struggle out. I played the groupie and sought autographs from Paddy and John on their CD's. They promised to come north to play again at Café Lena's in Saratoga. Standing in the driveway, twilight coming in, Tom and Paddy had one last discussion about Irish whistles. Tom was in his element, speaking to his idol about their music. Paddy asked to see one of Tom's whistles. When it was drawn from the bag, Paddy's eyes lighted and he brought it to his lips. Recognizing the song, Tom pulled out a smaller whistle. The two played *The Tar Road to Sligo*. Conversation died. The notes drifted around us as we stood still, caught once again in the spell of the music; drawing us together, touching the Irish in us all.

TOM—INTIMACY

My grandfather loved to fish. There are albums filled with his photographs of trout, rainbow and brown, lined up neatly in rows, framed by forest ferns on a background of day-old newspaper.

He would stand in the swiftly moving river outside his hunting camp, waders up to his thighs, casting and playing the line across the rapids, the shiny leaden sinkers flashing like lightening through the air, glimmering like silver in the ripples and eddies of the current.

My life is like that scene. It often moves swiftly, but occasionally it pools in the shallows; sometimes brilliantly beautiful, now and then dim and muddy, but always moving, inexorably to the end of the cascade, around the bend ahead, unseen and unknown.

My cares are like those silvery leaden sinkers. Any one of them a small, almost inconsequential weight, manageable in ones, or twos or threes. But taken all together, they can pull me down into the depths, the murky, choking depths, where there is no light, no sound, only the weight of them pulling me to the dark, silty, sucking bottom, full of pain and doubt.

When the weight of my fears and heartbreaks and regrets threaten to drown me, there is a recourse that buoys me up, allows me to float for a few moments, forces air into my lungs, and releases me.

Orgasms.

The touch, the taste, the feel of my lover as he moves along my body. Fingers, hands, lips, teeth. Touching, caressing, and tugging me down the slippery slope of passion. Muscles relaxing, then bunching, nerve endings tingling and leaping, skin hot then cool from his breath on the dampness of my throat, breasts and thighs. Invading my body, my mind and my soul.

Pleasure swirling through me, to my fingertips, to my toes, to the very roots of my hair, then gathering, centering at my core.

My thoughts are focused on that spot, that spot he is touching, that pleasure point he is tasting. Please, soon, please, almost, please, please, please. *Now*. Oh my God, yes, there, now!

Oblivion. No more thought, no more worry, no pain, no regret. Pleasure. Mind-numbing, soul-shattering pleasure. Light, brilliant light. And weightlessness. Soaring up to the light, calling on God, Jesus, Moses, my lover, as I move to the light. Then arching into it, almost in Heaven. Suspended there. Then floating, falling, drifting as though on a cloud back to my body, supine and sated, motionless except for the faint ripples on my thighs and abdomen. Gulping, gasping, dragging air back into my lungs. Laughter erupting.

Movement, pulling me up, turning me over, positioning me here or there. Then, filling me. Joining himself to me. Moving in me. Moving on him. Not alone, not now, two moving as one. One goal, one need, once more. Again, our pleas pounding on Heaven's door. Now? Yes? *Yes! Now!* We come together, we *come* together. *Sweet.*

After, with anyone, smiles, a giggle, a caress. Thanks for taking me *there*. I'll sleep tonight, dreamless, deep, sleep. But with Tom, even though it was happening with less and less frequency, when we came together, a deeper feeling, a belonging. I kept thinking, hoping, praying: maybe this will work.

TOM—WHAT I DID FOR LOVE

I did not swim the ocean or climb the highest mountain for love. I did not write a bestseller or record a Grammy-award winning song. I did not run into a burning building or face-off a rabid dog for love. At fifty-seven, overweight and with a new knee, I went to the Adirondacks with my boyfriend, Tommy Becker. Camping. In a tent.

Meacham Lake is almost too far north to be in the Adirondack Park. Just inside the Blue Line, it is about twenty miles south of Malone, where Tom and I grew up. As kids and teenagers, we all spent time at Meacham Lake: close to town, sandy beach, pretty vistas. And the loons.

The first and last time I camped at Meacham was in 1976. I was twenty-three. I was fit and trim. I was engaged, but not to Tom. My future husband and I stayed in a Winnebago. We did cook hot dogs over the campfire, and I showered in the bathhouse. But at night we slept in a real bed with sheets and doors that locked the wild animals out and kept the warmth inside.

When Tom initially suggested we spend most of his vacation week in July camping at Lake Meacham, I was cautiously agreeable. We were just past our one-year mark of reuniting and we were going to rent a pop-up trailer and share a campsite with Tom's brother, Dennis. Tom would get the week off and drive from Virginia to New York to pick up the camper, my dog Marley and me. Then the rental fell through. Dennis offered a tent. A tent! We would be staying, without the dog now, in a tent, for four nights.

Suffice it to say, I faced what had started out as a nice nature adventure with increasing trepidation. The yentas were astonished I was even contemplating such an outing and started making side bets as to whether I would actually make the trip; and, if by some miracle I did, whether I would last through the first night. No one bet I would stay Sunday night through Thursday morning—when I left my friends on Saturday morning, the bets were limited to what hour on Sunday night I would pack it in and head for civilization. I kept silent, knowing that I had only promised Tom I would stay for one night. In the tent. Then, if I didn't like it, I was heading for that rundown motel in Malone.

Tom arrived Sunday late morning after an all-night drive from Virginia. He was going to shower and take a short nap while I went to the market to shop for Marley and my daughter. He gave me one hundred dollars, and told me to pick up whatever I needed, but to get him a case of Genesee beer. *Genesee beer! Did they still make it?* Off I went to purchase chicken breasts for the dog, citronella candles for me, and Genesee. Hannaford did not carry the brew; neither did Price Chopper. Desperate, I called Georgeann, a beer drinker of some renown.

"Where do you buy Genesee?"

"Genesee! Jesus, do they still make that?"

"Tommy says he's had it up north and really wants some for this camping trip. But, the supermarket doesn't carry it."

"You'll have to try a beverage center, but good luck. Genesee? Who drinks that shit anyway?"

Off I went to Savemore Beverage Center, and, after a few turns around the place, I found a case of Genesee cans. For $14.99. My twelve-pack of Corona Light was the same price. I would not be sharing my Coronas with Tom, even at a two-for-one exchange rate. Arriving home, I dumped ice into my big cooler and Tom's two smaller ones, then tucked the beer into the ice in his coolers. My cooler was the refrigerator where all our perishable food was stored, including Hershey bars for the inevitable s'mores. My daughter pulled into the driveway just as we were loading my *new* secondhand bike onto the carrier next to Tom's. My daughter guffawed at the sight of my bike. I defensively proclaimed, "I can still ride a bike!" She derisively replied, "Yeah, but why would you?"

We arrived at Meacham in the late afternoon. It is a jewel of a lake and one of the prettiest of all the State campsites. Number twenty-seven was our address, but it was empty. No sign of Dennis and the tent, no sign of Tom's daughter, Emily. But there were echoes of activity floating up the camp road so we set out to find Dennis. The campsite next to ours was occupied by Emily. And her mother. And her grandmother. *This is awkward.* Tom introduced me to Emily, who gave me a friendly grin.

Then, Tom said, "This is Morgan," to Emily's mother, who did shake my hand. "Hey, how are you?" I bravely inquired.

"Good, nice to meet you," the mother of Tom's youngest daughter replied politely.

Emily's grandmother, the matriarch of the clan, was glaring at me suspiciously throughout this is exchange. She turned to Emily and asked, "Who is this?"

Emily, seemingly unaware of the tension, replied I was "Morgan, Tom's old friend."

That earned me a pointed glare from the grandmother. Tom was silent, not correcting the *friend* appellation. Though I understood his not wanting to make an issue in front of his daughter's grandmother, his failure to clarify I was his girlfriend, lover or even significant other, hurt more than I expected.

The ice broken but not thawed, we headed back to our site. Fortunately, not only had Dennis arrived but also, from Malone, Tom's two older daughters and his son-in-law. They all made short work of setting up our tarp over the picnic table and erecting a blue, dome-shaped tent. Tom inflated the queen-sized air mattress, and I set the welcome mat in front of the tent. Ice-cold beers in hand, we built a fire in the ancient fireplace and roasted hot dogs. *So far, so good.* No mosquitoes, mild temperatures, lively conversation with some good-natured teasing between daughters and dad. Dusk was falling when I broke out the fixings for s'mores. They disappeared as fast as they were made. Nothing says camping like charred marshmallows jammed between chocolate and graham crackers, washed down with a cold brew.

Amidst humorous comments about my lack of camping experience and semiserious advice about the woods at night, the Malone crew departed, and Tom and I were left alone with Dennis and Emily. We sat around the campfire and Tom's new lantern, drinking beer and sharing stories of growing up in Malone. Tommy and Dennis were fabulous storytellers and I laughed so hard, I had to pee.

When I asked where the bathroom was, Emily walked with me across the camp road, through some trees to a clearing, then a left turn onto a trail through the woods, to the bathroom. *Right. Like I am going to be able to make this trip in the middle of the night.* I led the way back with my flashlight trained on the ground, only making one wrong turn. *No more beer for you, my girl.*

Tom and I stumbled into the tent about midnight. I had made up the air mattress with sheets and a comforter. Tom draped a sleeping bag over the foot of the bed. Tired and more than a little drunk, we climbed into bed in our jammie bottoms and long-sleeved T-shirts. A kiss good-night, and we were instantly asleep; the distant sound of the loons a sweet lullaby.

The end of my nose was an icicle. It was the only thing protruding into the below-zero night air when I awoke. I had somehow wrapped part of the blanket around my head. Tom, never a cuddler, was glued to my side, dead to the world. The comforter and sleeping bag bunched around us. I was shivering from the damp cold permeating the tent. I knew I would see my breath if I could just get the nerve to lower the blanket from right under my nose. And I had to pee. I was too cold to move, but I inched my fingers to the edge of the mattress and reached out for my sweatshirt. Under the covers, I slipped it over my head and squirmed until it was in place.

Unfortunately the squirming had two negative effects: it jostled my too-full bladder, and it dipped the mattress on my side; so that in an instant, Tom rolled into me, and I ended up on the floor.

Okay, I might as well go to the bathroom since I'm awake and already cold. I clambered to my feet, awkwardly, stiff from my knee replacement and the bitter cold. I found my Crocs, my glasses, and my flashlight. Quietly, I unzipped the tent flap and stepped outside. I quickly zipped the flap back in place, although I abruptly realized, it was warmer outside the tent. The full moon lit the campsite in a dusty white light. A few red embers still glowed in the old stone fireplace, fanned into flame by the wind flowing around the towering evergreens and oaks. I breathed in the night air, scented with woodsmoke and pine. *I had no idea where I was.*

I knew I was at our campsite, but I was totally disoriented. I could not remember how to get to the bathroom. But lack of directions became a moot point as soon as I took a step. *I have to pee. Now.* Blindly, I looked from left to right. A trail entered the woods about ten feet to my right. I jerked the flashlight in that general direction and turned into the woods. The first tree on the right looked good but was too narrow to conceal the width of my white bottom, should the forest ranger come driving by on his nightly patrol. Waving the flashlight around, I spotted a huge pine about six feet ahead of me. Walking with my teeth clenched and my knees pressed together, I edged up and around the tree. I needed both hands to pull down my jammie bottoms, so I wedged the flashlight under my chin. My chest was brightly illuminated, but nothing else. My back against the tree, I crouched, yanking at my pants. *My knees were still locked together. What the hell?!* In a combination of movements that would have made a gymnast proud, I spread my knees, pulled my pants almost to my ankles, grabbed the extra fabric in one hand and the flashlight, sliding out from under my chin, in my other hand. *Thank you, God!* Blessed relief.

Propped against the tree for what seemed like an hour, peeing like a racehorse, I decided to look around. I aimed the light away from the growing puddle between me and the tree and out into the forest.

What was I thinking? It was the middle of the night, in the middle of the forest, and I'm looking to see who or what is nearby? Terror swept through me as I imagined all the pairs of yellow eyes peering at me from the underbrush. Rabbits, foxes, coyotes. Bears. Empty at last, knees starting to lock up, I scrambled into an upright position. My jammie bottoms held up in one hand, the flashlight in the other, I veered to the left and onto the path. In seconds I was back inside the tent, shaking as much from fear as from the cold.

Safe at last, I kicked off my Crocs and placed the flashlight next to the mattress. I took a few more moments to straighten the comforter and sleeping bag and pull on my socks, discarded at bedtime. Crawling under the covers, I snuggled next to Tommy, trying to capture some of his warmth. His arm crept around me as he pulled me close. *Love?*

Yup, that is what I did for love.

TOM—MEN IN KILTS

I now write romance novels and stories instead of dry legal arguments in appellate briefs. I love romance in all its forms and variations: stories, novellas and trilogies. I am in love with the soldiers, tycoons, pirates and firefighters that are the favorite heroes in most tales. But, in my heart of hearts, I truly melt for men in kilts.

I had come to the Highland Games and Celtic Festival at The Meadow, just outside of Richmond, Virginia. Tom's Celtic band was playing on the main stage for the first time. I had promised to make the long journey south to share in this experience with him, long before our relationship had begun to fade at the beginning of the summer, maybe even before, if I was completely honest with myself. Despite my misgivings about the possible outcome of the long weekend, I was happy to be back in Virginia. And I was thrilled to be part of the Games.

We arrived late on Friday evening, me from New York, Tommy from Lynchburg, and his brother Dennis from Connecticut. Tom had booked adjoining rooms—one for us and the other for Dennis—at a motel not far from the site of the Games. Dennis's company made dinner a fun time of storytelling and joking, followed by one of our now legendary Trivial Pursuit marathons and lots of beer.

Our room had two double beds. Late in the evening, after Dennis had staggered off to his room, I emerged from the bathroom in my Irish lace and lawn nightie to find both beds turned down. Tom was sitting on the edge of one, still fully dressed.

"You can take the bed by the bathroom, I'll sleep in the other one tonight."

"You will?" I asked it casually but my insides were twisting as a slow anger began burning in my gut.

"Yes, we have to get up so early tomorrow morning and we've both had a long day. We'll sleep better in our own beds." He rose to kiss me goodnight, the now-occurring-way-too-often-kiss-on-the-forehead, and disappeared into the bathroom.

I climbed into my bed, annoyed and hurt. And exhausted. I was asleep almost before I had time to wonder if the end had come.

The next morning, we were both groggy and stiff when we climbed into Tom's truck for the short ride to the State Fairgrounds. Tom was clad in his Buchannan plaid dress kilt and all the accessories. I had helped him dress with a mixture of pride and sadness.

Now, at the Fairgrounds, looking for Dennis who was off playing his bagpipes and the other members of Tom's band, I was surrounded by men in kilts. I was in Heaven.

The colors are vivid red, yellow and green in the Buchanan tartan, more colorful even than the intense red predominant in the Royal Stewart or the bright red and green combination belonging to Clan Bruce. Dazzling blue mixes with white and true green in the Gordon Highland tartan, the dark navy and darker green in the Black Watch plaid contrasts with the almost turquoise and aqua of the Campbell Clan pattern. The Caledonia tartan features brilliant purple and pure white, while the MacGregor Rob Roy was, I thought, almost garishly Halloween orange and black. Tom was pointing out the colors of the different clans to me as we made our way around the tents to the parade grounds.

Matching flashes encircle muscular or frail calves covered to the knee in heavy wool hose in cream or green or navy. Tucked into the hose, a *sgian-dubh* is often found, its blade hidden, only the hilt visible on the right leg. Sporrans of rabbit or fox dangle from simple silver chains, or more ornate decorated links of silver and gold hung low on the hips. These man-purses might feature full heads or have just one rabbit's foot in the center.

Above the plaids, the tops are as varied as the men. Jacobite full-sleeved blouses in cream or brown, lacings half way down the chest, or crisp business shirts, buttoned tight to the chin, with neckties in the clan's plaid are common. The traditional Argyle jacket in blue or heather green wool, silver or pewter buttons marching down the front is evident, especially among the older men. Military sweaters in olive drab or khaki were favored by the younger men.

Much to my delight I saw soldiers wearing service blouses, the sleeves rolled back to reveal muscular forearms, adorned with tattoos of Celtic knots and service insignias. They were enough to make me drool, especially given Tom's failure to walk next to me as we traversed the Fair Grounds. I almost gave up trying to keep up with him, in frustration and to enable me to peruse all the men surrounding me. Men in kilts.

Some wear the plaid draped across chest and one shoulder, held in place by a Scottish crest badge. Head coverings are also varied, with everything from tam o'shanters to Glengarry bonnets seen atop balding heads or perched jauntily over graying ponytails. From top to bottom, traditional wars with contemporary. The older men sport ghillie brogues or regular leather business shoes, other men wear combat boots or hunting boots. Sandals or sneakers are not a good look.

I finally grabbed Tom's arm to stop him.

"Who are those guys?" I asked, nodding at a group of young men who seemed to be from another world.

"They are the Scots wannabes." He snorted derisively and began walking away. Dark and foreboding, they look like refugees from some late-night Dungeons and Dragons computer marathon. Swirling black capes conceal the two-handed Highland claymore, strapped across frail white backs that, in the days of the Battle of Culloden, would not have been fit to carry even feed for the horses, much less the mighty weapon of Scots Highlanders. They flit and flicker along the periphery of the gathering, massing around the vendors selling dirks and swords, fingering the sharp gray blades with long nail-bitten fingers, stroking chins bereft of whiskers.

Above it all, the whine of the bagpipes echoed on the cool early morning air. We found Dennis, in full Highlander dress, coming off the field after his turn in the bagpipes competition. He at least seemed willing to walk next to me, and to answer my questions.

"Don't mind Tom, he's nervous about appearing at this gathering and is concerned he and his group members won't have enough time to set up and have a rehearsal before their set."

"It's like he wants me here but doesn't want me here."

"Yeah, he can be a dick sometimes, but he doesn't mean anything by it." Somewhat mollified by Dennis's kindness and explanations, I relaxed and looked around the next area we approached.

Southerners love their traditions; they seem to love those of the Old Country even more than those of their Confederate forbearers. And there was plenty of evidence of this mixed heritage at the Games. Vendors selling haggis and colcannon warred with those offering she-crab soup and barbeque. Confederate flags and Celtic knots adorned bumper stickers on a variety of pick-up trucks and Cadillacs. Southern drawls and the brogue of the Highlands drifted from the open doors of the cavernous Farm Bureau. And men in kilts. I was in my glory.

What is it about the sight of hundreds of men wearing kilts? Lines of men in Gordon or MacDougall or Stewart plaid, bagpipes or drums strapped to chests or waists, marched in order down the field, crisply stopping or turning at the Drum Major's whistle. Then, in twos and threes, they walked abreast over the field, almost always with a dark Irish beer in hand, even before the morning's mist had burned off. I watched them with real appreciation. The sway of the pleats below nicely shaped behinds wrested a longing sigh from me. Too many Scottish romance novels perhaps, but there has always been something about a man in a kilt. The oddly masculine swagger of a man in plaid, knees just peeking out, the sporran swinging low on the hips beneath the thick leather belt, and my heart quickens. And it is not just because I know what hides beneath those kilts if the men are dressed in *regimental* style. It takes a special man to wear a *skirt* in this day and age.

My admiration for them aside, I am enough of a realist to understand some of these men—no matter their pedigree—should not be wearing kilts. For example, under no circumstances should kilts be worn with regular black dress socks, the flashes circling thick ankles. Likewise, men should refrain from the miniskirt version of the kilt, no matter how pretty their legs are. While most pants can be worn beneath the bulge of protruding beer belly, kilts hung that low in front tend to ride up in back, a sight better left to the imagination. As I observed these men in kilts, I wondered if there is a book of kilt etiquette. There are numerous guides to appropriate Scottish attire: when and where the dress kilt as opposed to the hunting kilt should be worn, and when the Prince Charlie jacket is too dressy or the Argyle jacket too casual. But I have not found a book that tells men how to wear a skirt. Men need a guide that explains that it is *not* okay to bend over from the waist to pick up something on the ground; this is a situation that requires crouching. When sitting down, the proper way to ensure that one's kilt is tucked beneath what might be a bare butt, is to reach behind while sitting and smooth the fabric over the bottom; one should not plop down, lifting one leg and then the other to tug the fabric under, unless one is seated behind the wheel of one's pick-up truck. Finally, men must learn the proper position of their knees when sitting in a kilt. They do not need to be pressed primly together as the nuns instructed all of us, but they certainly should not be spread apart as if in a seated plié. Especially if one is wearing beneath the kilt the traditional Scottish undergarment—nothing.

I was seated at a table near the stage, listening to Tom's group finish their run-through. I was responsible for selling their CD's of Gaelic music, and business was brisk before the music started.

As I sat and watched the men in kilts from my vantage point beside the stage, it came to me that there are even more subtle rules for men who wear kilts. There is a romance surrounding a man in a kilt. Part of it is the tragic struggle of the Scots to be free of British rule; the men who followed Bonnie Prince Charlie on his fruitless quest; and men like Rob Roy and William Wallace who were fighters and lovers. And part of it is the romanticizing of the rough Highland lord with the tender and poetic heart. I watched a man in a kilt dancing with his lady, holding her tightly to him; I watched an older couple, he in full regalia, she in a long skirt and picture hat tied up with a plaid ribbon and rosette, holding hands in the folds of his kilt. I stared at the tall, dark and handsome young man who came striding through the crowd, his kilt swinging jauntily above legs clad in traditional hose and work boots, his khaki shirtsleeves rolled up to reveal muscular arms and mystical tattoos, his white teeth flashing in a ready grin, his eyes sparkling with the knowledge most female eyes were on him, and the promise of appreciation for all the feminine attention.

I looked at my own man in a kilt (the bright Buchanan plaid), and I realized part of my attraction to him was how his tush looks in a kilt and how his legs were so sexy, encased in dark green hose and flashes. Part of what drew me to him is his prowess with the mandolin. And his whistles softly blowing while his voice blends in the low harmony of a Celtic love song:

Come over the hills, my bonnie Irish lass. Come over the hills to your darling

You choose the rose, love, and I'll make the vow. And I'll be your true love forever.

Yes, men in kilts need a guidebook. Their love of history and clan, tradition and song, make unspoken promises to a woman, promises of love, honor and unity she will believe are her due.

Tom had been distant from me all weekend, near me but not next to me. How can a man who carries himself with pride and confidence through a crowd while wearing a skirt seem completely unaware the woman who follows behind him should be at his side?

As we met up with other musicians and other men in kilts, Tom had failed to introduce me or if he did, I was referred to as his friend. How can a man who takes care he does honor to his clan not realize such honor must also be bestowed on the woman who straightens his kilt and fastens his sporran?

Our love life was waning. Tom was affectionate but not passionate, not anymore. How could this man, who sings *Red is the Rose* with such passion, not realize the woman who lies beside him needs the rose and the promise and the love?

The song was ending. The last refrain and my realization Tom simply did not care enough about me to make my continued interest and the long trips south worthwhile, brought tears to my eyes. I was blinking them away when a masculine hand thrust a white cotton handkerchief in front of me. Startled, I looked up into the face of the handsome soldier who I had been admiring moments earlier.

"Are you all right, miss?" His dark eyes showed genuine concern.

"I'm fine, really. It's just that song; it always makes me cry." I dabbed my eyes with the proffered cloth and handed it back to him.

He stuffed the handkerchief into his sporran, as he nodded and said, "Aye, that is one of the sweetest and prettiest songs we have. But it's about true love and a lovely lass like yourself should not be crying about love, especially when it's your man who is doing the singing." He looked over at Tom, and with a parting smile, he was gone.

Men in kilts, gotta love them.

TOM—SEGUE

Tom was too buried in his own bullshit to see it coming. But as I followed him back to Lynchburg after the Highland Games, I knew we were over. I couldn't hate him. I had been almost in love with him, and I did love him, if even just for our many years of friendship. But I couldn't get inside his head, and I wasn't sure how far I had wormed my way into his heart. I was in his bed, but I might as well have been sleeping on the couch for all the warmth or intimacy we shared. There had been five visits, during the course of almost nine months, and we had made love fewer times than I had fingers on my right hand. I had tentatively broached the subject with him in the spring, and he blamed it on the alcohol he consumed nightly. I suggested less alcohol, and he agreed, but even that did nothing to rouse the passion in him. At least passion for me. I wondered if there was another woman. Certainly, we spent weeks apart, and there were always women around him. Tom is one of those men who is easy with women; he has no agenda, he has no ego, but I wondered if he found it difficult to say, "No."

That Sunday night in Lynchburg, exhausted from the weekend, I still hoped there would be something. He had been too tired and stressed while playing at the Highland Games to even sleep in the same bed with me. So, as we headed to bed back at his house on Sunday night, I asked, "What bed do you want me in?"

He seemed stunned by my question. "Mine, of course!"

"Just checking." I smiled, encouraged by his vehement response.

Still, after he turned out the light, he put his arm around me, drew my head to his shoulder, kissed me lightly on the lips and fell asleep. I spent the night tossing and turning in my frustration, disappointment, and ignorance. The next day, he worked and I wrote. We went to a local pub, where I wrote more while he played. The events of Sunday night replayed themselves once again in his bedroom. I was done.

The next morning, I arose early. The drive to New York was ten hours at best and I still needed to stop every two hours to stretch my recently replaced right knee. I showered and packed my bag, including the nightshirt I always left in his closet and my toiletries that had been stowed in the vanity in the bathroom. Tom awoke as I was loading my car. He didn't make a move to help me, and I didn't ask. Finally packed, I turned to him to say goodbye.

He hugged me and gave me a sweet, close-lipped kiss on the mouth. I pulled back from him and looked him in the eye. He looked surprised.

"Tommy, I think it's time to recognize what is: we're just good friends. Let's leave it at that before there is anger and hurt feelings."

"What do you mean? I still have such a crush on you. I adore you!" He seemed genuinely astonished at my words.

"You have a funny way of showing it; we haven't had sex in months."

"It's hard with all the time we spend apart, it takes a while each time to readjust. And then you're gone." I had heard this excuse before.

"Tom, even when I'm here, you're not with me. I flirt with you, and you change the subject. I proposition you, and you drink more beer." He had the grace to blush.

"I know. The drinking is a problem. I'll work on that." It was not enough.

"I'm heading out. We'll talk about it later." I kissed his cheek quickly and walked out to my SUV.

As I drove away, his doorway was empty. He had not waited to wave me goodbye or blow me a kiss. He called a few times to track my progress and give me the news of the day. I called him late that night to let him know I had arrived safely home. "Good-night, sweetheart. I adore you."

"Good-night, Tom."

I gave it another week. He didn't want to talk about it, about us, so I waited until late one evening when I could tell he had been drinking a bit more than usual.

"It's not working, darlin'."

"It's the distance."

"It's not the distance. It's something else that you won't talk about. But I went fifteen years without intimacy in my life. I am not spending the next fifteen years living like a nun."

"I don't have any answers. It's physical, mental, and emotional."

"You can fix physical. You can get help with mental and emotional…if it's not there, it's not there."

"I don't want to end this. I don't want to lose you again."

"You're not going to lose me—we're still friends."

"You told me at the beginning that if I broke your heart again, you would hate me."

Jesus, was that why he had stayed with me long after his interest had obviously waned?

"Don't worry, darlin', I would have had to give you my heart for you to break it. I never gave it to you. I came close, but I was waiting for a sign from you and I never saw it."

"I adore you." The easy stand-in phrase for "I am not in love with you, but I want to say something other than 'I care'."

"I adore you, too, and if you ever feel like you could make a commitment to me, I am open for any suggestions you might have."

"I'll miss you. And Marley." He had shown much more affection to my dog Marley, lately, than he had to me. At least we had that: I had helped him get over his fear of dogs by introducing Marley into his life. One of his favorite moments was when he took Marley for a ride in his pick-up truck: so Southern, so macho and so cute to see Tommy's elbow hanging out one window, Marley's head out the other, music blaring as they went to pick up beer and cigarettes. I would miss those moments.

And Tom had given me respite from Jamie's medical drama and absence, which had left a gaping hole in my life. Now, I was really alone again, the painting of the loon I had done for Tom's birthday hanging on my wall, the Irish music CDs gathering dust, and Marley sniffing hopefully at the travel bed Tom had given him. So many trinkets, so many memories, so many questions about our promising beginning, and so few answers for our sad little ending.

So I resolved to go on hiatus for a year to sort out my feelings, my needs and my life. No flirting, no dating, no trysts, no conquests. Just me, my family, my friends, and my words.

COCKTAILS

After eight years, almost eighty men, close to 800 margaritas and not nearly 8000 orgasms, where was I?

Older and certainly wiser. I started this adventure in my forty-ninth year. I stopped at fifty-eight to think, then to write and then to recover from a serious illness. I am now past sixty. Weight has been lost and regained, lost again. It takes a bit more product to get my hair this blond, and I have so many freckles and other spots I almost don't need my beloved spray tans any longer. With one new knee and a few more scars, I have aged physically at about the same rate and in similar manner to most women my age. But I now know something many women my age do not know or do not believe: men my age, and even younger, are not all interested in Eva Longoria or Angelina Jolie or any woman in her thirties or forties. Many are looking for women of their own age and experience. A woman, as my baby brother says, who knows who Grand Funk Railroad was. And while our wrinkles, sags, and gray hair may repulse us, they do not scare away most men. Just as we are not only interested in a Ben Affleck-look-alike-contest- winner, they are not only interested in Playboy Bunny wannabes. We seek the same person: a partner, a friend, a lover. Some for short-term, some for the long haul, some for a full range of experience, some for only physical intimacy, and some for just a platonic friendship. But we are all looking for a person, not an image.

I am poorer for the price, richer for the experience. One of my adventures cost me a great deal of money. A few of my lovers stole from me emotionally and physically, draining me until I was but a shell of myself for a time. Some interfered with my work, my friends, my family. But most, most made me smile, made me laugh, made me feel alive again. All gave me interesting times, human contact, and refuge from the loneliness my life had been. And stories, they gave me so many stories.

One, or a few, gave me the greatest gift of all: love.

From blue margaritas with Biff, to regional wines with Boyfriend Bob, from Coronas with lime at Mr. More's apartment to Beune Blanc in the Adirondacks with the Wine Critic, each man has been a new flavor, a quick buzz, a light-headedness I had not enjoyed in decades. And sometimes, just sometimes, the *cocktail* defined the man.

Nathan was as harsh and common as the Budweiser he always drank; a seemingly perfect way to quench any woman's hot thirst, which then left a bitter taste in the mouth and a roiling in the gut. Guinness ale is full-bodied; light and foamy on top, dark in the glass, full of hidden depths and, like Tommy, something you have to wait for and sip gradually before you fully appreciate the complexity. And, like Tommy, eventually proven to be too heavy for my tastes.

I never liked Manhattans. The taste was too strong and the drink belonged to an older generation. Like Jamie. Too strong a personality for me and too old, some would say. But, a Magic Drink is as unlike a Manhattan as Jamie is dissimilar to the typical *married man*. At my first sip, I fell in love with Magic Drinks, and I fell in love with Jamie almost as fast. I got as drunk on him as I did on his unique combination of rye, vermouth and bitters. That damn drink put eighteen pounds on my already generously padded frame that I have yet to lose.

Jamie got into my heart just as insidiously and remains there still. I do not begrudge him either the pounds or the heartache that are his responsibility. I am grateful to him for so many adventures and so many stories. And for proving to me, always a judge, my damaged heart had healed enough to fall in love again. And that I am, like him, a warrior strong enough to survive another broken heart.

So like the Greeks, beaten, bloodied but unbroken, I am ready to return to the battlefield of love, ready to return with my shield—or on it—as I seek to fall in love for the last time in my life.

EPILOGUE

After saying good-bye to Tom, I sat down to write the stories of my dating adventures.

As my memories became words on the computer screen, I relived the craziness that had been my fifties. I read many of the stories to my memoir writing class. Laughter, gasps and a few tears were often the response. But, also, words of caution. Did I really want to let the world into my boudoir, or, as the case may be, the backseat of my car, a Mexican bar and a number of hotel rooms? Why not write this book as fiction? An erotic contemporary romp?

Some of the essays that form these chapters were featured in readings at local bookstores and selected for regional memoir competitions. Initially, I was nervous about standing in front of a room filled mostly with strangers and revealing my encounters with John Number One, Critter and Jamie, and talking about intimacy, bad boys and phone sex. Afterward, I was relieved to have the ordeal over but still had some trepidation as audience members gathered round to ask questions and make comments. As I listened to the women who were gracious enough to share their thoughts with me, I was convinced if my stories were to make it to print, they had to be presented as nonfiction. To a woman, I heard over and over:

"Is this going to be a book? I have to get it for my sister-in-law (or cousin or friend). She was just divorced (or separated or widowed). She thinks there is no man out there who would be interested in her because she is in her fifties (or sixties) or she is overweight or she has not dated in twenty-five or thirty years.

Did you really date a lot of men? Did you fall in love? Can we find happiness with a man at our age?"

So, here it is. Obviously, I have changed the names to protect the innocent and not-so-innocent. A few of the characters are composites of two or three men who were similar, or who I knew in the same timeframe. And, though it may not seem so, I have left out many intimate details I did not feel were necessary to tell my story.

Am I afraid I may be cast as a fool, a slut, a drunk and a philanderer? I am. I am not proud of some of my encounters. I do not hold my judgment up as the wisest or the most cautious. But I was on a journey of self-discovery, though at first, I really did just want to get laid, just once. As I moved through the world of online dating, I found a new and different woman emerging from the shell of the woman I had been for years. She is not the woman I thought I would be at sixty, but she is real. And I am finally comfortable in her skin.

When I started dating, I had no confidence in anything other than my intelligence and my ability to write coherently. Though I was concerned about my weight, my age, my scars and my wrinkles, I determined to brazen it out and act as though I was as attractive as any woman half my age, half my weight. I learned, in fact, I was attractive to many men. I came to believe their compliments and began to personify the old adage "beauty is as beauty does." I never thought I was particularly funny, but I made men laugh, and when I wrote about them, I made audiences laugh. I was a control freak; I needed to control everything so no tragedy would ever happen again. I've learned to let go. There have been a few pretty bad moments over the years with these men. Now, I look at these bad times and ask myself, "Is it as bad as my husband dying? No, nothing is as bad as that. Okay, well, I survived his death. I can survive anything."

In the past ten years, I have fallen in love again, had my heart broken again, chalked up a multitude of orgasms and met some men who will always be my friends. And I would do it all, or at least most of it, again.

Boyfriend Bob dated one of my acquaintances for years. They broke up and he ended up dating a different friend of mine for a short time. I saw him a few years ago at a play. He has put on a few pounds, lost a little hair, but he is still a handsome man. We were not meant to be. But I wish him well.

Yalie and I correspond frequently, flirting and talking politics. He is back in our old hometown, still trying to change the world. And as much as I care for him, I know he is, ultimately and regretfully, not the man for me.

Critter calls when I think of him, still there is that invisible connection. In 2008, when I retired after thirty years from my job—amidst intense pressure and veiled threats—he hopped into a two-seat plane with a crazy coworker named Diego and flew all night to spend the day with me in a cozy little hotel. Once again, our twelve hours were filled with laughter and loving, conversation and cuddling—two old friends comfortable in each other's arms. At midnight, he was gone. But he is still just a phone call away.

Hot-Tub Ken has recently moved back to Albany. We met for dinner one night. Just dinner. We reminisced, and then we kissed. He is still an incredible kisser. And I still arouse him like no other woman. Where this will all lead, I do not know—but as I did in 2003, I may again someday meander down his path.

Tom got married in 2014, to a woman he began seeing about three weeks after I bid him farewell. I suspect they were involved long before my final visit, but I can't be sure. It really does not make a difference to me now. So I congratulated him on his nuptials. And I still love men in kilts.

Jamie. Well, Jamie is most in my thoughts when I am in the pool on a summer evening or when I drive along Interstate 90 or when I occasionally make a Magic Drink. After I said goodbye to Tom, Jamie resurfaced for a bit. His house in Kinderhook had finally been sold and he was trying to decide where he would live—Myrtle Beach or Bristol or someplace else. As we had once discussed, I told him he was still welcome to live with me, to resume our relationship, but only if he had a legal separation or divorce. I would not live with a married man. He sighed. He took my hand. His tired eyes were sad when he told me "I love you. A divorce would cost me millions. I am too old and too tired to pay that price. I just don't love you enough."

His honesty stung. But I had known that was where we were headed almost from the start: his money and my needs would always come between us. We kissed goodbye, and he was gone. I have not seen him in a year, but a trace of my feelings for him will always remain in my heart.

After this manuscript was finished, and I was busy writing a romance novel, I decided to try my luck online again. Reading or writing romance always gets me thinking and wanting. And there are so many new sites geared toward men and women in their fifties, sixties and seventies and more.

In the late summer of 2014, I signed up for *Our Time*. No provocative prose this time, no sexy picture. Just warm and witty and a bit wistful, wondering if love would find me again.

There was the usual flurry of responses—common whenever a new profile appears on any site. A few men caught my eye: interesting, nice looking, age-appropriate and grammatically correct.

But the two I liked best listed their status as "separated." Warning sign! Before writing them off, I made inquiries as to whether divorce was imminent. Alas, they both said, separated was where they were and where, for financial reasons, they would have to stay. I regretfully said I was not interested. I have learned that lesson, at least.

Then there he was. Oliver. He was funny, handsome, athletic and long-divorced. We winked and then we e-mailed. We quickly progressed to chatting on the phone. He had a sexy voice, and was interested in politics and history. Even better, he was a fan of the Yankees, lived in Saratoga and drove a red BMW. Oliver was looking for a fun and feisty woman who wanted to travel. I told him he had found her: I adore travel. He pleaded for me to meet him that first weekend. And I really wanted to, but I had a deadline for a first chapter and synopsis for the romance novel due on Monday. Oliver was fascinated that I was an author and asked to read some of my romance. On Sunday, I sent him a few snippets from the work in progress. Sadly, by Monday, he had decided I was too busy for him; he wanted a woman who had no ties and could be with him whenever he wanted her for dinner, movies and trips.

So I sold a book and lost a man. I think it was a fair trade. And I still believe the man for me, and for you, is waiting out there in cyber space, just an e-mail away.

THE END

UNANSWERED PRAYERS

BY

MORGAN MALONE

Summer of 2001. Naomi Stein was just praying for a little peace from her son, her ex-husband and her boss. Instead, she ends up following surly Country singer Sam Rhodes across the USA, covering his breakout tour for Rolling Stone.

Sam has had bad luck with women and Naomi is trouble from the start. He tries to keep the feisty, sexy blonde at arm's length…until Naomi pushes him over the edge. The hottest tor of the summer has just caught on fire. The music gets better and the romance steamier as they criss-cross the country.

Will their passion burn out as autumn approaches? Stubborn pride forces them apart until the tragedy of 9/11 compels them to face each other one more time.

QUESTIONS FOR DISCUSSION

- Do you agree with Morgan's choices of the men she would pursue a relationship with and the men she did not date or did not stay with? Why?

- How did Morgan's decision to start dating and the way she dated affect family, friends and work? Were these positive effects for Morgan? For her family, her friends and her work associates?

- Why did Morgan choose online dating over more traditional methods of meeting men? Do you think it was based on her desire to control the dating process? What would you do?

- For single parents deciding to start dating, how important is the approval of their children? Why was Morgan's son opposed the very idea of his mother dating while her daughter approved?

- Morgan wrote her stories as memoir instead of fiction. Do you think this was the best format? Why?

Questions contributed by: *Have A Life Book Group*

CONTEMPORARY ROMANCES BY
MORGAN MALONE:

Unanswered Prayers
Katarina—Out of Control

If you enjoyed Morgan Malone's *Cocktales,*
please consider telling others and writing a review.

ABOUT MORGAN MALONE

Morgan Malone was a published author at the age of eight. After that, everything that happened to her became material for a story she could write. So, of course, when she finally began dating after fifteen years as a widow, her adventures just had to be told. She has been writing memoir for the last eight years, after retiring from a thirty-year career as a judge and counsel at a New York State agency. Morgan lives near Saratoga Springs, New York, with her chocolate Labrador Retriever. When not writing memoir, Morgan can be found penning romance novels or painting watercolors. Visit her on Facebook, Twitter or at www.MorganMaloneAuthor.com.

Made in the USA
Lexington, KY
27 May 2018